READING THE GOSPELS WITH KARL BARTH

Reading the Gospels with Karl Barth

Edited by

Daniel L. Migliore

WILLIAM B. EERDMANS PUBLISHING COMPANY
GRAND RAPIDS, MICHIGAN

Wm. B. Eerdmans Publishing Co.
2140 Oak Industrial Drive N.E., Grand Rapids, Michigan 49505
www.eerdmans.com

© 2017 Daniel L. Migliore
All rights reserved
Published 2017

ISBN 978-0-8028-7363-7

Library of Congress Cataloging-in-Publication Data

Names: Karl Barth Conference (2015 : Princeton Theological Seminary), author. |
    Migliore, Daniel L., 1935– editor. | Princeton Theological Seminary, host institution.
Title: Reading the Gospels with Karl Barth / edited by Daniel L. Migliore.
Description: Grand Rapids : Eerdmans Publishing Co., 2017. | Papers presented at the 2015
    Karl Barth Conference, held June 21–24, at Princeton Theological Seminary on the theme
    of "Karl Barth and the Gospels: Interpreting Gospel Texts." | Includes bibliographical
    references and index.
Identifiers: LCCN 2016049801 | ISBN 9780802873637 (pbk. : alk. paper)
Subjects: LCSH: Barth, Karl, 1886–1968—Congresses. | Bible. Gospels—Criticism,
    interpretation, etc.—Congresses.
Classification: LCC BX4827.B3 K363 2015 | DDC 226.6/06092—dc23
    LC record available at https://lccn.loc.gov/2016049801

To Jürgen Moltmann

Contents

Acknowledgments   x

Abbreviations   xi

Introduction   xii

1. The Election of Grace   1
   Barth on the Doctrine of Predestination
   JÜRGEN MOLTMANN

2. Revelatory Word or Beloved Son?   16
   Barth on the Johannine Prologue
   RICHARD BAUCKHAM

3. The Gospel within the Commandment   34
   Barth on the Parable of the Good Samaritan
   ERIC GREGORY

4. A Rich Disciple?   56
   Barth on the Rich Young Ruler
   WILLIE JAMES JENNINGS

CONTENTS

5. The Compassion of Jesus Christ — 67
   Barth on Matthew 9:36
   PAUL T. NIMMO

6. The Journey of God's Son — 80
   Barth and Balthasar on the Parable of the Lost Son
   DANIEL L. MIGLIORE

7. Parabolic Retelling and Christological Discourse — 106
   Julian of Norwich and Karl Barth on the Parable of the Lost Son
   KENDALL COX

8. The Riddle of Gethsemane — 124
   Barth on Jesus's Agony in the Garden
   PAUL DAFYDD JONES

9. The Passion of God Himself — 155
   Barth on Jesus's Cry of Dereliction
   BRUCE L. MCCORMACK

10. The Self-Witness of the Risen Jesus — 173
    Karl Barth's Reading of the Emmaus Road Story
    BEVERLY ROBERTS GAVENTA

11. The Sum of the Gospel — 187
    Barth's Intracanonical and Intertextual Interpretation of paradidōmi
    SHANNON NICOLE SMYTHE

12. What's in Those Lamps?   204
   A Sermon on Matthew 25:1–13
   FLEMING RUTLEDGE

Contributors   210

Index of Authors   213

Index of Subjects   218

Index of Scripture References   224

Acknowledgments

My hearty thanks are extended to all who assisted in planning and organizing the Karl Barth Conference held in Princeton in June 2015. Special thanks go to the staff of the Center for Barth Studies at Princeton Theological Seminary, and above all to its expert and energetic curator, Kait Dugan, and her equally able assistant, Sara Misgen, who together guided every practical and technical aspect of the conference with grace and skill.

Thanks also to Craig Barnes, president of Princeton Theological Seminary, for his strong support of the project and good advice on many matters; to Amy Ehlin, director of conferences and hospitality, for her efficiency and cheerfulness in overseeing the undertaking; to the facilities and technical teams of the Seminary for readying its buildings—including its stunning new library—for four days of rich theological discussion, an all-Mozart concert, and a fascinating slide lecture on Matthias Grünewald's Isenheim Altarpiece by Professor Karlfried Froehlich; and to Kate Skrebutenas, Princeton Seminary's reference librarian, for her invaluable help on all matters bibliographical. Finally, a special thanks to the plenary lecturers and to the presenters and moderators of afternoon discussion sessions whose able leadership and spirited interactions with conference participants assured its success.

This volume is dedicated to Jürgen Moltmann in grateful recognition of his seminal contributions to theology and church for more than half a century.

Abbreviations

CD   Karl Barth, *Church Dogmatics*, 4 vols. in 13 parts, trans. G. W. Bromiley and T. F. Torrance (Edinburgh: T. & T. Clark, 1936–1975)

KD   Karl Barth, *Kirchliche Dogmatik*, 4 vols. in 13 parts (Zollikon-Zürich: Evangelischer Verlag, 1932–1967)

KJV   King James Version

NRSV New Revised Standard Version

WW   Karl Barth, *Witness to the Word: A Commentary on John 1; Lectures at Münster in 1925 and at Bonn in 1933*, ed. Walther Fürst, trans. Geoffrey W. Bromiley (Grand Rapids: Eerdmans, 1986)

Introduction

In the course of his multivolume *Church Dogmatics*, Karl Barth not only cites thousands of texts of Scripture but also offers extensive exegetical discussion of numerous passages. These biblical references and small-print exegetical explorations did not function for him as "proof texts" and certainly not as mere window dressing. Instead, his purpose was to present some of "the exegetical background to the dogmatic exposition."[1] When Barth famously wrote that dogmatics "does not ask what the prophets and apostles said but what we must say on the basis of the prophets and apostles," he differentiated biblical and dogmatic theology while also affirming their intimate relationship.[2] Constructive dogmatic reflections are both rooted in and tested by whether they are in agreement with the witness of the prophets and apostles contained in Scripture.

Even though Barth's intention to base his theology on the witness of Scripture is beyond question, his arresting readings of biblical texts have met with both praise and demurrers. In defense of Barth's readings of Scripture, Paul Dafydd Jones argues that "it is attention to the biblical record that stimulates Barth's formulation of finely grained theological claims."[3] By contrast, after examining Barth's use of Scripture in his contested doctrine of election, Stephen N. Williams concludes we must "part company

---

1. *CD* II/2, ix.
2. *CD* I/1, 16.
3. Paul Dafydd Jones, "The Heart of the Matter: Karl Barth's Christological Exegesis," in *Thy Word Is Truth: Barth on Scripture*, ed. George Hunsinger (Grand Rapids: Eerdmans, 2012), 190.

Introduction

with [Barth] in the way he relates Scripture to dogmatics."[4] Mary Kathleen Cunningham summarizes well the complexity of any evaluation of Barth's theological exegesis: "Few contemporary theologians have been as self-consciously concerned to do theology in accord with Scripture as Barth. In his *Church Dogmatics*, he consistently pairs theological claims with often lengthy exegetical excursuses. These passages bristle with highly inventive and frequently controversial claims about biblical texts and their significance for theological reflection. Sometimes adhering to the canons of historical criticism, sometimes diverging from these procedures in dramatic ways, Barth astounds critics and supporters alike with his exegetical ingenuity."[5]

Why Study Barth on the Gospels?

To say there is a sizable literature on Barth's doctrine of Scripture and his hermeneutical principles is an understatement. In his judgment, however, far more valuable than abstract debates about methods of exegesis are careful readings of particular scriptural texts. As Barth wrote in a letter to Hermann Diem, "Hermeneutics cannot be an independent topic of conversation; its problems can only be tackled and answered in countless acts of interpretation—all of which are mutually corrective and supplementary, while at the same time being principally concerned with the content of the text."[6] It is a positive development, therefore, that detailed studies of Barth's distinctive, rich, and sometimes controversial readings of particular biblical books and passages are on the increase. Some representative works include studies of Barth's interpretation of Genesis 1 and 2, 1 Samuel 25, the book of Job, the prophet Isaiah, Mark 10:17–31, the Gospel of John, and the Sermon on the Mount.[7] Given the scope of Barth's exegetical labors, much of his work in

---

4. Stephen N. Williams, *The Election of Grace: A Riddle without a Resolution?* (Grand Rapids: Eerdmans, 2015), 198.

5. Mary Kathleen Cunningham, *What Is Theological Exegesis? Interpretation and Use of Scripture in Barth's Doctrine of Election* (Valley Forge, PA: Trinity Press International, 1995), 11.

6. See Eberhard Busch, *Karl Barth: His Life from Letters and Autobiographical Texts* (Philadelphia: Fortress, 1976), 349.

7. Johann-Friedrich Konrad, *Abbild und Ziel der Schöpfung: Untersuchungen zur Exegese von Genesis 1 und 2 in Barths Kirchlicher Dogmatik III, 1* (Tübingen: J. C. B. Mohr, 1962); Gerhard Bergner, *Um der Sachewillen: Karl Barths Schriftauslegung in der Kirchlichen Dogmatik* (Göttingen: Vandenhoeck & Ruprecht, 2015), 241–49; Susannah Ticciati, *Job and the Disruption of Identity: Reading beyond Barth* (London: T&T Clark, 2005); Mark S. Gignil-

INTRODUCTION

this area remains to be explored. It was with this conviction that the 2015 Karl Barth Conference, held at Princeton Theological Seminary, took as its theme, "Karl Barth and the Gospels: Interpreting Gospel Texts." The aims of the conference were: to examine both carefully and critically a selection of Barth's readings of passages in the Gospels to determine the ways in which his readings are distinctive or novel; to explore how they influence and are influenced by the inner logic of his theology; to set his interpretations in conversation with other ways of reading the texts; and to suggest what contribution his readings of Gospel texts might make to church, theology, and ethics in our own time.

Why focus on Barth's readings of the Gospels? Two reasons can be given, the first being quite obvious. At the center of the Christian message is the person and reconciling work of Jesus Christ. Who he is and what he has done for sinful humanity is the object of Christian faith, love, and hope, the focus of Christian worship and service, and in Barth's words, "the heart of the Church's dogmatics."[8] Since it is in the four canonical Gospels that the singular identity and reconciling activity of Jesus Christ on our behalf is most fully and concretely set forth, Barth's interpretation of Gospel texts is of special interest.

The second reason for the 2015 Conference theme requires a bit more explanation. Barth's earliest exegetical efforts concentrated on the letters of Paul, and most particularly on Paul's epistle to the Romans (2nd ed., 1922). During his pastorate in Safenwil, his preaching included, of course, sermons based on texts from the Gospels as well as from the Old Testament and the Pauline Epistles. Moreover, in the first decade and a half of his university teaching, he lectured not only on Ephesians and Colossians and wrote commentaries on Philippians and First Corinthians but also gave courses on James, 1 John, and the Sermon on the Mount as well as a series of lectures on John 1 and Luke 1.[9] Still, it is fair to say that the Pauline corpus had a

---

liat, *Karl Barth and the Fifth Gospel: Barth's Theological Exegesis of Isaiah* (Burlington, VT: Ashgate, 2009); *Karl Barth: Der Reiche Jüngling*, edited with introduction by Peter Eicher (Munich: Kosel, 1986), 13–46; John Webster, "Karl Barth's Lectures on the Gospel of John," in *What Is It That the Scripture Says?*, ed. Phillip McCosker (London: T&T Clark, 2006), 211–30; Paul Nimmo, "Exegesis, Ontology, and Ethics: Karl Barth and the Sermon on the Mount," in *Christology and Scripture: Interdisciplinary Perspectives*, ed. Andrew Lincoln and Angus Paddison (London: T&T Clark, 2007), 171–87.

8. *CD* IV/1, 3.

9. Karl Barth, *The Epistle to the Philippians*, trans. James W. Leitch, 40th anniversary edition with introductory essays by Bruce L. McCormack and Francis B. Watson (Louisville:

privileged place in Barth's earliest endeavors in theological exegesis, and with some notable exceptions, his close readings of the Gospels awaited his work on the *Church Dogmatics*.[10]

It is not surprising, then, that when the word *exegesis* is placed alongside Barth's name, the first thought that may come to mind is not exposition of texts from the Gospels but the second edition of Barth's Romans commentary. In this work Barth departed dramatically from the sort of commentaries dominant in nineteenth- and early twentieth-century biblical scholarship. He took sharp issue with biblical scholars who casually dismissed some of the central themes of Paul's letter as curious ancient artifacts or considered them scandals to modern thought. In the prefaces to the book, he insisted on the responsibility of the interpreter to wrestle theologically with the biblical texts, however strange and disturbing, and to ask to what extent they continue to address readers and hearers today with a disruptive yet life-renewing word of God. Responding to critics who labeled him an enemy of responsible historical-critical study of the Bible, Barth replied that he had no objection to such study in principle and considered it an important preliminary step in serious interpretation of the Bible. His call for robust theological exegesis was not a call for a less but a "more critical" reading of the Bible.[11] Beyond what is supposedly self-evident in the texts, there remains a world of meaning that "subtly escapes both understanding and interpretation, or which, at least, awaits further investigation."[12]

Barth's reading of biblical texts in his later Pauline commentaries and especially in the *Church Dogmatics* continued to grow beyond the interpretive practice and powerful rhetoric of the Romans commentary. Nevertheless, he remained firm in his commitment to the theological interpretation of Scripture. In his farewell to his Bonn students before being expelled from Germany, Barth gave this charge: "Listen to my last piece of advice: exegesis, exegesis, and yet more exegesis! Keep to the Word, to the Scripture that has

---

Westminster John Knox, 2002); Barth, *The Resurrection of the Dead*, trans. H. J. Stenning (Fleming H. Revell, 1933, reprinted by Wipf & Stock, 2003); Barth, *Witness to the Word: A Commentary on John 1* (Eugene, OR: Wipf & Stock, 2003); Barth, *The Great Promise: Luke 1* (New York: Philosophical Library, 1963).

10. For dates and order of Barth's earliest exegetical works, see Bruce L. McCormack, "The Significance of Karl Barth's Theological Exegesis of Philippians," in Karl Barth, *The Epistle to the Philippians*, v-vi.

11. Karl Barth, *The Epistle to the Romans*, trans. Edwyn C. Hoskyns (Oxford: Oxford University Press, 1933), 8.

12. Barth, *Romans*, 12.

been given us."[13] In *Church Dogmatics* I/2, Barth identifies three phases of theological exegesis: *explicatio* (literary-historical investigation), *meditatio* (thinking through what is said in the text), and *applicatio* (appropriating what is said and its impact on our entire existence). What is crucial at *every* phase of the interpretive process, Barth insists, is "fidelity in all circumstances to the object [the subject matter, *die Sache*] reflected in the words of the prophets and apostles."[14]

In one of his last writings Barth summarized the task of biblical interpretation in shorthand fashion as requiring both "minute attention" to the texts and "bold imagination."[15] Of course, by bold imagination Barth meant something quite different from rendering the text in any way one pleases. Far from a free-wheeling exercise, use of the imagination of the responsible biblical interpreter is, according to Barth, disciplined. It presupposes that the distinctive subject matter of Scripture must always be the focus of its interpretation; that the diverse texts of Scripture have an inner unity rather than being a collection of largely unrelated writings; that this unity is to be found in the history of God's covenant with the people of Israel and the fulfillment of the covenant in the person and work of Jesus Christ; that Scripture constitutes a canon or rule of faith in the life, worship, preaching, and mission of the Christian community; and that the faithful reading of Scripture occurs always with the recollection and expectation of encountering afresh the living Word of God and in the context of the prayer *Veni Creator Spiritus!*

So how does Barth's practice of theological exegesis play out in his reading of texts from the Gospels in the *Church Dogmatics*? What are the fundamental features of Barth's interpretation of Gospel texts and to what extent do they enliven the theological endeavor today? My hope is that readers of the chapters in this volume will find a number of helpful answers to these questions as well as considerable stimulus for further study and discussion. In this brief introduction, I will venture only a few comments on some features of Barth's readings of Gospel texts.

First, in his readings Barth is consistently *christocentric*. This observation should surprise no one. After all, in a frequently cited passage—repeated in a variety of ways many times over in the *Church Dogmatics*—Barth speaks of his christocentric reading of the Bible with force and clarity:

---

13. Busch, *Barth*, 259.
14. *CD* I/2, 725.
15. Karl Barth, *Evangelical Theology: An Introduction* (Grand Rapids: Eerdmans, 1963), 186.

Introduction

> The Bible says all sorts of things, certainly; but in all this multiplicity and variety, it says in truth only one thing—just this: the name of Jesus Christ, concealed under the name Israel in the Old Testament, revealed under His own name in the New Testament, which therefore can be understood only as it has understood itself, as a commentary on the Old Testament. ... The Bible remains dark to us if we do not hear in it this sovereign name, and if, therefore, we think we perceived God and humanity in some other relation than the one determined once for all by this name.[16]

Christocentrism, however, can have more than one meaning. Barth was fully aware of this fact already in his first cycle of lectures in dogmatics in Göttingen when he critiqued the "christocentrism"—or more accurately the "Jesus-centrism"—of nineteenth-century liberal Protestant theology with its concentration on the recovery of the "historical Jesus."[17] His criticism of this enterprise in no way reflects a questioning of the full humanity of the incarnate Lord, as he makes clear in all phases of his dogmatic work and perhaps most compellingly in *CD* IV/2, §64.3, "The Royal Man." The point of Barth's criticism of the "historical Jesus" project is that it is not the figure of Jesus supposedly lying behind the Gospel texts and reconstructed by modern historians who is the object of Christian faith, the center of Christian theology, and the proper focus of interpretation of the Gospels. Rather, it is the living Jesus whose identity and work is narrated, confessed, and proclaimed most explicitly in the canonical Gospels. It must be added that for Barth interpreters of the Gospel texts are no more justified in anxiously imposing the church's orthodox christological doctrines on the texts than they are in imposing their own ideas or those of a cultural or political movement. Barth's reading of the Gospels, as his reading of Scripture generally, is characterized by an "unmistakable intensity to listen to the text ... to give the fullest possible play to what the text is after."[18] We must ask again and again to what extent and in what way the God of the gospel decisively revealed in Jesus Christ speaks anew through these texts of God's judgment and grace, and of his patience and faithfulness despite our sin and unfaithfulness.

A second notable feature of Barth's reading of the Gospels is his atten-

---

16. *CD* I/2, 720.

17. Karl Barth, *The Göttingen Dogmatics* (Grand Rapids: Eerdmans, 1991). Barth criticized the separation of the "historical Jesus" from his "theological content," and for that reason said dogmatics must dare to be "less christocentric," i.e., more trinitarian (91).

18. James A. Wharton, "Karl Barth as Exegete and His Influence on Biblical Interpretation," *Interpretation* 28, no. 1 (1972): 7.

tion to the *narrative form* their witness frequently takes. Form and content for Barth are inseparable both in the event of revelation and in the proper interpretation of biblical texts. If the person and work of Jesus Christ is central in a right understanding of Scripture, the identity of the one who bears this name is properly rendered not by a set of ideas or doctrines, however sophisticated and impressive they may be, but in the retelling of the particular history narrated in Scripture. The scriptural witnesses tell of God's covenantal love for Israel culminating in the history of Jesus Christ, sent by the Father and obedient to the Father in the power of the Spirit for the reconciliation of the world. As Barth puts it in his doctrine of election, it is the history in which God "takes on Himself man's lowliness in order that man may be exalted. . . . [A]ll this is history . . . Who and what Jesus Christ is, is something which can only be told, not a system which can be considered and described."[19] Barth makes the same point in his doctrine of reconciliation: "The atonement is history. To know it, we must know it as such. To think of it, we must think of it as such. To speak of it, we must tell it as history. To try to grasp it as supra-historical or non-historical truth is not to grasp it at all. . . . But the atonement is the very special history of God with man, the very special history of man with God. As such it has a particular character and demands particular attention."[20] It will be noted that many of the Gospel passages discussed in the following chapters are narratives. Barth not only takes this narrative form into account but also reads each passage as part both of the wider narrative of each Evangelist and of the overarching biblical narrative.

A third feature of Barth's reading of Gospel texts is closely related to the preceding. In his exegetical practice he assumes both the rich *diversity* and the deep *unity* of the biblical witnesses. In all their diversity—their "extremely polyphonic," not "monotonous" testimony to the work and word of God[21]—the Scriptures are deeply interconnected. In brief, Barth characteristically explores this differentiated unity rather than reading Scripture piecemeal. He does not pick out a single text isolated from its context in the biblical book in which it is found or from the still larger context of the entire message of Scripture. Theological exegesis of Scripture involves for him a kind of pilgrimage, migrating "from the Old Testament to the New and return[ing] again, from the Yahwist to the priestly codex, from the psalms of

---

19. *CD* II/2, 188.
20. *CD* II/2, 157.
21. *Evangelical Theology*, 33.

Introduction

David to the proverbs of Solomon, from the Gospel of John to the synoptic gospels, from the Letter of Galatians to the so-called straw epistle of James, and so on continually."[22] According to Barth, this continuous movement of interpretation corresponds to the fact that "the work of God . . . is an ongoing and at all points differentiated history in the course of which God continually wills and does particular things and therefore has always something particular to say, even though he always speaks of His present, past and future rule and action."[23] As the following chapters show, Barth's prizing of the diversity and unity of Scripture is evident in his reading of the Gospels. To give only one example, in an exegetical excursus in *CD* I/2, Barth characterizes the difference between the Synoptic Gospels and the Gospel of John as a diversity in unity, with the Synoptic Gospels bearing witness that Jesus is the *Christ* and *Son of God* while the Gospel of John bears witness that the Word and Son of God is *Jesus*.[24] In sum, in its differentiated unity, Scripture for Barth contains a rich history of God with humanity and of humanity with God, a history that culminates in the incarnation, ministry, crucifixion, and resurrection of Jesus Christ. His atoning work is a history both of God's self-humbling and self-expenditure and of human justification, sanctification, and exaltation to fellowship with God.

Not least among the features of Barth's interpretation of Gospel texts is that he assumes the *actuality* and *contemporaneity* of the primary subject of their story. The One whose saving work they attest is not imprisoned in the past but continues to address each person and all people here and now. Scripture in all its parts, and especially in the Gospels, bears witness to the *living* Word of God. Barth here reiterates one of the great themes of Reformation readings of Scripture: *Tua res agitur* (the subject matter concerns you). Readers, hearers, and interpreters of Scripture are addressed and claimed by the living Word in the totality of their existence, personally and corporately, socially and politically. Moreover, because the living Word is ever new, no single interpretation of a text can be considered exhaustive. The interpreter must listen to each text afresh and in the company of other interpreters. Listening afresh means openness to the new. This is why Barth not only honors the child's "naïve" hearing of the Gospel stories;[25] he also speaks of the importance of a "tested and critical naivety" on the part of the

22. *Evangelical Theology*, 34.
23. *CD* IV/3.2, 577.
24. *CD* I/2, 15–25.
25. *CD* IV/2, 112–13.

mature interpreter.²⁶ "Tested and critical naivety" clearly does not signify a return to the uncritical. Instead, it is the practice of a "post-critical" interpretation that passes through the fires of criticism but does not close itself to what is new beyond the presuppositions and viewpoints every interpreter inevitably brings to the text.²⁷ Post-critical interpretation or "tested and critical naivety" in the approach to the Gospels—as in the interpretation of all biblical witnesses—is a radical openness to the ever new light that shines from these texts. Jesus of Nazareth, the incarnate and crucified Son of God and Son of Man, is the living Lord, and the radiance of his reality attested in Scripture illumines our lives and our world here and now in the power of the Holy Spirit.

An Overview of This Volume

The contributors to this volume are women and men from diverse backgrounds: biblical studies, systematic theology, ethics, and church leadership. Their theological perspectives vary. While their responses to Barth's theology are deeply appreciative, they are far from uniform. What they have in common is an understanding of the importance of vigorous theological reflection today for church, academy, and the wider culture; the inseparability of such reflection from responsible and creative interpretations of biblical texts; and the stimulus that Barth's legacy of "minute attention" and "bold imagination" in the readings of Scripture gives to biblically funded theological work.

Chapter 1. Jürgen Moltmann was asked to write the lead chapter: "The Election of Grace: Barth on the Doctrine of Predestination." It seemed fitting to start with this topic because of the prominence Barth assigns to a christocentric reinterpretation of the doctrine of election in his theology and biblical interpretation. Moltmann begins his reflections on Barth's renewal of this doctrine by recalling how as a young theologian he greeted Barth's momentous achievement with "gratitude and deep relief." In contrast to

---

26. *CD* IV/2, 479.
27. On "post-critical" interpretation see Rudolf Smend, "Nachkritische Schriftauslegung," in *Parrhesia: Karl Barth zum achtzigsten Geburtstag*, ed. Eberhard Busch, Jürgen Fangmeier, and Max Geiger (Zürich: Evangelischer Verlag Zürich, 1966), 215–37; and George Hunsinger, "Postcritical Scriptural Interpretation: Rudolf Smend on Karl Barth," in *Thy Word Is Truth: Barth on Scripture*, ed. George Hunsinger (Grand Rapids: Eerdmans, 2012), 29–48.

Introduction

the fearful doctrine of double predestination—a source, Moltmann says, of "many misunderstandings and much mental and spiritual damage"—Barth contends that the doctrine of predestination does not have to do with an arbitrary eternal divine decree by which some are elected and others are rejected. Instead, it declares God's eternal election of grace in Jesus Christ. From all eternity God wills not to be alone and self-sufficient as he might be, but chooses to be God with and for us. When understood in this way, the election of grace cancels the idea of a "horrible decree" and becomes, in Barth's words, "the sum of the gospel." While grateful for Barth's christocentric renewal of this doctrine of election, Moltmann nevertheless raises two fundamental questions: whether Barth's way of thinking about the relationship of God's freedom and God's love veers toward voluntarism, and whether Barth properly describes the relationship of God's will and God's nature. In the concluding section of his chapter, Moltmann puts his own characteristic stamp on Barth's reinterpretation of the doctrine of election by arguing that it should be brought into dialogue with the concerns of political theology and understood as inseparable both from the proclamation of the universal scope of God's grace and from a call to resistance to all injustice.

Chapter 2. In "Revelatory Word or Beloved Son? Barth on the Johannine Prologue," Richard Bauckham carefully examines the similarities and differences between Barth's 1925–1926 lectures on the Johannine prologue and his exegesis of the passage in the *Church Dogmatics*. Bauckham's chapter appropriately follows Moltmann's since Barth frequently appeals to John 1:1–14 and Ephesians 1:3–5 in support of his christocentric reconstruction of the doctrine of election and his insistence that Jesus Christ is the electing God as well as the elected human being. Barth reads John's term "Word" (*logos*) in verses 1 and 2, whose provenance and meaning are variously interpreted by scholars, as functioning not as a reference to an abstract and indefinite aspect of the divine life but as a "placeholder" (*Platzhalter*) for the concrete person of Jesus Christ who will be specifically identified in later verses of the prologue as Jesus Christ (1:17), the Word become flesh (1:18). Bauckham shows that in comparison with his early lectures on John, Barth's reading of the prologue in the *Church Dogmatics* is primarily concerned to reject the idea of a *logos asarkos* mysteriously lurking behind or different from the Word made flesh. Considering Barth's exegetical work "far ahead of his time," and in broad agreement with Barth about the importance of a theological exegesis that dares to go beyond philological and historical observations, Bauckham nevertheless thinks Barth's reading of the prologue has some serious omissions, especially in failing to attend sufficiently to the relationship of

INTRODUCTION

John 1 and Genesis 1 and in overlooking the importance in John's Gospel of the term *monogenēs* (only Son, v. 18) of the Father. Bauckham's tightly argued chapter underscores the value of critical and constructive conversation between dogmatic theologians and biblical scholars.

Chapter 3. In "The Gospel within the Commandment: Barth on the Parable of the Good Samaritan," Eric Gregory examines Barth's interpretation of the parable of the Good Samaritan against the background of a lack of sustained attention to Barth in the field of Christian ethics today and particularly of his use of Scripture in his ethical reflection. Gregory contends that Barth swims against the stream of commonplace interpretations of the parable of the Good Samaritan that would view it simply as an appeal to care for the neighbor in need. Such moralistic interpretation enshrines the drive of the modern liberal mentality to remove all of the world's sufferings, often ending in "compassion fatigue." Kantian duty replaces the liberating good news of the gospel. By contrast, Barth emphasizes the "grace in the commandment," and understands the parable of the Good Samaritan as bearing witness in the first place not to our duty but to the surprising grace of God. The grace decisively embodied in the person and work of Jesus Christ is reflected in the Samaritan—the stranger who comes to the rescue of the one lying injured on the road. At the same time, the injured and needy person of this parable confronts us, as in the parable of Matthew 25, with the poverty and wounds of Christ and thus not primarily with a task but a hidden gift and blessing. Gregory is careful to point out that Barth's reversal of common understandings of the parable does not result in ecclesiocentrism. According to Barth, the witness of Jesus Christ is present in and beyond the church, in neighbors near and far. While Gregory recognizes real limitations in Barth's contributions to ethics, he nevertheless underscores the importance of Barth's prioritizing of grace in relation to law and his "aversion to an ethical system that cranks out solutions" but leaves us bereft of the message of good news.

Chapter 4. In his chapter "A Rich Disciple? Barth on the Rich Young Ruler," Willie James Jennings sets Barth's exposition of the story of the rich young man in the context of Switzerland during the early years of World War II, where banks dutifully managed resources of the Nazi economy and Jewish refugees were at the Swiss border seeking to escape from genocide. In reminding us of this context, Jennings's point is that Barth's exposition of this Gospel story does not occur in a vacuum but in the concrete reality of the Switzerland of his time. By extension, Barth's reading of the rich young man's encounter with Jesus continues to speak with power to self-sufficient

Introduction

and complacent Western Christians who offer Jesus "ritualized obedience" and do not realize how risky it is to ask Jesus what they must do to inherit eternal life. As Barth understands the plight of the rich young man, there is, in Jennings's words, "a formation in the faith that thwarts faith." The masters are unaware that their mastery is in fact a crippling captivity. Yet Jesus's response is not condemnation; instead, it is love, and especially love for the poor and the needy, precisely what the self-enclosed man who questions Jesus about eternal life is unwilling to risk. Jennings brings home his deeply insightful reading of Barth's exposition by noting how the rich young man's (and our) assumed theological mastery is resourced by financial mastery. In addition, Jennings notes how Barth's reading of the subsequent discussion of the disciples exposes their hidden desire to be the rich man. All this challenges readers of Barth's exposition of the story to realize the extent to which our existence is "enfolded in banking interests" and to ask whether we are truly open to be part of the new Adam rather than the old Adam.

Chapter 5. In "The Compassion of Jesus Christ: Barth on Matthew 9:36," Paul T. Nimmo first places Barth's treatment of this text in the wider context of his comprehensive doctrine of reconciliation. According to Barth, Jesus is both Son of God humbled and Son of Man exalted for our salvation. As the royal human being, Jesus realizes and manifests the true, new, exalted human being. This new humanity has many striking aspects, according to Barth, among which is the singular "compassion" of Jesus for the "crowds." Jesus's compassion for them is from the depths of his being—from his very heart, or literally, from his very "bowels." He enters into complete solidarity with them and is for them just as God is for them. Nimmo deftly draws out insights and doctrinal trajectories of Barth's analysis of Jesus's compassion for the crowds in the areas of theological anthropology and atonement theory. Our anthropology is deepened when we acknowledge that all human beings belong to the crowds on whom Jesus has compassion. Likewise, atonement theory is enriched when it takes into account the compassion of Jesus for the crowds. Jesus's life and death is not of restricted scope; its embrace is universal. Jesus takes human sin and misery into himself and in him humanity is liberated for new life and community.

Chapter 6. In "The Journey of God's Son: Barth and Balthasar on the Parable of the Lost Son," the present writer examines Barth's provocative exposition of this beloved parable and compares it with glosses on the parable by Hans Urs von Balthasar. For Barth, the journey of the son of the parable is a distant analogy to—a "faint reflection," a "copy," but also a "caricature" of—the self-humbling journey of the Son of God into the far country of fallen humanity and his joyful homecoming as the exalted Son of Man. Equally provocative are Balthasar's glosses on the parable, according to which the willingness of the father of the parable to give his all to the son is an analogy to or reflection of the "primal kenosis" in the eternal life of the triune God whereby the Father in begetting the Son gives him everything and holds nothing back. This primal act of kenosis or self-emptying is, according to Balthasar, the basis of all the self-giving acts of God in relation to the world. Concluding that Balthasar's fertile analogical reading of the parable crosses at points into the zone of trinitarian speculation, I also ask whether Barth's christocentric reading leaves underdeveloped the astonishing humility of the father of the parable and his suffering the loss of the son as well as rejoicing in his return. In brief, if this parable has any bearing on the relationship of Father and Son in the eternal triune life, it would question whether this relationship is, as Barth often contends, best described as one of "command" and "obedience." Also at work in Barth's and Balthasar's readings of the parable are different understandings of human freedom. Whereas Balthasar emphasizes human freedom as freedom of choice, and ultimately the freedom to say Yes or No to God, Barth describes true human freedom as the free and joyful Yes to God's extravagant freedom to love that is concretely extended to humankind in Jesus Christ and enlivened in us by the power of the Holy Spirit.

Chapter 7. Kendall Cox takes a different tack on the same parable in her chapter, "Parabolic Retelling and Christological Discourse: Julian of Norwich and Karl Barth on the Parable of the Lost Son," comparing the readings of the parable by Karl Barth and Julian of Norwich. She begins by noting that Barth's interpretation of the parable is often thought to be "unprecedented, and even idiosyncratic." She then shows that, on the contrary, there is a striking precedent to Barth's reading in the visionary writer Julian of Norwich. Setting the exegesis of the parable by Barth and Julian alongside one another uncovers unexpected and remarkable congruencies between the two. Just as Barth finds an analogy between the journey of the lost son of the parable and the journey of the Son of God for human salvation, so Julian discerns that outwardly the son of the parable is a fallen human and at a distance from God, but inwardly he is "the godhed," the "deerwurthy son . . . even with [equal to] the fader." Both Barth and Julian focus on the structure of the parable—the departure and the homecoming; both set it in a broader scriptural framework, and both anchor their readings in the doctrines of election and Trinity. Of equal significance in a comparison of their readings, both point to the possibility of doing Christology in the mode of parable rather than limiting the work of Christology to the abstract conceptualities to which we have become accustomed. Parable, Cox argues, complements the value we have learned to assign to narrative in theological discourse generally and in Christology in particular. Parable "facilitates a bifocality befitting the subject matter. In the parabolic form, we have an apt parallel to the content of incarnation and atonement. It corresponds to the ontologically irreducible doubleness of the person and work of Jesus Christ."

Chapter 8. In "The Riddle of Gethsemane: Barth on Jesus's Agony in the Garden," Paul Dafydd Jones examines Barth's discussion of Jesus's struggle in prayer prior to his arrest and crucifixion. Jones begins by noting that, according to Barth, the drama of Jesus's ministry narrated in the Synoptic Gospels moves from a stage in which Jesus is the acting subject, through a stage in which he not so much the actor as the one acted upon, to the final stage in which Jesus the crucified is raised from the dead. The Gethsemane prayer "not my will but thine be done" occurs crucially at the point of transition from the first to the second stage, and it has long posed the disturbing question to interpreters whether a fracture is discernible, if only for a moment, in the hypostatic union of divinity and humanity in the person of Jesus Christ. After tracing the interpretations of the Gethsemane prayer in the thought of Maximus the Confessor, John Calvin, and Friedrich Schleiermacher, Jones offers an in-depth analysis of Barth's daring treatment of this passage in *CD* IV/1. According to Barth, the "riddle" of the prayer is not limited to the questions surrounding the hypostatic union. It also and most decisively encompasses the horrible coincidence in Jesus's dark hour of the divine will and the forces of evil. Neither Barth nor Jones shies away from the confession that in his free compliance with the Father's will Jesus draws into himself the full force of God's judgment on human sin for the sake of our salvation. Jones's chapter is a masterful study of Barth's vivid depiction of the full humanity of Jesus, his "vulnerability" and his "permeability" to sin and judgment in his mission in obedience to the Father's will.

Chapter 9. Bruce L. McCormack's chapter, "The Passion of God Himself: Barth on Jesus's Cry of Dereliction," opens with the Portuguese novelist José Saramago's dramatic retelling of the Gospel narrative. The point of this retelling is that the Christian God—a God who feels no remorse for creating a world in which evil and misery are inescapable—is morally repulsive and unworthy of belief. McCormack responds to Saramago's challenge not by invoking the standard arguments of theodicy but by presenting Barth's interpretation of Jesus's cry of dereliction as the decisive expression of "the passion of God Himself." In God's identification with us in Jesus Christ—and preeminently in Jesus's experience of God-abandonment on the cross—sin, suffering, and death are taken up and overcome in the very life of God. According to Barth, in this event God accepts responsibility for the evil we have done, adding to himself what would not otherwise have been his. McCormack walks with Barth a long way but thinks we must go beyond Barth in responding to the protest-atheist challenge of Saramago. If creation is for the sake of redemption, and if redemption presupposes something to be redeemed from, then "the negative side of reality belongs to the overall positive aim as its shadow side." Describing God as "self-giving, self-donating, self-emptying love," and contending that "if God is indeed self-emptying love, then the love of God 'necessarily' overflows," McCormack offers his conclusion as a difficult personal confession of faith: Christians worship a God "whose very love for us brings us pain and suffering."

Chapter 10. In "The Self-Witness of the Risen Jesus: Karl Barth's Reading of the Emmaus Road Story," Beverly Roberts Gaventa draws attention to the fact that in Barth's exposition of the story of the two disciples unknowingly meeting and dining with the risen Jesus, it is not simply the breaking of bread that in and of itself constitutes the moment of the revelation that the crucified Jesus is risen. It is the fact that the living Jesus reveals himself in this moment; the disciples do not come to this conclusion by themselves. Gaventa also underscores the fact that Barth looks through the lens of the Emmaus episode back to the preface to Luke's Gospel and forward to the book of Acts. Comparing and contrasting Barth's exposition with that of current Lukan scholarship, she finds that Barth's emphasis that Jesus, not the disciples, is the primary agent of the Emmaus story proves to be very helpful in understanding the sequel to Luke's Gospel. Whereas many scholars suggest that in the book of Acts the activity of Jesus recedes and is replaced by the activity of the church and its leaders, Gaventa argues that Jesus is indeed present and active according to the witness of this book and that the so-called "leaders" of the church are better described as "witnesses" to the living Jesus in the power of the Holy Spirit. Cautioning that Barth's use of the Emmaus story is not a key to open all doors, Gaventa nevertheless concludes that "there is a sense in which Barth gets at the subject far better than most exegetes have done."

Chapter 11. In "The Sum of the Gospel: Barth's Intracanonical and Intertextual Interpretation of *paradidōmi*," Shannon Nicole Smythe offers an overview of Barth's remarkable exposition of the *paradidōmi* passages of the New Testament: God's "handing over" of sinners to their sinfulness; Judas's "handing over" (betrayal) of Jesus; and apostolic "handing over" of the gospel to the followers of Jesus. She argues that all this is anchored in the eternal divine election according to which the triune God determines to give himself in his Son for the sake of human salvation. Smythe explores the implication of this for an understanding of the doctrine of justification and gives special attention to the ethical implications of the "handing over" theme for Christian mission today. God's electing grace is not to special privilege or simply to future heavenly existence. It is election to participation in the apostolic witness, to join in God's missionary work in the world by handing over the gospel to all humanity.

Chapter 12. In her many years as preacher and writer, Fleming Rutledge has often found help in the theology of Karl Barth. Her sermon "What's in Those Lamps? A Sermon on Matthew 25:1–13" was delivered at the 2015 Barth Conference several days after the murders of nine black church members engaged in Bible study in the Emanuel African Methodist Episcopal Church in Charleston, South Carolina. Rutledge's timely sermon on a familiar parable of Jesus shines a bright light into the darkness of that event, and is reminiscent of the power and relevance of many of Barth's sermons in crisis situations. As indicated in the title of one of her books—*The Bible and the New York Times*, Rutledge takes seriously Barth's oft-quoted comment that the work of theology involves having the Bible in one hand and the newspaper in the other.

1 The Election of Grace

Barth on the Doctrine of Predestination

JÜRGEN MOLTMANN

In 1942, in his preface to vol. II/2 of the *Church Dogmatics* Karl Barth wrote:

> I would have preferred to follow Calvin's doctrine of predestination much more closely, instead of departing from it so radically. . . . [But] as I let the Bible itself speak to me on these matters, as I meditated upon what I seemed to hear, I was driven irresistibly to reconstruction. And now I cannot but be anxious to see whether I shall be alone in this work, or whether there will be others who will find enlightenment in the basis and scope suggested.[1]

Between 1950 and 1952, I worked on my dissertation on the seventeenth-century Calvinist doctrines of predestination in Calvin, Beza, Gomarus, and Moyse Amyraut,[2] and ever since I have been among the "others" who greeted Karl Barth's "reconstruction" gratefully and with deep relief, and who have been "enlightened" by the reasoning and scope of his christological renewal of the doctrine of predestination.

In this chapter I propose to consider Barth's section 32 under the heading "Predestination or Election of Grace?" and shall then look at section 33 in the light of the question "Double Predestination in Jesus Christ?" I shall

---

1. *CD* II/2, x.
2. Jürgen Moltmann, "Prädestination und Heilsgeschichte bei Moyse Amyraut. Ein Beitrag zur Geschichte der reformierten Theologie zwischen Orthodoxie und Aufklärung," *Zeitschrift für Kirchengeschichte* 65/66 (1953/1954): 207–303.

emphasize Barth's reconstructions, and shall then draw on Martin Luther and the Lutheran Paul Gerhardt in order to reinforce the Barthian doctrine of the election of grace. Finally, I shall deal with God's electing and rejecting in the reign of Christ, to bring Barth's theology and political theology into dialogue.

Predestination or God's Election of Grace? The *Decretum Horribile*[3]

Ever since Calvin and Theodor of Beza, the Reformed doctrines of predestination have given rise to many misunderstandings and have done a great deal of mental and spiritual damage. Max Weber called the doctrine "emotional inhumanity."[4] "I may go to hell, but such a God will never command my respect," was already John Milton's cry.[5] "It represents the most holy God as worse than the devil, as both more false, more cruel, and more unjust," John Wesley disgustedly complained.[6]

And it is true: the idea that the almighty God should from eternity choose some persons and damn the others is a hellish message. What it evokes is not faith; it is fatalism. This is a cruel, arbitrary God, who plunges his human beings into the torments of hell by making them ask: Am I among the elect, or am I damned?

Yet according to Theodor of Beza, Calvin's successor in Geneva, God actually shows his "sublime glory" by predestining the one to eternal bliss and the other to eternal damnation; and out of this idea he developed a whole dogmatics on a single page, not on ten thousand, like Barth.[7] It begins with divine election and rejection, and finishes with human blessedness and damnation. It begins by affirming that God's ways are unfathomable, and ends: "How incomprehensible are his judgments! Who has given him and repaid him anything beforehand and requited him?" (Rom. 11:33, 35). That is the Calvinist doctrine of decrees which Barth struggles with and which he formulated afresh in his doctrine of the election of grace.

What experience lies behind the ancient doctrine of predestination? It is the experience that one and the same proclaimed Word of God awakens

---

3. "Dreadful decree." See John Calvin, *Institutes of the Christian Religion* III.23.7.
4. Max Weber, "Die protestantische Ethik und der Geist des Kapitalismus," in *Gesammelte Aufsätze zur Religionssoziologie*, vol. 1, 4th ed. (Tübingen: Mohr, 1947), 17–206.
5. Quoted in Barth, *CD* II/2, 13.
6. John Wesley, Free Grace Sermon 128, 1740.
7. Heppe/Bizer, *Die Dogmatik der evangelisch-reformierten Kirche* (Neukirchen: Neukirchener Verlag, 1958), 119.

faith in one person and unbelief in another.[8] The believer hears the call of the gospel, and knows that he is chosen, justified, and sanctified. The unbeliever does not hear any call from God, so he is necessarily not chosen, not justified, and not sanctified. Just as the believer owes his faith not to himself but to God's gracious election, in the same way the unbeliever has to put his unbelief down to God's non-election. That is the conclusion of the circular argument of double predestination: The believer has been elected—whoever has been elected, believes. The person who is damned does not believe— whoever does not believe is damned.

This dualism of belief and unbelief is rather harmless in our liberal and secular societies, and without consequences. Everyone can believe or not believe what he wants. We have the "freedom of religion." In the Islam-interpretation of the terror-organization ISIS in Iraq and Syria this division of the world into believers and unbelievers has murderous consequences: Whoever does not believe must die.

It is the invaluable merit of Karl Barth to have overcome this dualism of belief and unbelief in Christian theology. Islamic theology can also overcome this dualism, if they start with Allah, the "All-merciful" (ar-Rahman) instead of debating the true identity of a "good Muslim."[9]

However: Before we speculate about the election of the one and the rejection of the other we have to look at God and at God's self-determination. Before God elects and condemns human beings, God elects himself. That is God's election of grace. Before God says, "You shall be my people," he says, "I will be your God."

Election as the Sum of the Gospel

At the beginning of II/2, Barth starts his chapter 7, "The Election of God," with a section (§32) titled "The Problem of a Correct Doctrine of the Election of Grace." The introductory paragraph comprises these four sentences:

> [1] The doctrine of election is the sum of the Gospel because of all the words that can be said or heard it is the best: that God elects man; that God is for man too the One who loves in freedom. [2] It is grounded in the knowledge of Jesus Christ because He is both the electing God and

---

8. See H. Otten, *Calvins theologische Anschauung von der Prädestination* (Munich, 1938).
9. M. Khorschide, *Islam ist Barmherzigkeit* (Freiburg: Herder, 2012).

elected man in one. [3] It is part of the doctrine of God because originally God's election of man is a predestination not merely of man but of Himself. [4] Its function is to bear fundamental testimony to eternal, free and unchanging grace as the beginning of all the ways and works of God.[10]

I have inserted numbers for these four sentences because I now propose to look at each of these sentences as Karl Barth intended them to be understood, interpreting them in his own words.

1. Barth shifted the discussion of predestination from the explanation of why there are believers and unbelievers into the universal proclamation of the gospel. Unbelievers do not need a theological explanation of why they are not believing or why they cannot believe; they need only the testimony of the gospel. Believers do not condemn unbelievers; they pray for them because God is the God of hope for unbelievers as well as believers.

The gospel of Jesus Christ proclaims God's election of grace: God turns toward human beings in Christ. That is pure grace, merciful love, patient hope. It is the overflowing love that accords with God's being. It is founded on God's primal decision to live in community with another than himself. Barth calls this an "election," thereby basing the Reformed doctrine of decrees on this one primal divine decree. "God in His love elects another to fellowship with Himself. First and foremost this means that God makes a self-election in favour of this other. He ordains that He should not be entirely self-sufficient as He might be. He determines for Himself that overflowing, that movement, that condescension."[11] This "election of grace" is the gospel in a nutshell. It has its sole foundation in God's freedom and is not a reaction on God's part to human sin. In this sense Barth's doctrine of the election of grace is in dogmatic terms supralapsarian. Just as the word "grace" describes God's commitment, the word "election" describes God's freedom. Barth is so acutely aware of his "revision" that he devotes many pages of small print to a discussion of the Reformed tradition—a rarity with him.

2. God's election of grace is manifest only in Jesus Christ. In accordance with the doctrine of the two natures, Barth calls Jesus Christ "the electing God" and "the elected human being" in one. Jesus Christ is "God in His commitment to the human being" or, to be more precise, to all human beings represented by the one human being, Jesus of Nazareth. Here Barth does not yet distinguish between Israel and the nations, but talks about "*das Menschen-*

---

10. *CD* II/2, 3.
11. *CD* II/2, 10.

volk" (all people). What Barth says is dominated by strict christocentricism: "Everything which comes from God takes place 'in Jesus Christ.'"[12] This is "the primal history which is played out between God and this one man": "The general (the world or man) exists for the sake of the particular," i.e., Jesus Christ.[13]

3. God's election of grace belongs to the doctrine of God, and only after that to human soteriology. God is not only "almighty" as the Reformed doctrines of predestination stress; he is first of all determinative of himself. Barth expresses this through the concept of God's primal self-determination. In choosing the human being, God first of all chooses himself on behalf of the human being. It follows: God's Yes to the world is based on God's self-affirmation. He desires this creation as truly as he wills himself. He affirms human beings with the power of his self-affirmation.

4. That means, fourthly, that the function of the doctrine of predestination is nothing other than to be "the fundamental testimony to free and enduring grace as the beginning of all God's ways and works." At this point Barth does not as yet say anything about the end of all God's ways and works.

No one has brought out better or in a finer way what Barth develops theologically in *CD* II/2, §32 in discussion with the Reformed tradition than the Lutheran theologian Paul Gerhardt in his well-known Christmas hymn:

> Als ich noch nicht geworden war,
> da bist du mir geboren
> und hast dich mir zu eigen gar,
> eh ich dich kann erkoren.
> Eh ich durch deine Hand gemacht,
> da hast du schon bei dir bedacht,
> wie du mein wolltest werden.

> Thy love, O Lord, before my birth
> Thou didst elect to show me,
> And for my sake didst come to earth
> Before I e'er did know Thee.
> Yea, long before Thy gracious hand
> Created me, Thy grace had planned
> To make Thee mine forever.[14]

---

12. *CD* II/2, 8.
13. *CD* II/2, 8.
14. *Evangelisches Gesangbuch* 37, 2; *Evangelical Lutheran Hymnary* (St. Louis: Morning Star, 1996), Hymn 129, Stanza 2, trans. Harold R. Vetter.

The election of grace—"and as Thine own hadst chosen me"—comes from the heart of God and is not motivated by the sin of human beings. In the prevenient birth of Jesus Christ it will become flesh and blood and will be manifested "ere ever I began to be"—"ere Thee I knew"—"before I by Thy hand was made." The person who perceives this finds himself or herself already present in Jesus Christ and God's election of grace. In God's election of grace, God runs ahead of him or her. The history of Christ is the miracle of God's revealed election of grace. The universal gospel is the medium through which the overflowing love of God desires to reach all human beings.

That brings us to two theological problems raised by §32 of the *Church Dogmatics*: God's freedom and God's love, and God's will and God's nature.

God as the One Who Loves in Freedom

"God is . . . the One who loves in freedom." Is not that a matter of course? How should God love in any other way than in freedom? Even among human beings love is a freedom. No one can be compelled to love. God—the One who loves in freedom. Is not that a tautology? Are not freedom and love two sides of the same thing?

Barth adheres here to the concept of freedom of choice. God chooses human beings out of his love. God chooses himself. Has he any choices where he himself is concerned? As Barth writes: "In so far as God not only is love, but loves, in the act of love which determines His whole being, God elects."[15] It is true that Barth laments the "absolutising of the concept of electing, or of its freedom,"[16] but at the same time he adheres to his insistence on God's freedom of choice "that God should not be entirely self-sufficient as He might be."[17] But according to Barth, we know nothing about any such state in God before his election of grace. Yet the concept of "free decision" presupposes a state of this kind. It brings the "before" and "after" of time into God's eternity, and that introduces a contradiction into God.

Is *freedom of choice* really the sole or the supreme concept of freedom? According to a German saying, "*Wer die Wahl hat, hat die Qual*": "the person who must choose has the torment of choice." Freedom, I believe, is not an attribute of a subject; it is a concept of relation. It belongs to the realm

---

15. *CD* II/2, 76.
16. *CD* II/2, 25.
17. *CD* II/2, 10.

of relationships. I would assign freedom of choice to the relationship between *subject and object*, whereas the relation between *subject and subject* is dominated by a *communicative freedom*. I experience liberation when I am accepted, respected, and loved by another; I practice freedom when I for my part accept, respect, and love another. I participate, and experience participation. That is why the Reformed Federal theologians, such as Caspar Olevian, author of *De substantia foederis gratuiti inter Deum et electos* (Geneva, 1585), introduced the concept of covenant at this point. The covenant of grace is between God and the elected. It is a *covenant between subjects*.[18] The root of the German term for freedom (*Freiheit*) is relational and the same is true of the word for friendliness (*Freundlichkeit*), as the words *gastfrei* (hospitable) and *freigebig* (generous) show. Friendship (*Freundschaft*) is the concrete term for freedom.[19]

God's Will and God's Nature

Is God's will absolutely free in the election of grace? There are no external grounds that could set limits to his freedom, but are there internal ones? Barth starts from the will of the divine subject. That God "chooses," Barth argues, determines his nature. But does not God's nature also determine his will? After all, God does not choose one possibility out of an infinite number of possibilities, in an arbitrary fashion. He chooses that which corresponds to his nature. He loves because he is love. "He is faithful. He cannot deny himself" (2 Tim. 2:13). Later, Barth himself introduces the concept of "correspondence" at this point: God is free, but he corresponds to himself. He does what he desires to do, but what he desires to do is in conformity with his essential nature. So we cannot proceed solely from God's will if we want to understand his essential nature; we must also start from God's essential nature if we want to know his will.

---

18. G. Schrenk, *Gottesreich und Bund in alteren Protestantismus* (Gütersloh: Bertelsmann, 1923); J. Wayne Baker, *Heinrich Bullinger and the Covenant: The Other Reformed Tradition* (Athens: Ohio University Press, 1980).

19. See Jürgen Moltmann, *The Trinity and the Kingdom: The Doctrine of God* (San Francisco: Harper & Row, 1981), 54–55; W. Huber, *Von der Freiheit* (Munich: Beck, 2012).

JÜRGEN MOLTMANN

Double Predestination in Jesus Christ?

The following section (§33) in *CD* II/2 is titled "The Election of Jesus Christ." In discourse regarding the election of human beings, the phrase "double predestination" is traditionally used to mean not just their election but both their *election and rejection*. Do we detect in the election of Jesus Christ not just the election of human beings but their rejection as well? Let us see! The introductory paragraph for this section says:

> The election of grace is the eternal beginning of all the ways and works of God in Jesus Christ. In Jesus Christ God in His free grace determines Himself for sinful man and sinful man for Himself. He therefore takes upon Himself the rejection of man with all its consequences, and elects man to participation in His own glory.[20]

What does God elect Jesus Christ for? For suffering and dying: "The election of the man Jesus means, then, that a wrath is kindled, a sentence pronounced and finally executed, a rejection actualised."[21]

Karl Barth's doctrine of predestination is his *theology of the cross*: "The rejection which all men incurred, the wrath of God, under which all men lie, the death which all men must die, God in His love for men transfers from all eternity to Jesus Christ in whom He loves and elects them, and whom He elects at their head and in their place."[22] Our eternal Judge makes himself the one condemned for us. "God wills to lose, in order that man may gain. There is a sure and certain salvation for man, and a sure and certain risk for God."[23]

"Double predestination"—that is to say election *and* rejection, predestination to salvation *and* to perdition—are so entwined in the suffering and dying of Christ that out of the acceptance of the sinful and condemned human being there issues the election of the sinful and condemned human being. "In the election of Jesus Christ, which is the eternal will of God, God has ascribed to man, election, salvation and life; and to Himself He has ascribed the latter, reprobation, perdition, and death."[24]

What significance does this have for an understanding of God's election of grace? God chose our condemnation in his suffering and his death. "He

20. *CD* II/2, 94.
21. *CD* II/2, 122.
22. *CD* II/2, 123.
23. *CD* II/2, 162.
24. *CD* II/2, 163.

elects the cross of Golgotha as His kingly throne. He elects the tomb in the garden as the scene of His being as the living God."[25] Barth was not afraid to call the divine event on the cross the true justification of God in the face of the evil and suffering in the world of human beings: the true *theodicy*! And the election of rejected human beings is nothing other than the *justification of the sinner*!

Belief in predestination thus means "faith in the non-rejection of man, or disbelief in his rejection. Man is not rejected. In God's eternal purpose, it is God Himself, who is rejected in His Son. The self-giving of God consists, the giving and sending of His Son is fulfilled, in the fact that He is rejected in order that we might not be rejected. Predestination means that from all eternity God has determined upon man's acquittal at His own cost. It means that God has ordained, that in the place of the one acquitted He Himself should be perishing and abandoned and rejected—the Lamb slain from the foundation of the world."[26] Predestination in Jesus Christ is the non-rejection of the human being—of all human beings.

Barth finds the positive element, which he circumscribes through the expression non-rejection, in "God's overflowing glory."[27] For in the outward flowing of God's glory, the human creature is predestined to blessedness and the promise of eternal life. "The suffering borne on the cross of Golgotha by the son of man in unity with the Son of God . . . is a stage on the road, an unavoidable point of transition, to the glory of the resurrection, ascension and session."[28] Just as Christ was sacrificed for our sins and raised for our justification (Rom. 4:25), so he is rejected and raised for our election and glorification.

It is remarkable that Barth complements his concept of free will, the election of grace, by way of the neo-Platonic concept of "God's overflowing glory." In the progressive logic of his ideas, we should actually expect in place of the negation of the negation, non-rejection, the positive concept of "election" or "election of grace." Barth, however, goes beyond this with "God's overflowing glory," a concept of being. For we are not talking here about the simple concept of election, but about an election that proceeds from the substitutionary assumption of rejection. Consequently the initial concept "election of grace" is too general. This is a position that proceeds

---

25. *CD* II/2, 165.
26. *CD* II/2, 167.
27. *CD* II/2, 170, 173, and frequently.
28. *CD* II/2, 173.

from the negation of the negative and is consequently irrefutable and certain (cf. Rom. 8:31–39).

Martin Luther had already sought and found in a pastoral context what Karl Barth so impressively describes in dogmatic terms. Talk about double predestination has always evoked more fear than assurance. Everyone who takes this idea seriously thinks of his own rejection: being damned to all eternity. Ever since the Middle Ages two fears have made themselves felt in this sector: The *tentatio de indignitate*: am I sufficiently worthy that God should choose me? And the *tentatio de particularitate*: many are called, but few are chosen. Why me? Why should I be among the few chosen?

These anxieties drove the young Luther mad; he felt the hellish torments of the damned. Johann von Staupitz, the general prior of his Augustinian order, then gave him the wise counsel: *Si vis disputare predestinatione, incipe a vulneribus Christi. Tunc cessabit simul omnia disputatio de predestinatione* (If you wish to think about predestination, begin with the wounds of Christ. Then all your uncertainty about predestination will immediately vanish).

What does the person who has been plunged into the torments of hell discover in the wounds of Christ? He finds the one who was even more completely forsaken by God and who suffers the torments of the deepest hell. He will become "like in form" to the Christ, who suffered from God, and this *conformitas Christi*—this "con-formity" with Christ—saves him.

> "Verissimum itaque signum predestinationnis et immediatum est conformitas passionis Christi."

> The true and direct token of predestination is conformity with the sufferings of Christ.

The person who perceives his sufferings in the sufferings of Christ will become "like in form" and enters into fellowship with him. He then recognizes that Christ has overcome for him his damnation and his hellish torments and is taking him with him on his way to resurrection and eternal life. That is why Luther translates 1 Corinthians 15:55 as *"Hölle, wo is den Sieg?*—Hell, where is thy victory?"

Luther found Johann von Staupitz's advice consoling and liberating, and in 1519 passed it on himself in his "Sermon on the Preparation for Dying":

> Thou needest not contemplate the hell and eternity of torment, not in thyself, nor in those who are damned, nor must thou concern thyself with

so many persons in the whole world. Look upon the heavenly picture of Christ, who for thy sake descended into hell and was forsaken by God as one, who was eternally damned, as he said on the cross: "Eli, eli lema sabachthani." See, in that picture thy hell is overcome and thy uncertain predestination made sure. . . . Seek thyself only in Christ and not in thyself, and then thou willst find thyself eternally in him.[29]

It is only in the crucified and risen Christ that God's rejection and election become manifest to human beings. Karl Barth is in good company. For Calvin, too, Christ was the mirror of predestination: Christ is the "*speculum electionis,*" the mirror of election, in which the Calvinist believer in the seventeenth century detects his election, not his bank account, as Max Weber mockingly said about the Calvinists and their *syllogismus practicus.*

Electing and Rejecting in the Reign of Jesus Christ

I am adding a chapter of my own to the presentation of Karl Barth's christological doctrine of predestination to bring Barth's theology into dialogue with political theology, and I hope my effort is in his spirit.[30] Barth has shown us how God has taken the rejection and damnation of sinful humankind upon Godself in the suffering and death of Christ on the cross, in order to give us his election of grace, the overflowing of his glory. This leads to the question of how election and rejection are working in the reign of the risen Christ.

Different from the missionary tradition, the prophetic traditions of the Bible do not speak of God's electing and rejecting in view of personal belief or unbelief, but in view of human injustice and godless violence in God's beloved world. Whom does the God of Israel and of Jesus Christ elect and whom does this God reject and with what purpose does the Lord elect and reject?

Luke 4:18 reports that Jesus preached the gospel of the kingdom not to everybody in general, but especially "to the poor," the "captives," the "blind," and the "broken-hearted," to set at liberty all "who are bruised." The

---

29. Martin Luther, *WA* 2, 690. See Ernst Wolf, *Staupitz und Luther* (Leipzig, 1927); E. Vogelsang, *Der Angefochtene Christus bei Luther* (Göttingen, 1932).

30. See Jürgen Moltmann, *On Human Dignity: Political Theology and Ethics* (Philadelphia: Fortress, 1984).

"Damned of This Earth," as Frantz Fanon put it, those who are excluded by a self-righteous society and who are humiliated by a violent class, are the ones God has elected to hear the gospel of the kingdom. The jobless and the homeless and the migrants in this unjust world receive the "election of grace." The lost will be found, the last will be the first, and hope is coming to the desperate.

When Mary became pregnant she believed God had seen the low estate of his handmaiden and had chosen her to be mother of the Savior of the world, and she felt "blessed" and sang the well-known song:

> He has put down the mighty from their seats,
> and exalted them of low degree.
> He has filled the hungry with good things,
> And the rich he has sent empty away. (Luke 1:52–53)

In the injustice of this world, God's "election of grace" is obviously one-sided and partial. God has mercy on the miserable, and the miserable are the first to experience the overflowing glory of the Lord.

The apostle Paul demonstrates the one-sided and preferential "election of grace" with the situation of the first congregation in Corinth:

> See your calling, brethren:
> not many wise men after the flesh,
> not many noble are called,
> but God has chosen the foolish things of the world
> to confound the wise,
> and God has chosen the weak things of the world
> to confound the things that are mighty. (1 Cor. 1:26–27)

Why this preference? What is the purpose? "That no flesh should glory in his presence" (1:29). This is the negative formulation of the universal truth: before God all humans are equal and belong to one human community. To reach this universal solidarity God is electing "the base things of the world, and things which are despised" (1:28) and is rejecting and confounding "things which are mighty." In other words, God chooses the side of the poor, not because of revenge or retaliation against the rich, but because of hope. God has chosen the poor in order also to redeem the rich. God has chosen the victims in order also to liberate the violent.

But how are the rich redeemed and the violent liberated? By their turning around and being reintegrated into the human community they left when they exalted themselves and began to live at the cost of others.

The prophet Isaiah announced this in a great picture:

> Every valley shall be exalted,
> and every mountain and hill shall be made low . . .
> and the glory of the Lord shall be revealed,
> and *all flesh* shall see it *together*. (Isa. 40:4–5)

The purpose and the universal goal of God's electing and rejecting in the reign of Christ is clear: The poor are not at stake, nor the rich, neither the victims nor the perpetrators. Instead, God is electing and rejecting in order to bring all humans into God's "Beloved Community." All flesh shall see the glory of the Lord *together*!

Inequality in human society is hindering God's revelation; the "beloved community" hastens redemption. The true alternative to poverty is not prosperity; the true alternative to poverty and prosperity is: *community*.

Martin Luther King underscored his great dream of the "Beloved Community" in Washington, DC, in 1963 with this prophetic vision of Isaiah 40:4–5 and declared: "This is our hope"—a hope of the universal solidarity of humankind.[31]

Predestination and Perseverance: "God is faithful"—"Resist!"

There is yet a third temptation connected with predestination, and that is the fear that one's faith and one's fight for justice may prove to be too weak to withstand the persecutions and seductions of this world. This was called the *tentatio de infirmitate fidei*. In the second Reformation period the Catholic Counter-Reformation began. In France the Huguenots were persecuted, in Austria the Lutherans, and in Italy the Waldensians. Meanwhile refugee congregations gathered together in the Protestant cities of Geneva and Strasbourg. At this time steadfastness and endurance in faith became the existential theme of the Protestant faith. It is against this historical background that we have to understand the Calvinist doctrines of predestination.[32]

---

31. Martin Luther King Jr., *I Have a Dream: Writings and Speeches That Changed the World*, ed. James M. Washington (San Francisco: Harper, 2003), 101–6.

32. Jürgen Moltmann, *Prädestination and Perseveranz: Geschichte und Bedeutung der Reformierten Lehre "de Perseverantia Sanctorum"* (Neukirchen: Neukirchener Verlag, 1961).

The assurance of election provides comfort and courage: "God is faithful, by whom you were called" (1 Cor. 1:9). "For his steadfast love endureth for ever" (Ps. 100:5). "He who began a good work in you will bring it to completion at the day of Jesus Christ" (Phil. 1:6). The spearhead of the doctrine of predestination is not the elite of believers in a mass of unbelievers (Augustine) but the *perseverance of believers* in persecution, expulsion, and martyrdom. "God is the God of the eternal election of His grace. In the light of this election, the whole of the Gospel is light," wrote Karl Barth.[33] That is the true assurance of salvation: God has elected me. I can never again be lost to God. The faithfulness of God awakens steadfastness in faith and in the love for justice.

Assurance of election is not a vainglorious self-assurance; it is a humble assurance in God. But what are the theological reasons for it? Calvin had based the faith of the community on Christ. Belief means faithfulness to Christ and in temptations and persecutions, participation in the patience of Christ (see Heb. 10:32; 12:2; James 5:7; Rev. 1:9; 2:2; 13:10). In other words, faith includes acceptance of suffering for Christ's sake, and acceptance of that suffering with Christ. "He who endures to the end will be saved" (Matt. 10:22). What is "the end"? It is the coming parousia of Christ, the kingdom of God. That is the reason why the "patience of Christ" is always at the same time a "steadfastness of hope" (1 Thess. 1:3). According to Calvin, faith in Christ is the foundation on which hope rests, but hope for its part strengthens and nourishes faith.[34] With the biblical witness, Calvin teaches that we are called to endure until all things are perfected. But how can one hold fast to faith if one becomes weak in the allurements, persecutions, and seductions? Calvin's answer: "There can be no doubt that when Christ prays for all the elect, that he implores for them the same thing as he did for Peter: that their faith may never fail (Luke 22:32). From this we infer that they are out of danger of falling away because the Son of God, asking that their godliness be kept constant, did not suffer a refusal."[35]

In the course of the second Reformation period, the assurance of not being lost for God even in persecutions and temptations, and even in spite of one's own grave sins and disappointments, is given a trinitarian foundation:

1. In the faithfulness of God the Father who does not abandon those who are his;

---

33. *CD* II/2, 14.
34. John Calvin, *Institutes of the Christian Religion* III.2.43.
35. *Institutes* III.24.6.

2. In the intercession of Jesus Christ, "that your faith may not fail";
3. In the indestructible seed of the Holy Spirit, so that there are still live embers beneath the ashes.

Believers are, Calvin writes, "sealed with the Holy Spirit." "However deficient or weak faith may be in the elect, still because the Spirit of God is for them the sure guarantee and seal of their adoption (Eph. 1:14; cf. 2 Cor. 1:22), the mark he has engraved can never be erased from their hearts."[36] The indwelling of God's Spirit is an indestructible seed, the "seed of life" (*semen vitae*) that can never be lost.[37]

In the state of Christianity today, the point throughout is that we should learn endurance in faith and in the struggle for justice. Just as we should never give up faith, so we should never give up the fight for justice.

There is a little town in the south of France by the name of *Aigues-Mortes*. In this town there is a tower called *la Tour de Constance* where the Huguenot Marie Durand endured thirty-eight years of captivity. She comforted her fellow-sufferers with a word she engraved at the exit: that word is *Résistez!—Resist!*[38] That is a good and convincing word for the doctrine of predestination!

---

36. *Institutes* III.2.12.
37. *Institutes* III.2.11.
38. D. Benoit and A. Favre, *Marie Durand* (Bienlefit, 1945).

2 Revelatory Word or Beloved Son?

Barth on the Johannine Prologue

RICHARD BAUCKHAM

Barth gave a series of lectures on the Gospel of John in Münster in 1925-26. Like many lecturers on John, he lingered disproportionately long over the Prologue, and he never got past chapter 8. He repeated the lectures in 1933 in Bonn, but they were never published in his lifetime.[1] They were published in 1976, and an English translation of the commentary on chapter 1 only by Geoffrey Bromiley appeared in 1986.

Barth's exegesis of the Prologue (John 1:1-18), which actually amounts to not much less than half of the whole commentary, is of great interest, both in itself but also because most of Barth's exegesis of parts of the Prologue in the *Church Dogmatics* is taken more or less directly from this earlier work in which he undertook a continuous exegesis of the whole Prologue. For Barth, the Johannine Prologue was a passage of key theological significance, as it had been for the Fathers especially. Barth's interest was naturally theological, but the commentary is notable for his attention to matters of text and philology, as well as theology (he recognizes that the theology cannot be separated from these more basic aspects of exegesis) and notable also for his detailed interaction with the major commentaries available in German at the time.

In this chapter I shall confine myself to Barth's commentary on selected parts of the Prologue only, those to which he also gives detailed exegeti-

---

1. These details are from Walther Fürst's preface to the 1976 German edition, translated in Karl Barth, *Witness to the Word: A Commentary on John 1; Lectures at Münster in 1925 and at Bonn in 1933*, ed. Walther Fürst, trans. Geoffrey W. Bromiley (Grand Rapids: Eerdmans, 1986) (henceforth *WW*), ix-xii.

cal attention in the *Church Dogmatics*. We shall look at verses 1–2, verse 3, and, from verse 14, the phrase "the Word became flesh." In each case I shall explain key features of Barth's exegesis in the commentary and then what he makes of the same material in the *Church Dogmatics*. This will enable a somewhat more nuanced understanding of the way he developed his theological interpretation of the Johannine Prologue than if we were to confine ourselves to the passages in the *Church Dogmatics* alone. Finally, I shall offer an assessment of Barth's exegesis of the Prologue from my own perspective as a New Testament scholar working toward writing a theological commentary on the Gospel of John.

The Word (*Logos*) as Placeholder (*Platzhalter*) (vv. 1–2)

Barth takes the unusual step of discussing verse 1 in some detail without enquiring into the meaning of the term *ho Logos*, for which, at this stage, he uses simply the transliterated form "the Logos" (*WW*, 19–22). He justifies this procedure by claiming that in none of the three clauses of this verse, in each of which the Logos is the subject, does the emphasis fall on the Logos. Moreover, he observes that "this concept . . . obviously plays for the author the role of a *locum tenens*. It is simply the provisional designation of a place which something or someone else will later fill." This explains why the term occurs only once more in the Prologue (at v. 14) and never thereafter in the Gospel.[2] At least in the Prologue as a whole, if not already in verse 2 (see below), it is clear that the term "is a substitute for Jesus Christ. His is the place which at one and the same time is occupied, reserved, and delimited by the predicates which are ascribed to the Logos" (*WW*, 22–23).

Only now does Barth enquire why the author should have selected precisely this term for the role of placeholder. He cites the various proposals that had been made about the historical background of the term, but, while agreeing that John certainly "is borrowing a well-known term current in the popular philosophical and religious vocabulary of his day," he maintains that it is impossible to know "in what specific form the Evangelist took over the concept," especially since we also do not know how far he refunctioned it for his own use. Barth does not in principle disallow this kind of historical investigation, but he does insist that, when we ask about the meaning of the

---

2. As Barth also notes, elsewhere in the New Testament it is found only in Rev. 19:13 ("the Word of God").

concept in the Gospel, then, "of course, we turn not to Philo or the Mandaeans, but exclusively to John himself" (*WW*, 24).

In effect, this ensures that we do not import into the Gospel any of the ancient usages in which "the Logos is essentially and primarily a principle, whether in epistemology or in the metaphysical explanation of the world" (*WW*, 24). In the context of the Johannine Prologue, which mentions but does not linger over the cosmogonic role ascribed to the Logos in verse 3, "the Logos is the principle of revelation, not of being, as that which challenges all that is and all being by the divine address" (*WW*, 25). Jesus Christ, for whom the Logos is here a provisional substitute, is himself "in his whole manifestation" the Word, the Revealer who reveals himself. At this point Barth abandons the use of the transliterated form "Logos"[3] (which, of course, may mean more or other than "word"):

> In John Logos means Word, and perhaps we do best not to add to this, not even perhaps to make the addition Creator-Word which recollection of Gen. 1:1 suggests. (*WW*, 26)

Accordingly, *ho Logos* in the Johannine Prologue is "like the x in the equation whose value will appear only when the equation is solved" (*WW*, 27). This analogy might prove misleading if it suggests that the term is a mere cipher with no meaning at all until Jesus Christ replaces it. It does mean "word," and, as *the* Word, "the Word of all words" (*WW*, 26), it is spoken by God. The x in the equation is in fact not a cypher with no meaning at all, since in the context of the equation we do know that it stands for a number. As Barth says, it "gives the unknown factor its place, its relation to the other numbers." Similarly, in the Johannine Prologue, the term "word" stands in for some kind of divine revelation, as does the term "light" in verses 2–8. Verse 1 puts what it calls "the word" *in its place* in relation to God, while subsequent verses prior to verse 14 put it *in its place* in relation to "the world, humanity, the witnesses, believers" (*WW*, 27). In this sense *ho Logos* is the verbal placeholder for Jesus Christ, who is not named until verse 17.

Barth's distinctive interpretation of verse 2 of the Prologue reinforces the notion of the Word as placeholder. At first sight this verse (*houtos ēn en archē pros ton theon*) seems merely to repeat what has already been said in the first two clauses of verse 1. Barth complains that the commentators,

---

3. He does not do this consistently through the rest of the commentary, but he uses "Word" predominantly and "Logos" only occasionally.

most of whom say that it is just such a recapitulation, do not explain why a recapitulation should be necessary. Adolf Schlatter alone advances an explanation that Barth finds convincing. This is that the demonstrative pronoun *houtos*, usually thought to refer back to the immediately preceding mention of *ho Logos*, not only refers backwards but also points forwards to the name Jesus Christ that appears only much later in the Prologue (*WW*, 28–29). It means "this person"—the person who is the subject of the whole Prologue, though not named until verse 17. The view that the whole Prologue is about Jesus, on which all exegetes agree, Barth says is based on the impression the whole Prologue makes, but exegetically "its correctness can be demonstrated only if the *houtos* of v. 2 does not refer back[4] to the *ho logos* of v. 1c but is a first and purely indicatory filling of the place that is marked out by the term Logos and its predicates in v. 1" (*WW*, 28). (It may be that here Barth is aware that, if *houtos* did merely refer back to *ho Logos*, then it would supply precisely that emphasis on the Logos as such that Barth finds missing in verse 1.)

We should note that, in making this rather eccentric exegetical choice, Barth is not engaged in purely theological eisegesis, but makes an ordinary exegetical case for it and relies on the fact that it had already been proposed by a significant biblical scholar. But it is clearly for him a theologically very important point of exegesis, and he was to repeat it again and again in the *Church Dogmatics* (at least eight times).[5]

In the context of the commentary, its theological value is that it necessitates understanding verse 1c (*theos ēn ho logos*) "as an identification by nature of two distinct persons. For alongside the person denoted by *ho theos* the *houtos* that partakes of the same *theotēs*, the Logos, has also come in *person*" (*WW*, 29). (Barth is doubtless aware that, if *houtos* merely refers back to *ho logos*, it need not have a personal sense. The masculine noun *logos* would require the masculine pronoun *houtos*.)

In the context of the commentary, the notion that the whole Prologue is about Jesus Christ is probably understood by Barth in no stronger terms than the traditional understanding of the hypostatic union, according to which there is continuity of hypostasis between the preincarnate Logos and the incarnate one. He is not yet concerned to claim that we cannot know the *Logos asarkos*, but only the *Logos ensarkos*, who is Jesus Christ, the God-

---

4. Barth seems to oscillate between saying that *houtos* refers both backwards and forwards and saying that it refers only forwards.

5. *CD* I/1, 137, 401; I/2, 133; II/2, 98; III/1, 54; III/2, 66, 483; IV/2, 33.

human. This seems clear from a comment on verse 4 ("In him was life and the life was the light of humans"):

> Inasmuch as every word here relates to Jesus Christ, it also relates to the Logos as the Revealer of God who announces himself before *and even apart from* Jesus of Nazareth. . . . What the author wants to say is that whatever was revelation, the light of life, redemption for men, was so only in him . . . in the same Word that took flesh in Jesus Christ, alongside which there never was or can be any other Word. (*WW*, 43; my italics)

The only divine Word is the Word who became incarnate as Jesus Christ, but the revelatory activity of this Word can be envisaged as occurring apart from Jesus Christ. Barth here appeals to the *Extra Calvinisticum*.

Verses 1–2 *in the* Church Dogmatics

The remarkable fact about Barth's exegesis of the first two verses of the Johannine Prologue is that it passes unchanged into the *Church Dogmatics*, but acquires there a significance it does not have in the commentary. In the commentary, in the light of Barth's unusual exegesis of verse 2, he can say that Jesus Christ was in the beginning with God, and those familiar with Barth's mature theology will inevitably think of his doctrine of election, that is, of the election in eternity of the God-human Jesus Christ as God's self-determination to be, in him, the God who creates, loves, and redeems the world. But in the commentary Barth says nothing of this. In the commentary Barth stays with the self-revelation of God to the world and does not raise the issue of its basis in God's eternal self-determination. The theological significance he there finds in his exegesis of verse 2 is that it helps to establish the doctrine of the Trinity by making it clear that the Word is a personal subject, not an impersonal principle. His view that the term Logos serves only as a verbal placeholder for Jesus Christ highlights the incarnation as the real subject of the whole Prologue. It means that what is said of the Word before incarnation is said only for the sake of the light it throws on the incarnation itself. But the continuity between the Word in the beginning and the Word made flesh is not here said to lie in an eternal divine choice to become human. It lies in what is much more obvious in the text of the Prologue itself: the continuity of divine subject before and in incarnation.

In the *Church Dogmatics* Barth puts the same exegesis to a different theological use, mainly just by inserting it into a specific theological context. This happens in *CD* II/2, §33.2, the section titled "Jesus Christ, Electing and Elected." Here Barth reproduces the whole of his exegesis of John 1:1–2 from the commentary (95–98).[6] He omits hardly anything, other than some references to commentators, and makes only a few substantial additions. It is clear that he now understands the exegesis he had developed in the commentary as the scriptural basis for the distinctive doctrine of election that he expounds in this section.

However, among the additions he makes to the text lifted from the commentary are a few that serve to orientate the exegesis in the direction of the theological use to which he is now putting it. Of special interest are two that speak of the relation of eternity to time. Of the threefold "was" (*ēn*) of verse 1, Barth says:

> It points to an eternal happening and to a temporal: to an eternal in the form of time, and to a temporal with the content of eternity. (97)

This seems to mean that "the beginning" to which verse 1 refers designates the transition from eternity to time, so that what the verse says of the Word, i.e., of Jesus, is true in both eternity and time. It is an event in both eternity and time. Commenting on verse 2, and following his unusual claim that *houtos* there refers to Jesus, Barth says:

> we have no need to project anything into eternity, for at this point eternity is time, i.e. the eternal name has become a temporal name, and the divine name a human. It is of this name that we speak. (98)

These comments draw out the implications of saying that Jesus Christ was in the beginning with God in a way that is not explicit in the commentary but makes a connection with the concerns of Barth's understanding of election.

By way of exegesis of verse 3 of the Prologue, Barth does not here follow what he said in his commentary, but instead connects that verse with the various other New Testament texts that relate Jesus Christ to creation in order to make again the general point that these texts speak not of a Word or Son of God *in abstracto*, but, *in concreto*, of Jesus Christ (98–99). He is not

---

6. This exegetical section continues with comment on verse 3 (98–99), but this consists of little more than relating that verse of John to the other New Testament texts that relate Jesus Christ to creation. It owes nothing to his comments on verse 3 in the commentary.

at this point especially interested in the relationship of Christ to creation, but in the point that his exegesis of verse 3 of the Prologue made: that *Jesus Christ* was in the beginning. So

> in this person we are called upon to recognize the beginning of the Word and decree and election of God, the conclusive and absolute authority in respect of the aim and origin of all things.... We are not thinking rightly of God Himself if we do not take as our starting-point the fact which should be both "first and last": that from all eternity God elected to bear this name. Over against all that is really outside God, Jesus Christ is the eternal will of God, the eternal decree of God and the eternal beginning of God. (99)

Moreover, as Barth goes on to develop this doctrine of election in its two aspects—Jesus Christ as the electing God and as the elected man—he continues to claim that it derives from John 1:1-2 (*CD* II/2, 104, cf. 117, 145).[7]

Mary Cunningham claims that, in connection with his doctrine of election in the *Church Dogmatics*, Barth mounts "a spirited *exegetical* assault on the notion of a *Logos asarkos*."[8] Within this exegetical assault, the first few verses of the Johannine Prologue play a particularly prominent part. Without an understanding of Barth's particular exegesis of these verses, this may seem very odd, since the Prologue is precisely the passage that states that "the Word became flesh," implying, surely, that the beginning of the Prologue speaks of the Word before the Word became flesh, i.e., of the *Logos asarkos*. In Barth's understanding of the first two verses, however, the Word is already, in the beginning, identified with Jesus Christ, the God-human. Barth is clearly not denying the reality of the temporal becoming of verse 14. What he means by his reading of the opening verses has two levels. In the first place, it relates to our knowledge of God. Jesus Christ, the incarnate Word, is completely and exclusively God's self-revelation. Thus we know only the Word *ensarkos*. But also, secondly, Barth means that Jesus Christ

---

7. David Gibson, *Reading the Decree: Exegesis, Election and Christology in Calvin and Barth* (London: T&T Clark [Continuum], 2009), 53, observes that "the Prologue exegesis is not there *in the first instance* to make the immediate point that Christ is the subject of election." This is true, but Barth certainly claims that his continuing argument, especially for Jesus Christ as the electing God, is based on John 1:1-2 (*CD* I/2, 104).

8. Mary Cunningham, *What Is Theological Exegesis?: Interpretation and Use of Scripture in Barth's Doctrine of Election* (Valley Forge, PA: Trinity Press International, 1995), 23 (my italics).

was in the beginning because the incarnation was God's eternal purpose: from all eternity he elected to bear the name Jesus Christ. This is why we know God only in the Word *ensarkos*. The Word *ensarkos* is who and what God is for us.

It is only Jesus Christ who gives content to the otherwise purely abstract idea of God's self-revelation. This is what Barth meant by calling the term *ho Logos* merely a verbal placeholder. It is what he means when he speaks of a *Logos asarkos* or even an eternal divine Son as *in abstracto*, as opposed to the concrete person, Jesus Christ. However, it is quite consistent with this view that Barth does not reject the notion of a *Logos asarkos* completely. He says that it

> has shown itself necessary to the christological and trinitarian reflections of the Church. Even today it is indispensable for dogmatic enquiry and presentation, and it is often touched upon in the New Testament, though nowhere expounded directly. (III/1, 54)

He surely means that the notion of the incarnation itself would be unintelligible unless we could, in a purely theoretical way, think the divine Logos apart from the human nature he assumed. Precisely as an abstraction, but only as an abstraction, the notion of the *Logos asarkos* is necessary. It is, so to speak, an element in the concept of the *Logos ensarkos*, but this does not justify making it an independent object of theological reflection.[9]

This presumably makes sense of the following rather surprising exception to Barth's general rule that the New Testament never refers to the second person of the Trinity apart from the man Jesus:

> The event attested in Jn 1[14] is one to which the whole Prologue looks back. So, then, the whole Prologue *(with the possible exception of the first phrase of v. 1)*—although it certainly speaks of the eternal Son—speaks also of the man Jesus. (IV/2, 33; my italics)

The fact that Barth can even contemplate a *possible* exception here is significant. The exegetical logic of this possible exception, which Barth does not explain, can perhaps be reconstructed. Barth's exegesis of verse 2 depends on arguing that it cannot simply recapitulate what was already said in verse 1,

---

9. Cunningham, *What Is Theological Exegesis?*, 38, argues that the minimal role Barth allows to the *Logos asarkos* serves to emphasize the freedom of God's decision.

which it would do if *houtos* merely referred back to *ho Logos*. It must therefore refer forward to Jesus Christ. But if this is, so to speak, the *plus* of verse 2 in relation to verse 1, then does it not follow that verse 1, before the *houtos* of verse 2, refers to the Word in itself, not yet as Jesus Christ? There would then be, so to speak, a moment in which readers contemplate the divine Word as such before immediately recognizing that it is identical with the figure of Jesus Christ. Barth does not take this option, but it shows that his rejection of the *Logos asarkos* was not so absolute as to rule out this exegetical option.

Creation through the Word (v. 3)

In commenting on verse 1, Barth had made it very clear that the Word is "the principle of revelation, not of being" (*WW*, 25). This distinguishes the Johannine Word from the Logos that functions as an element in a metaphysical explanation of the world, as in Stoicism and in Philo. He did allow that the Logos is given a cosmogonic role, a mediating role in creation, in verse 3, but that "in the total context of the Prologue" this is "obviously an episode, a subordinate element in the picture" (*WW*, 25). A key question to be faced in his exegesis of verse 3 would therefore seem to be how this subordinate element is related to the overall theme of the Prologue, which is God's self-revelation in Jesus Christ.

Barth allows that what is said in verse 3 (along with other New Testament passages that say that the world was created "through" [*dia*] Jesus Christ[10]) does parallel the role not only of Philo's Logos but also of other mediating figures in the religious systems of the time. This widespread notion of cosmological mediation was popular because it was a solution to "the riddle of the world": how the transcendent God can relate to this world. Of the notion of a Revealer who alone can bind God and the world together, Barth says: "Natural and revealed theology do not disagree but agree on this point." He does not hesitate to say that on this point the New Testament writers affirm a thought that was common in their day. He even observes, more generally, that many of the New Testament's "most important statements may be heard everywhere [in the world of their time] in a more or less clear form, that the time ... seemed to have a general awareness of what needed simply to be given its proper name and proclaimed as a reality by the Christian church" (*WW*, 31). This is Barth's theological accommodation of the kind of approach to the New Testament that was characteristic of the *religionsgeschichtliche Schule* of his time.

10. 1 Cor. 8:6; Col. 1:16; Heb. 1:2.

However, Barth does also distinguish the New Testament writers from the non-Christian parallels in that their interest in the concept of a mediatory figure such as the Logos was primarily christological. Their "aim is to give Jesus Christ his place, and then to give God and the world their places" (*WW*, 32). But he goes on to find the specific intent of the verse in the distinction between the Logos and all created things, such that nothing in the created world enjoys the immediate relationship with God that the Logos has. Creation's existence depends on the Logos. It is notable that, although Barth has previously stressed that the Mediator is Jesus Christ, in this discussion of creation and mediation he speaks only of the Logos, not of Jesus Christ. He has not really been able to integrate this verse into his understanding of the whole Prologue as concerned with the self-revelation of God in Jesus Christ. That the Word is the placeholder for Jesus seems at this point to make little difference.

Verse 3 *in the* Church Dogmatics

Whereas Barth was able to take over the whole of his exegesis of the first two verses of the Prologue into the *Church Dogmatics*, in the case of his exegesis of verse 3 far less of it survives into the *Church Dogmatics*. He has, indeed, an important passage in *CD* III/1, §41.1 ("Creation, History and Creation History"), presented as a discussion of all the New Testament passages that relate Christ to creation (51–56),[11] that begins with the same observation that began his treatment of John 1:3 in the commentary: "the notion of a second divine being assisting in the work of creation had become general" in the period of the New Testament writers. For this notion he borrows the description he had composed for the commentary, but he also adds much more detail about the Old Testament and Jewish figure of Wisdom. Barth still allows that the New Testament writers were referring to this widespread notion, but insists that they did not borrow it (52). The distinctiveness of what they had to say is considerably sharpened, by comparison with the commentary. It turns out to be actually contradictory. Barth says that they

> were the bearers of the objective, shattering message of the kingdom of God drawn near, and the consequent end of all mediating philosophy, theosophy and cosmology. As against the views of their contemporaries,

---

11. Much of the argument here is presented again, more briefly, in *CD* II/2, 83–84.

which seemed to be so similar, they could not have spoken more critically than they did when they described Jesus Christ as the One "through whom" or "in whom" God had created all things. (53)

A key difference is that Jesus Christ is the Mediator between God and humanity, but he is so as being both God and man, not as "an intermediate being, a third between the two" (53).

Thus in place of the convergence of natural and revealed theology that Barth entertained in the commentary, he now envisages an "apocalyptic" confrontation. He is able to do so because, in this context, he is working consistently with the conviction that it is to Jesus Christ, the God-man, that the New Testament writers refer in these passages about creation. Jesus Christ "existed in the counsel of God and before all creation" (51) as God's self-determination to love the world. It is in this sense, therefore, that God created the world "through him": he, Jesus Christ, is "the actual divine ground of creation" and "the peculiar creative causality." Whereas in his commentary on verse 3 Barth was evidently able to think of the eternal Logos in relation to creation without reference to his identity as Jesus Christ, he now insists that we must, like the New Testament writers in the passages under discussion, think "more inclusively and more concretely" of the Word made flesh. They did not think of the Logos *in abstracto* or as *Logos asarkos* (54).

With reference to the Johannine Prologue, he again adduces his identification of *houtos* in verse 2 as Jesus Christ, and again finds it decisively important: "We shall misunderstand the whole Johannine Prologue if we fail" to recognize this point (54). On the other hand, he also claims that it "is not difficult to prove that" John 1:3 and all the other passages under discussion "refer to Jesus the Christ," true God *and also true human* (55).

The Word Became Flesh (v. 14)

Here Barth initially focuses on the verb "became" (*egeneto*), pointing out that the word has hitherto in the Prologue been used of created beings (vv. 3, 6, 12). It is what we should least expect to hear of the "divine, creative, redeeming, revealing Word, whose sovereign being and action vv. 1–13 depicted." Thus Barth claims that "the well-known paradox" of this verse [the Word became flesh] lies already in the *egeneto*. "What the predicate [*sarx*] seeks to say is proclaimed already in the copula [*egeneto*]" (*WW*, 86). This is primarily because of the antithesis (an antithesis that he says idealism is right to recognize as an antithesis) between the eternal being denoted by the *einai* of verse 1 and the concrete, contingent, historically singular coming to be that is denoted by the *ginesthai* of verse 14. Without discarding the former "and all its specific content" the Word now adds the latter "with its express and different specific content." For all their antithesis, the text requires us "to see them as definitions of one and the same subject" (87).

Turning to the word "flesh" (*sarx*), Barth allows that it can have a neutral sense (John 17:2), but aligns its use in verse 14 with passages in which it refers to "human nature in its exclusively hostile opposition to God or the Spirit, in its inability to comprehend them" (1:13; 3:6; 8:15), since this is the sense in the immediately preceding verse (v. 13) (*WW*, 87–88). Therefore the meaning of the phrase "the Word became flesh" is not primarily that the Word became a man, nor that he assumed human nature in general, though these points are included. Rather the emphasis is that the Word assumed "the fallen and corrupt human nature which needs to be sanctified and redeemed" (*WW*, 88).

As well as interpreting the word "flesh" in the negative sense, Barth is also reading verse 14 in the context of what has preceded, where a contrast was set up between the Word, on the one hand, and, on the other, the darkness, the world's failure to know him and his own people's failure to accept him (vv. 3, 10–11). This antithesis is overcome in verse 14 by "a third inconceivable thing," namely, that the Word has put himself on the side of his opponents and "is there as others are, in the midst of darkness" (*WW*, 89). Only because the Word is in this way what we are, accessible to us, can it be "God's Word as his revelation of life to us" (*WW*, 90).

Verse 14 *in the* Church Dogmatics

Much of this exegesis reappears in *CD* I/2, §15.2 ("Very God and Very Man"), where Barth's discussion of the incarnation is structured as an unpacking of the meaning of the statement: "The Word became flesh." This discussion is not itself presented as exegesis of the Johannine text, but there are passages of exegesis (151, 159–60) that consist largely of material from the commentary, while the discussion itself is certainly indebted to exegesis.

It is notable that, while repeating the commentary's reflections on the occurrences of the verb "became" (*egeneto*) in the Prologue, he substitutes for "paradox" the word "problem": "The whole problem of Jn. 1^{14} is thus expressed in this copula *egeneto*" (159). Another small difference is that, whereas in the commentary he referred to idealism only to confirm it as right in seeing the eternal being of the Logos as antithetical to historical becoming, here he is concerned explicitly to deny that the opposites are to be thought together in a Hegelian way: "we are not challenged to combine the two concepts in a third higher concept and so to abolish their object. In this case there can be no higher object in which the opposition between the two concepts would disappear. In place of this higher concept stands the name of Jesus Christ" (160).

With regard to the meaning of "flesh," Barth gives much more attention than he did in the commentary to the implications that the commentary did not deny—that the Word became human in a general sense and also a particular human being (147–51)—but he also continues to maintain the negative meaning: "Flesh is the concrete form of human nature marked by Adam's fall" (151). Exegetically, his account here is less satisfactory than that in the commentary, since he does not refer to the specific meanings of "flesh" in the Gospel of John, but only to what the "New Testament calls *sarx*." But he repeats from the commentary the argument from the preceding context of John 1:14 that the Logos in incarnation adopts the situation of what is opposed to him and thus overcomes it (151).

A Johannine Scholar's Assessment of Barth's Interpretation

With Barth's general approach to exegesis I find myself in broad agreement. I think, for example, that he is right to consider only the final form of the text and not to pursue the wild goose chase of reconstructing a source, different from the text of the Prologue that we have. In this respect, Barth was in fact far ahead of his time, adopting an approach that is now not uncommon at a time when source criticism was all the rage. I also agree with him that attempts to illuminate the Prologue by viewing it against the background of various concepts of the Logos in religious and philosophical traditions of the ancient world have not proved very helpful. There is insufficient evidence in the text to show that it intended reference to any of these concepts. In my case, at least, this is not a question of ruling out the relevance of such historical backgrounds in principle, simply a judgment that in this particular instance they are not relevant or of only minor relevance. I would make one general criticism of Barth's exegetical methods: his failure to attend at all to the literary structure of the Prologue. There are unmistakable signs that the Prologue has a quasi-poetic structure, which is of interest not merely for aesthetic reasons but because it has a role in making the text's meaning. It is an important aid to exegesis that Barth neglects.

Relationship to Genesis 1:1–5

A major criticism of Barth's interpretation of the Prologue that I would make is that he gives hardly any attention to the way the first five verses of the Prologue allude to the first five verses of Genesis. They are a christological reading of the Genesis 1 creation narrative. The fact that the Prologue begins with precisely the same phrase as the opening words of Genesis ("In the beginning") makes this obvious to any reader familiar with the Old Testament. The Prologue therefore situates itself in the context of Jewish interpretations of these key verses of the Hebrew Bible, to which contemporaries of John gave considerable attention. This (not Philo or Stoicism) is the relevant background to which the Prologue itself clearly points. So the Word to which John refers is initially that word by which God created the world, not in some metaphysical cosmology, but according to Genesis 1, which, while it does not use the word "word," repeatedly says that God spoke. Scripture itself summarizes this account with the words: "By the word of the LORD the heavens were made" (Ps. 33:6). In that case, the term *ho Logos* is not a mere verbal placeholder. It has some specific content of its own. It is the divine word of which Genesis 1 speaks. It is both creative and revelatory, for God in creating the world at the same time reveals himself to his creation. Similarly, the activity of Jesus Christ in John's Gospel is both revelatory and creative, revealing who God is at the same time as giving new life.

Barth's notion of a placeholder serves the purpose of not allowing Jesus to be defined by preexisting categories, which would threaten the absoluteness and exclusivity of revelation in Jesus Christ. But, even in his own terms, Barth seems here to have thrown out the biblical baby with the hellenistic bathwater. The beginning of the Hebrew Bible is not really, for him, in the same category as Stoicism or Mandaeism. It is a preliminary part of God's self-revelation in Jesus Christ. But I think we see here a problematic aspect of Barth's christological absorption of the Old Testament which deprives the latter of even a preliminary integrity of its own. He seems unable to accommodate the idea that the Prologue's strategy is to say to its Jewish readers: "This Word you already know about from Genesis is the Word that has become flesh in Jesus Christ."

The Reference of houtos (v. 2)

Barth's particular interpretation of verse 2 is, as he recognizes, very important for the plausibility of his idea that *ho Logos* in verse 1 is merely a placeholder. That the term refers forward to a figure who will be properly introduced later in the Prologue is, in his view, established already in verse 2 by the pronoun *houtos*, interpreted in the way that he found Adolf Schlatter had interpreted it. Barth must have found this interpretation theologically appealing, but, as we have seen, he offers a quite ordinary kind of exegetical argument for it, which can therefore be assessed as such. It is an interpretation that most commentators on John fail even to mention as a possibility, and I was surprised to find that one recent commentator, Francis Moloney, does adopt it. He translates *houtos* as "this man," but then rather inconsistently says that it both points backwards to *ho Logos* (which, as a masculine noun, requires a masculine pronoun) and forwards to "a figure with a human story."[12] Nevertheless, despite this recent support, Barth's interpretation cannot be maintained. In the first place, the use of *houtos* as a personal pronoun, virtually equivalent to "he" or "it," and referring back to a person or thing just mentioned, is Johannine style and occurs frequently in the Gospel (1:7; 3:2; 4:47; 6:50, 58, 71; 7:40, 41; 9:8; 12:21; 21:24). Secondly, when *houtos* is used to refer forward, what it refers to follows almost immediately.[13] I cannot find a parallel to the kind of reference forward across several verses that Barth's interpretation here requires. Barth's view of this verse seems to me linguistically impossible.

Barth argues that, if *houtos* refers back to *ho Logos*, then verse 2 simply recapitulates the first two of the three clauses of verse 1. It would therefore be redundant. However, the repetition is less surprising when we recognize the quasi-poetic style of this passage. There is a similar repetition in verse 3. The repetitions have the effect, as Barth himself remarks, of making verses 1-2 and verse 3 each a kind of closed circle (*WW*, 29). Furthermore, what verse 2 stresses (that the Word was in the beginning with God) forms an *inclusio* with the words at the other end of the Prologue: "God the only Son

---

12. Francis J. Moloney, *The Gospel of John*, Sacra Pagina 4 (Collegeville: Liturgical, 1998), 35; cf. Francis J. Moloney, *Belief in the Word: Reading John 1-4* (Minneapolis: Fortress, 1993), 30.

13. The use of *houtos* ascribed to John the Baptist in v. 5 of the Prologue, to which Barth attaches considerable importance, is not a real parallel. This verse anticipates 1:30, where John the Baptist is imagined actually pointing to Jesus who is standing near to him. The *houtos* does not point forward in the text, but spatially in the visualized scene.

who is in the bosom of the Father" (v. 18). What we first know as the divine Word's relationship with God we find, by the end of the Prologue, is the divine Son's relationship with his Father.

As we have seen, Barth attached considerable, even decisive importance for the understanding of the Prologue to his interpretation of verse 2. Without it, one can certainly argue that the whole Prologue is about Jesus Christ, but not in the very strong sense that Barth maintained, especially in the *Church Dogmatics*. One cannot simply substitute Jesus Christ for *ho Logos* in the first two verses as though that is just precisely what they mean.

The Point of the Prologue

My last criticism has quite far-reaching implications for a different reading of the Prologue from Barth's. Barth explains the use of the term *ho Logos* up to and including verse 14, together with the fact that it is never thereafter in the Gospel used for Jesus, by supposing that it is a mere placeholder for Jesus Christ, the incarnate One. This seems to me to miss the fact that it is not the name Jesus Christ that is stressed in verses 14–18 of the Prologue, but the term *monogenēs* ("only Son"[14]). The incarnation of the Word enables us to know him not merely as the Word but as the Son. The term *ho Logos* serves, in my view, not as a placeholder but as a preliminary indication of his identity. In Jesus in his relationship with his Father, the Word is revealed to be and to have always been the only Son of the Father. The eternal love relationship in God is now revealed, as it had not been in Genesis 1 or anywhere in the Hebrew Bible. Thus the Prologue adumbrates the central role of the Father-Son relationship through the rest of the Gospel. We should notice again the correspondence between the beginning of the Prologue and the end. In the beginning the Word is with God and is God. At the end the only Son is in the bosom of the Father. The relationship of God to the Word is replaced by—is revealed by the incarnation to be—the Son in intimate relationship with the Father.

Barth seems to me to have missed much of what the Prologue is actually saying about the incarnation. The point of the incarnation is not just that God is revealed in the God-human Jesus Christ, but that Jesus Christ, in his concrete human life and work, is the Son of the Father. It is as the Son that

---

14. The word itself means "unique one," but was often used to designate an only child, and in this context, where it is related to "the Father," this is clearly the sense.

he reveals the Father, and in so doing reveals God to be Father and Son, united in their love within the identity of the one God. Most of the time in the *Church Dogmatics* Barth simply treats Word and Son as parallel terms, whether as ways of saying that Jesus reveals God or as designations of the second person of the Trinity.[15] Strangely, despite his view of *ho Logos* in the Prologue as merely a verbal placeholder, in his accounts of the doctrines of the Trinity and of revelation, which of course are closely connected, it is Jesus as the Word of God that is dominant, rather than Jesus as the Son of the Father. Presumably this is connected with Barth's denial that the persons of the Trinity are personal subjects in interpersonal relationship. As has sometimes been argued, it is only when he constructs the doctrine of reconciliation that he speaks of the relationship of the Father and the Son within the Trinity in terms that seem, to some at least, hard to square with his original understanding of the Trinity.[16]

But finally, in *CD* IV/3, Barth says what I have missed from his earlier discussions, though he presents it, not as interpretation of the Johannine Prologue (hence the absence of this passage from the earlier parts of this chapter) but as part of a long overview of Jesus as the Revealer in the Gospel of John as a whole (IV/3, 231–37). "What," he asks, "does Jesus reveal according to the Fourth Gospel?" His answer, in brief summary, is that Jesus reveals the love between the Father and the Son. "This love is the content of the Word or declaration of Jesus, the positive thing which He makes known to the world." This love between the Father and the Son is the "inner divine mystery"—a claim that surely means more than God's self-determination to be the man Jesus Christ.

Barth writes:

> But the revelation of this mystery can and does take place only because it does not remain this inner divine mystery, but discloses itself within the reality distinct from God, the Word being made flesh, the Son who loves and is loved by the Father becoming identical with the man Jesus, so that Jesus is the One who is in the Father and the Father in Him. (235)

---

15. E.g., *CD* I/1, 434: "We are saying the same thing when we say either 'Son of God' or 'Word of God.'"

16. E.g., Rowan D. Williams, "Barth on the Triune God," in *Karl Barth: Studies of His Theological Method*, ed. Stephen W. Sykes (Oxford: Clarendon Press, 1979), 146–93, especially 175–82.

That passage, which is Barth's summary of what the whole of John's Gospel says about the revelation of God in Jesus Christ, seems to me to be precisely what is already said in the *Prologue* to the Gospel. It is what Barth had failed to notice in the Prologue. That the incarnation reveals God to be Father and Son in loving relationship is the main overall point that the Prologue seems designed to make.

3 The Gospel within the Commandment

Barth on the Parable of the Good Samaritan

ERIC GREGORY

This chapter focuses on Karl Barth's evangelical reading of the parable of the Good Samaritan (Luke 10:25–37). More briefly, it considers implications of this reading for contemporary discussions of global justice with respect to what human beings owe one another. In a global age, once-distant neighbors are fast becoming near neighbors, to borrow Barth's own terminology.[1] Should concepts of neighbor and obligation, so indebted to a theological heritage, change with the globalization of the neighborhood? Barth's theological interpretation of the parable is both extensive and illuminating. Surprisingly, his exposition has received little commentary in either Barth studies or Christian ethics.

Barth and Contemporary Christian Ethics

Karl Barth is the unwitting, and often repressed, father of modern Christian ethics in the Anglo-American tradition. It is striking, for example, to compare his prominence in the classic twentieth-century texts that gave shape to the field with his relative neglect in works of the past thirty years. I might hazard a further generalization: unlike Dietrich Bonhoeffer or Reinhold Niebuhr, it is the rare syllabus in Christian ethics or doctoral program in religious ethics that now includes sustained attention to Barth. Barth's use of Scripture is particularly absent. As a field, Christian ethics converses

---

1. *CD* III/4, 285–323.

more with philosophy and the social sciences than either theology or biblical studies. For example, note the resurgent pairing of Christian ethics and Peter Singer on a range of issues, especially the demandingness of moral obligations in the face of material abundance and extreme poverty.[2]

To be sure, Barth remains a conversation partner, even if as rhetorical foil rather than generative resource. Modern political theology can be interpreted as an implicit (and sometimes explicit) debate over the legacy of Barth's account of the state's participation in the mission of Jesus Christ and secular parables of the kingdom. Likewise, several recent monographs on Barth's ethics are notable. The renaissance of studies in Barth's ethics suggests increasing dialogue between "ethicists" and scholars of Barth's theology, especially in terms of noncompetitive relations between divine and human action, freedom and responsibility, and reason and revelation. Placing Barth in constructive relation to Aquinas and Hegel is one notable feature of this renaissance.[3]

In general, however, there remains a strange disconnect between developments in Barth studies and Christian ethics. As Gerald McKenny puts it, "Barth's approach to ethics is neither well understood nor widely appreciated."[4] McKenny, of course, is one of the growing tribe of ethicists trying to read Barth's insistence on the priority of God's self-revelation in Christ in ways that overcome what he creatively describes as a current situation where "certain heirs of Kant face off against certain heirs of Schleiermacher."[5] We could name names (Gustafson and Hauerwas), but I begin here not to enter into the complicated story of Barth's reception or failed reception in Christian ethics, not to mention philosophy and religious thought more generally. Parts of that story are told in detail elsewhere. These include critical accounts of Barth's misunderstanding of casuistry, practical reason, and virtue, as well as the perceived conservatism of his theological anthropology. Broader shifts in intellectual culture also shape the sociology of Barthian

---

2. See, for example, Charles C. Camosy, *Peter Singer and Christian Ethics: Beyond Polarization* (Cambridge: Cambridge University Press, 2012), and John Perry, ed., *God, the Good, and Utilitarianism: Perspectives on Peter Singer* (Cambridge: Cambridge University Press, 2014).

3. See, for example, Daniel L. Migliore, ed., *Commanding Grace: Studies in Barth's Ethics* (Grand Rapids: Eerdmans, 2010), and Kevin W. Hector, *Theology Without Metaphysics: God, Language, and the Spirit of Recognition* (Cambridge: Cambridge University Press, 2011).

4. Gerald McKenny, *The Analogy of Grace: Karl Barth's Moral Theology* (Oxford: Oxford University Press, 2010), vii.

5. McKenny, *Analogy of Grace*, 139.

reception as fideistic intuitionism for those unsure what to do with ethics as dogmatics and ethics as sin.

Augustine, by contrast, has no disciplinary home because he can be found throughout a university curriculum. Barth is not homeless in this sense, but his influence is often confined to a select number of seminaries and divinity schools. C. S. Lewis spoke for many when he described "Barthianism" as "a flattening out of all things into common insignificance before the inscrutable Creator."[6] I might add that he also spoke for many when he admitted, "Barth I have never read, or not that I remember."[7]

My focus is set against this background, but in a more narrow way. One topic that persists throughout modern Christian ethics is Christian love. The relation between two love commandments itself is a massive topic indebted to Augustine and the Scriptures themselves. Under the influence of Anders Nygren, even the modern literature is vast.[8] Nygren has met severe criticism. Like Barth, Nygren is read, if it all, more in courses on the history of Christian ethics than normative ethics. Yet Barth's discussion has played an influential role. For example, Barth was the only figure to warrant a chapter in Gene Outka's influential 1972 text, *Agape: An Ethical Analysis*.[9]

As the title suggests, Outka's treatment focused on issues that preoccupy Christian ethics, including the normative content of agape in relation to concepts like equal regard, eros, and mutuality. Outka argued that Barth's distinctively covenantal account rests "on the sense in which agape lives in but not by the opposition to eros."[10] He stressed Barth's "preference for 'self-giving' rather than 'self-sacrifice,'" his affirmation of "a creaturely freedom . . . that is more than pure reception and yet not a matter of nefarious human spontaneity," and the notion that "man's response to God is embodied necessarily if not exhaustively in his regard for the neighbor."[11] Most of

---

6. C. S. Lewis, *English Literature in the Sixteenth Century, Excluding Drama* (Oxford: Clarendon Press, 1954), 449. Lewis admits he is using the term loosely. It is also anachronistic since he invokes the label primarily as a characterization of certain puritan reactions to Thomas Hooker's account of reason.

7. C .S. Lewis, Letter to Corbin Scott Carnell (1958), in *The Collected Letters of C. S. Lewis*, vol. 3: *Narnia, Cambridge, and Joy 1950-1963*, ed. Walter Hooper (New York: HarperCollins, 2007), 980.

8. Anders Nygren, *Agape and Eros*, trans. Philip Watson (Philadelphia: Westminster, 1953).

9. Gene Outka, *Agape: An Ethical Analysis* (New Haven: Yale University Press, 1972), 207-56.

10. Outka, *Agape*, 228.

11. Outka, *Agape*, 209, 215, and 220.

Outka's critical attention was placed on Barth's refusal to identify agape with a universal love of humanity, a love modeled on the parable of the Good Samaritan rather than the fellowship of the Last Supper. According to Outka, it is a refusal that raises "crucial difficulties," despite Barth's theocentric affirmation of a radical sociality.[12] For Outka, equal respect and impartiality serve as analogues of divine love. I will return to the reasons for Barth's refusal, both scriptural and phenomenological.

Outka's chapter traveled between Barth's entire theology of grace and the relations of love and justice, rightness and goodness, and rules and virtues. But he did not engage Barth's scriptural exegesis in any sustained way. There is no mention of Barth's interpretation of the Good Samaritan. Perhaps because it has become such a commonplace, relatively few scholarly discussions of love, despite the turn to narrative, focus on the parable or its relation to Mark 12, Matthew 22, and of course, Deuteronomy 6 and Leviticus 19.

The salience of Barth's theological interpretation of the parable has been recognized. Paul Nimmo, in fact, suggests it is a "possible archetype" for the "practical casuistry" of *CD* III/4.[13] Yet, like many preachers and ethicists, few scholars seem sure what to do with the parable once invoked. Ethicists rarely turn to *CD* I/2 given their tendency to be more at home in the "ethical" portions of *CD* II/2, III/4, and the lecture fragments of IV/4.[14] Most discussions in Christian ethics follow Outka's lead in neglecting it. In Barth studies, the relevant passages serve primarily as a route into Barth on the Trinity, election, ecclesiology, and the logic of analogy. For example, while there are brief references, I could find no discussion of the parable in works by William Werpehowski, George Hunsinger, John Webster, David Haddorff, Matthew Rose, or Gerald McKenny.[15] Several chapters provide

---

12. Outka, *Agape*, 211.

13. Paul Nimmo, *Being in Action: The Theological Shape of Barth's Ethical Vision* (London: T&T Clark, 2007), 84n175.

14. For a compelling account of the ethical and ecclesial importance of *CD* I/2, see Derek Alan Woodard-Lehman, "Freedom and Authority: The Ethics of Revelation in Karl Barth" (PhD diss., Princeton Theological Seminary, 2014), and "Reason after Revelation: Karl Barth on Divine Word and Human Words," *Modern Theology* (special issue, November 2016).

15. William Werpehowski, *Karl Barth and Christian Ethics: Living in Truth* (Burlington, VT: Ashgate, 2014); George Hunsinger, *Disruptive Grace: Studies in the Theology of Karl Barth* (Grand Rapids: Eerdmans, 2000); John Webster, *Barth's Ethics of Reconciliation* (Cambridge: Cambridge University Press, 1995); David Haddorff, *Christian Ethics as Witness: Barth's Ethics for a World at Risk* (Eugene, OR: Cascade, 2010); Matthew Rose, *Ethics*

intriguing commentary, but they stand as exceptions and tend to refer to it in footnotes.[16]

The neglect is striking given the importance of the parable for current discussions of personhood, global ethics, and humanitarianism. It is one of the few biblical narratives positively invoked in the context of emerging recognition of global interdependence. From earthquakes to genocides to Syrian refugees, we confront the wounded and the broken on a global scale, often paralyzing us with compassion fatigue and overwhelming moral conflicts. Indeed, given the power of modern technology and various secular ideals of moral perfection, the stringency of duties of mutual aid owed to an extensive class of potential beneficiaries in acute distress is increasingly *the* central topic of moral and political philosophy. Recent work in theological ethics has argued for the limits of ethics in the face of these pervasive obligations.[17] I return to that issue at the end of this chapter in light of Barth's account of the crisis of human judgment.

The Parable in Modern Scholarship and Barth's Exposition

Few Gospel texts—indeed few biblical stories or characters—are as memorable and as popular as the parable of the Good Samaritan. In this case, familiarity has not bred contempt. It appeals as a story about the virtue of boundary-breaking universalism and the vice of religious hypocrisy. The

---

with Barth: God, Metaphysics and Morals (Burlington, VT: Ashgate, 2010); and McKenny, *Analogy of Grace*.

16. See, for example, Joseph Mangina, "The Stranger as Sacrament: Karl Barth and the Ethics of Ecclesial Practice," *International Journal of Systematic Theology* 1, no. 3 (November 1999): 322–39; David Clough, "Eros and Agape in Karl Barth's Church Dogmatics," *International Journal of Systematic Theology* 2, no. 2 (July 2000): 189–203; Paul Molnar, "Love of God and Love of Neighbor in the Theology of Karl Rahner and Karl Barth," *Modern Theology* 20, no. 4 (October 2004): 567–99; and John Webster, "Response to [Caroline J. Simon] 'What Wondrous Love Is This?'," in *For the Sake of the World: Karl Barth and the Future of Ecclesial Theology*, ed. George Hunsinger (Grand Rapids: Eerdmans, 2004), 159–64.

17. See, for example, Ted A. Smith, *Weird John Brown: Divine Violence and the Limits of Ethics* (Stanford: Stanford University Press, 2015). Smith argues that most secular and religious ethics since Kant construe obligations as a universal code that absorbs the whole of moral reasoning "entirely within immanent networks of cause and effect" (5). His account of a higher law negates absolute obligations in "ways that invite a *free response* in history that is *permeated by the presence of God*" (117). Smith appeals to Walter Benjamin and Charles Taylor rather than Karl Barth in his effort to chasten certain accounts of ethics for the sake of both law and freedom, but the similarities are notable.

moral of the story is taken to be a moral one: to put it uncharitably, confirmation of post-Kantian bourgeois ethics about the identity of a neighbor and our ethical liability, or more charitably, a radical disruption of natural tendencies to prefer people like us, a disruption that has sponsored great movements of social reform like the abolition of slavery and the promotion of international law. Readings of this kind, which have origins in the ethical vision of liberal Protestant exegesis, populate Western cultural imagination across a vast landscape of sermons, political speeches, literary works, papal encyclicals, and even contemporary philosophy. Scholars as diverse—and as secular—as John Rawls, Judith Thomson, and Amartya Sen invoke the parable in their accounts of moral obligation. The invocation, however, often denigrates love in the name of respect or justice. Allusions to the parable also pervade concrete discussions of humanitarian intervention, immigration, abortion, health care, and global poverty. This paradigmatic expression of Christian love—enshrined in hospitals, NGOs, and nightly news stories—even has been incorporated as a legal requirement in some continental European systems of positive law.[18]

Despite an apparent soteriological frame—set by its placement between the mission of the seventy and the story of Mary and Martha and the lawyer's opening question, "what must I do to inherit eternal life?"—biblical scholars often confirm these secular ethical readings. They consider it an example story focused on the action of Luke 10:34, which is taken to define neighborliness, compassion, and social responsibility. For many, the parable's account of the relation between love of God and love of neighbor simply is the essence of New Testament ethics. Of course, interpretations admit a wide spectrum of liberationist and conservative readings, all keen to appropriate Christian love.

Variously described as the parable of the compassionate, the merciful, or the good Samaritan, it appears only in Luke's Gospel, the Gospel with more parables than any other Gospel. Even the Jesus Seminar colors it red, indicating authenticity, with some debate about Lukan redactions from Markan parallels. Biblical scholars do lament modern readings stripped of literary, social, and historical context in ways that avoid the broader contours of Lukan theology and questions of audience in the first-century Mediterranean world.

---

18. See John Kleinig, "Good Samaritanism," *Philosophy & Public Affairs* 5, no. 4 (Summer 1976): 382–407, and Laura Valentini, "Social Samaritan Justice: When and Why Needy Fellow Citizens Have a Right to Assistance," *American Political Science Review* (November 2015): 1–15.

Modern parables scholarship has produced an array of interpretations: parable as example, metaphor, symbol, or allegory (sometimes called "typological," "figural," or "spiritual"). These are all set in relation to a distinctive Lukan interest in sharing possessions and identifying the community faithful to Yahweh. In fact, for some scholars, the parable is not primarily moral. It is an existential "speech-act which draws us into identification with the injured man, and which transforms our expectations, our horizons, by presenting the neighbor to us in the shape of the enemy."[19] Emphasizing more the doer than the deed, John Dominic Crossan argues that "the whole thrust of the story demands that one say what cannot be said, what is a contradiction in terms: Good + Samaritan," confronting and judging the hearer with "the necessity of saying the impossible and having their world turned upside down . . . *just so* does the Kingdom of God break abruptly into human values."[20] As another exegete puts it, "far from inculcating morals, Jesus's parables often undermine them."[21] This sharp distinction between moral and existential interpretation of reversal eludes me. Yet even the most technical discussions find it difficult to resist isolating the universalizing ethical message, which, Crossan argues, arises only later in a Gentile environment "where terms like 'Samaritan' had no meaning."[22] These readings abound: "the example of the despised halfbreed was intended to teach him that no human being was beyond the range of his charity";[23] "the point of the story is . . . a neighbor is anyone in need with whom one comes into contact";[24] and, the parable "challenges us to move beyond our social and religious constructs; it subverts our tendency to divide the world into insiders and outsiders."[25] Preachers who imaginatively replace the Samaritan with an al-Qaeda or IRA terrorist, a black male, or a Mexican immigrant tap into this tradition of admonition and example.

For my purposes, the contrast between example and allegory is most salient. Ancient Christian interpreters like Origen, Irenaeus, and Clement

---

19. Mike Higton, "Boldness and Reserve: A Lesson from St. Augustine," *Anglican Theological Review* 85, no. 3 (Summer 2003): 447–56, at 449.

20. John Dominic Crossan, *In Parables: The Challenge of the Historical Jesus* (New York: Harper & Row, 1973), 64–65.

21. Matthew Rindge, "Luke's Artistic Parables: Narratives of Subversion, Imagination, and Transformation," *Interpretation* 68, no. 4 (October 2014): 403–15, at 404.

22. Crossan, *In Parables*, 64.

23. Joachim Jeremias, *Parables of Jesus* (London: SCM, 1954/2003), 205.

24. Joseph Fitzmyer, *The Gospel according to Luke: X–XXIV* (New York: Doubleday, 1985), 884.

25. John R. Donahue, SJ, *The Gospel in Parable* (Minneapolis: Fortress, 1988), 134.

of Alexandria, while far from neglecting ethics, interpreted the parable allegorically. This tradition appears to date back to the earliest Jewish-Christian communities. On this reading, Jerusalem stood for paradise, Jericho the world after the Fall, the wounded man sinful humanity, the robbers as the devil and his angels, the priest and the Levite as the law of Moses, the two denarii as the old and new covenant, the inn as the church, the innkeeper as either Paul (Augustine) or the Holy Spirit (Irenaeus), and most fundamentally, the Samaritan as Jesus who promises to return.

Augustine frequently emphasized the ethical import of the parable, especially in *De Doctrina Christiana* where edifying love is the purpose of exegesis. His sermons affirmed the universality of Christian love by appeal to the parable.[26] Yet Augustine took for granted multiple senses of a text. His allegorization displays mastery of rhetoric and beautiful speech. It is also subject to modern biblical critics anxious about coded theologies and ideologies. As Mike Higton notes, "whenever critics gather to discuss examples of patristic eisegesis, of allegorical interpretation run wild, someone will turn to Augustine's reading of the parable of the Good Samaritan."[27] Augustine's outline is similar to others, likely drawing from Ambrose, but with further interpretation. For Augustine, Adam himself travels the Jericho road of mortality, beaten into sin, the oil and wine is the sacrament of baptism, the beast is the flesh of Christ, the two denarii are the two precepts of love, and, remarkably, the additional payment that the Samaritan promises is Paul's counsel of celibacy.

Adolph Julicher considered such interpretations, which squeeze gospel into parable, to be "tasteless."[28] Even C. H. Dodd, with his realized eschatology, called Augustine's reading "quite perverse."[29] Augustine's critics hold that these interpretations tell us more about Christian doctrine than the proclamation of Jesus. They tell us more about the interpreter's theology than the text. To be sure, ancient exegesis tells us about the interpreters: Irenaeus's and Origen's battle with Gnosticism, or Augustine's conflict with Pelagians. It is also telling that the interpretations of this parable often travel with a fraught anti-Judaism. Medieval sermons frequently point to the unlov-

---

26. See Roland Teske, "St. Augustine on the Good Samaritan," in *Augustine the Exegete*, ed. Frederick Van Fleteren and Joseph Schaubelt (New York: Peter Lang, 2001), 347–67.

27. Higton, "Boldness and Reserve," 447.

28. Cited by Riemer Roukema, "The Good Samaritan in Ancient Christianity," *Vigilae Christianae* 58, no. 1 (February 2004): 56–74, at 57.

29. C. H. Dodd, *The Parables of the Kingdom* (New York: Charles Scribner's Sons, 1961), 2.

ing character of Jewish tribalism and legalistic purity in support of a strong supersessionism. Modern exegesis, while rejecting the popular reading of fear of impurity, can trade on these stereotypes by depicting the lawyer as "clearly baiting Jesus"[30] or "wanting to ... make his job easier."[31] G. B. Caird is representative by arguing that the lawyer wanted "moral duties limited and defined with a rabbinic thoroughness."[32] For Caird, the parable "perfectly illustrates the difference between the ethics of law and the ethics of love."[33]

Opposition to allegory appeals to the integrity of the Hebrew Bible and this shameful past. Ironically, however, the purely ethical reading typically renders the characters of the New Testament story themselves superfluous.[34] There has been, once again, a resurgent call to integrate "theology" and "exegesis." If parables are ethics and theology in story form, transforming how the reader thinks, feels, and lives, then as Barth knew, historical criticism is only the beginning of the reading of the text.

Perhaps to his credit, Barth does not work as hard as Augustine on hyper-figural interpretation.[35] But if a choice is to be made between example and allegory, between ethics and theology, it is clear on which side he would stand. Yet, as with Augustine, it is a choice that Barth characteristically refuses. The deep connection between revelation and reconciliation in Barth's Christology "takes ethics into itself."[36] Exegesis, like dogmatics, is ethics.

Barth's Exposition of the Parable

Barth mentions the parable in various parts of the *Church Dogmatics*. The fullest discussion occurs in *CD* I/2, §18.3, on "The Praise of God," which I

---

30. David Lyle Jeffrey, *Luke* (Grand Rapids: Brazos, 2012), 148.

31. Robert A. J. Gagnon, "A Second Look at Two Lukan Parables," *Horizons in Biblical Theology* 20 (1998): 1–11, at 5.

32. G. B. Caird, *Luke* (New York: Penguin, 1964), 148.

33. Caird, *Luke*, 148.

34. Bruce Longenecker effectively shows how the "ethical" reading marginalizes the role of the innkeeper. See Bruce Longenecker, "The Story of the Samaritan and the Innkeeper (Luke 10:30–35): A Study of Character Rehabilitation," *Biblical Interpretation* 17 (2009): 422–47.

35. While generally praising the lessons we might learn from Augustine's exegesis, Higton also highlights the danger that Augustine's approach obscures "an account of the abiding humanity of Christ's participation in the divine life, precisely as human and creaturely and particular and finite," in Higton, "Boldness and Reserve," 453.

36. *CD* I/2, 371.

The Gospel within the Commandment

read as the climax of the section on "The Life of the Children of God." It builds upon themes found in the sections on "True Religion" (§17.3), "Man as a Doer of the Word" (§18.1), and "The Love of God" (§18.2).

In these prior sections, Barth counsels that the Christian life consists in love and praise, our being and our doing, the two concepts proper to theological ethics. For Barth, "love is the essence of Christian living."[37] It is the "fulfillment of the law" (Rom. 13:10) and the "goal of the command" (1 Timothy 1:5). Of course, Barth is quick to reject "a natural love to God which is proper to us apart from divine revelation."[38] The commandment to love is therefore not given to humanity in general. It is given "to the true Israel, the Church of Jesus Christ."[39] In *CD* IV/2, Barth famously will develop this claim by arguing that "however irksome this may be to those who regard Christian love as a human virtue—it is still a closed circle . . . the circle of the community of Jesus Christ gathered by the Holy Spirit from Jews and Gentiles, and ruled and quickened by Him."[40] I will return to the fluidity of this closed circle, a porous one tutored by the parable.

According to Barth, however, God's love does not leave human love dead in its tracks. Self-love is never justified, let alone commanded. It is judged by neighbor-love. Barth here finds Augustine's "invention of a commandment to love oneself" to be "a cardinal error."[41] Nevertheless, in ways that signal his coming interpretation of the parable, Barth argues that love "does become an event in an act or acts of human self-determination: it is a creaturely reality."[42] In this sense, his reading of the love commands will be eudaimonistic. The law, at least in part, is the way to the human good. It is proper to our human well-being, even as accomplished in Christ, to love God and neighbor. The praise of God is obedience to this commandment. In the freedom of obedience is the freedom of our good. Neighbor-love is a

---

37. *CD* I/2, 372.

38. *CD* I/2, 373. Barth here misleadingly cites, by contrast, Thomas Aquinas, *Summa Theologica* I.II, q65.5.1. The citation is found in the objection rather than the reply.

39. *CD* I/2, 381.

40. *CD* IV/2, 804. Barth admits the restriction of the closed circle "cannot be theoretical and definitive, but only practical and provisional" (*CD* IV/2, 808). David Clough finds here a salutary ambiguity—even equivocation—one that "affirms the value and legitimacy of special relationships, while also recognizing that any person or group, near or distant, may become the neighbor Christ commands us to love as ourselves" (Clough, "Eros and Agape," 201). See also David Clough, *Ethics in Crisis: Interpreting Barth's Ethics* (Burlington, VT: Ashgate, 2005), 85–87.

41. *CD* I/2, 388.

42. *CD* I/2, 373.

parable of love to God, living out redemption, drawing happiness into the space of the Law through becoming "what we already are."[43]

Barth emphasizes that Christian love is not a theory or generic concept. Love also is not God. It is the particular drama of the utter solidarity of God with humanity. Our participation in the perfection of God's love is "not a law which crushes and kills."[44] But it does chastise. As Barth puts it, only angels know each other freed from the law.[45] Yet, as witness, the command to love is the "Gospel in the Law."[46] There is no judgment apart from Christ. Service to others is neither achievement nor burden: "in relation to our neighbor, then, the road does not lead, as we are often told, from Law to Gospel—there is no road that way—but from the Gospel to Law."[47] This is "the Gospel within the commandment."[48]

If John 1 is the *locus classicus* of the incarnation of God's love for us, Luke 10 is the *locus classicus* of a proper human love. For Barth, there are not two absolute commandments existing "side by side."[49] But neither are they identical. Their identification, Barth proclaims, is a "damnable confusion and blasphemy."[50] God is not neighbor. Neighbor is not God. Love to God is supreme. Provocatively, Barth claims humanity has no independent value or inherent dignity apart from God. Humanitarianism, far from embodying Good Samaritanism, does not realize the radical lostness of humanity apart from God. The claims of the neighbor cannot be justified by the idea of humanity, or even posited by the history of creation. Love of neighbor is determined by the singularity of revelation.

Yet neighbor-love is not "at a lower stage of the divine commanding."[51] Love of neighbor is not a commentary on love of God. There is neither subordination nor competition. In the distinction of the love command there is a "definite connexion."[52] There is even something like a unity of the commandments. Both commands speak to our hidden twofold existence, living in time and eternity under one absolute Lord. That which comes has priority over that

---

43. *CD* I/2, 389–90.
44. *CD* I/2, 396.
45. *CD* I/2, 438.
46. *CD* I/2, 396.
47. *CD* I/2, 438.
48. *CD* I/2, 452.
49. *CD* I/2, 402.
50. *CD* I/2, 403.
51. *CD* I/2, 406.
52. *CD* I/2, 406.

which passes: love to God "for the child of God in his completed existence in Jesus Christ" and love to neighbor "in his not yet completed walk."[53] Love of neighbor, then, reflects the era of "free human reflection and decision."[54]

The neighbor for Barth is a sign of our assured future. We should not be confused, Barth warns, by the language in Scripture of "serving, helping, doing good, sacrificing ourselves."[55] The poverty of the neighbor is not what commands attention. Barth worries that Luther's influential advice about finding the neighbor within orders of society—advice that harkens back to Augustine and Aquinas on concentric circles of obligation—"might lead us to the idea that the neighbor is one to whom we have a definite duty, who has a claim upon us."[56] Augustine's *ordo amoris* was less definite than Aquinas's characteristic rigor in hierarchical mapping of what we owe family, friends, co-religionists, fellow citizens, or distant strangers. Part of this indeterminacy lies in the centrality of the parable for Augustine's account of a moral cosmopolitanism. It also registers concern about the law itself.

Barth would not deny that Christians have duties. According to Barth, however, "we cannot possibly think of our neighbor as Holy Scripture does if we think of him from that standpoint as the embodiment of the Law."[57] New Testament neighbor-love is not the content of an ethical mandate. A mandate exists. The moral order that presents the neighbor is itself part of divine goodness. But the true form of the neighbor is not "as a representative of the mandate, or as an authority to which we owe obedience and service."[58] Rather, for Barth, "the primary and true form of the neighbor is that he faces us as the bearer and representative of the divine compassion."[59]

The neighbor who comes to us as Law comes only as veiled form. In the veil, "where he is Law," he "means confusion, accusation, the discovery of our wickedness and helplessness, wrath and judgment."[60] Here, Barth arrives at the parable.

Barth admits the lawyer is trying to "tempt" Jesus, but he is not "necessarily guilty of subjective insincerity."[61] Like some who follow the "New

53. *CD* I/2, 409.
54. *CD* I/2, 411.
55. *CD* I/2, 416.
56. *CD* I/2, 416.
57. *CD* I/2, 416.
58. *CD* I/2, 416.
59. *CD* I/2, 416.
60. *CD* I/2, 416.
61. *CD* I/2, 417.

Perspective" on Paul, Barth suggests that by placing the two commandments on the lips of the lawyer the story emphasizes that the scribe belongs sociologically to the community of Yahweh.[62] But, for Barth, the lawyer is not simply asserting covenantal membership. He does wish "to justify himself" (Luke 10:29), and so he "does not know that only by mercy can he live and inherit eternal life."[63] As such, the lawyer does not see the intimate relation of the two commands, the passion of giving and receiving mercy. Barth writes that Jesus might have said to the teacher of the Law, "this Samaritan did not ask questions like you."[64] Instead, Jesus asks which of the three proved to be neighbor. It was the Samaritan who showed mercy who proved to be neighbor. In *CD* III/2, Barth points out that the dramatic Greek verb used to describe this merciful compassion, literally to be moved in the bowels, is used only of encounters with Jesus and two closely related figures: the magnanimous king in Matthew 18 and the father in the story of the prodigal son in Luke 15. Such divine love discloses the heart of God.[65] It shows a divine grace that "wills not only to love us but to be loved by us in return."[66]

The lawyer is confronted not by the poverty of the wounded man, but "by the anything but poor Samaritan."[67] For Barth, the lawyer had "first to see that he himself is the man fallen among thieves and lying helpless by the wayside."[68] The story is not about conceptual classification or a moralizing pattern for Christian ethics. It is a parable of grace in the form of the law. The mercy that has met the lawyer, unlike the priest and Levite, summons him to "bring comfort, help, Gospel to someone else."[69] He is to be a benefactor as he was benefited. This "is only Law because it is first Gospel"; on the lips of

---

62. See Colin M. Ambrose, "Desiring to Be Justified: An Examination of the Parable of the Good Samaritan in Luke 10:25–37," *Sewanee Theological Review* 54, no. 1 (2010): 17–28. Ambrose's reading aims to hold together the sociological, ethical, and soteriological elements of the parable. For Ambrose, the lawyer's question "was an attempt to appear in the right to the crowd and Jesus by asserting his confirmed membership in the covenantal community" (27). Jesus's reversal is *"not to define who is a member, but rather to define what it means to be a member"* (28).

63. *CD* I/2, 417.

64. *CD* I/2, 418.

65. On this theme in Barth's theology, see Paul Dafydd Jones, "The Heart of the Matter: Karl Barth's Christological Exegesis," in *Thy Word Is Truth: Barth on Scripture*, ed. George Hunsinger (Grand Rapids: Eerdmans, 2012), 173–95.

66. *CD* I/2, 395.

67. *CD* I/2, 418.

68. *CD* I/2, 418.

69. *CD* I/2, 419.

Jesus, go and do thou likewise means, "Follow thou me."[70] Indeed, the good Samaritan "is not far from the lawyer.... He stands before him incarnate."[71] Like the incarnation itself, the parable for Barth is a showing. It is a vivid, earthy enactment of the gospel.

This is the high christological and soteriological point of Barth's reading. But he returns to press his prior case against humanitarianism. The story shows that the biblical neighbor is not a fellow human being as such. Here Calvin's exegesis of the parable, Barth insists, is "obviously wide of the mark."[72] Calvin, like Augustine, taught that a central meaning of the parable was all persons are neighbors because of a common nature. Barth retorts, "this is more a Stoic than a New Testament doctrine."[73]

The neighbor is not a member of some group. On the contrary, "my neighbor is an event which places me in the existence of a definite man definitely marked off from all other men."[74] The neighbor is my particular neighbor. *This* singular neighbor is also my benefactor. This meaning is not self-evident without divine mercy.

Christ's intercession has its analogue in human love. Remarkably, Barth argues, "the bearer and representative of this temporal as well as eternal mercy of God is simply my neighbor."[75] On this sacramental interpretation, the neighbor is rendered christologically as blessing rather than task. The compassionate neighbor "is seen in the reflection of the sign which gives to the great sign of the Church, in all its meaning for humanity generally, its origin, basis and stability, in the reflection of the human nature of Jesus Christ."[76] "Man himself now becomes a sign," not by innate capacity but "because the Son of God has made Himself my neighbor in His incarnation and revealed Himself my neighbor in His resurrection."[77]

We are not alone. We are aided and summoned to aid, though in doing so not putting our neighbor under the Law. The neighbor is our sacrament of grace. How does this remarkable power emerge in history? "It is the Church," created by Word and Spirit, Barth declares, "which introduces the Good Samaritan."[78]

70. *CD* I/2, 419.
71. *CD* I/2, 419.
72. *CD* I/2, 419.
73. *CD* I/2, 419.
74. *CD* I/2, 420.
75. *CD* I/2, 421.
76. *CD* I/2, 424.
77. *CD* I/2, 424.
78. *CD* I/2, 421.

Is this ecclesiocentrism? No, says Barth. The church is not the Good Samaritan. Where it has the form of the priest and Levite, church is not church. Church, as representative of Christ's reconciliation, is always on pilgrimage as a witness between near and distant neighbors. "As the Bible sees it," Barth writes, "service of the compassionate neighbor is certainly not restricted to the life of the Church in itself and as such.... Humanity as a whole can take part in this service."[79] As Frei put it long ago, "humanity at large is the neighbor given to the church, through whom Christ is present to the church."[80] This neighbor is already in Christ. The neighbor, by virtue of the reconciliation brought by Jesus, is summoned with us to fellowship with God.

In fact, according to Barth, "the Samaritan in the parable shows us incontestably that even those who do not know that they are doing so, or what they are doing, can assume and exercise the function of a compassionate neighbor."[81] The church does not turn inward for its identity. All of humanity finds its identity under the promise of Christ. According to Barth, because anyone can be a Samaritan, even the outsider must be regarded within the church, what he later terms "the brother of tomorrow."[82]

Barth's Christian conception of humanity is not based on an assumed common nature or capacity. Those bases—which readily can be translated into contemporary secular proposals—are too easily corroded by skepticism about capacities and shared nature. There is no biblical language of a universal love. But it is a universality through particularity, concretized in the mission of the church as representative of human destiny: "it is only in the Church or from the Church that there has ever been a free, strong, truly open and confident expectation in regard to the natural man, a quiet and joyful hope, that he will be my neighbor."[83] This humanity—because of the visibility of the church—reminds us of the humanity of the Son of God even where we do not see the visible church. Jesus is present to us in this hidden neighbor. Joseph Mangina helpfully describes these passages as reflecting "the pronounced secular character of Barth's ethics."[84]

We expect to find the witness of Jesus Christ in every person. Barth records the many strangers in redemptive history, outsiders who come from

79. *CD* I/2, 422.
80. Hans W. Frei, *The Identity of Jesus Christ* (Eugene, OR: Wipf & Stock, 1997), 192.
81. *CD* I/2, 422.
82. *CD* IV/2, 809.
83. *CD* I/2, 423.
84. Mangina, "The Stranger as Sacrament," 336.

"unexpected distances right into the apparently closed circle of divine election": Balaam, Rahab, Ruth, Hiram, the Queen of Sheba, the Syrian captain Naaman, the Persian King Cyrus, the wise men from the East, the centurion of Capernaum, the Syro-Phoenician woman, the centurion at the cross, the centurion Cornelius at Caesarea, and Melchizedek, King of Salem, "the hermeneutic key to this whole succession."[85] This record does not speak to a general revelation, but through them "Jesus Christ proclaims Himself to be the great Samaritan: as it were, in a second and outer circle of His revelation, which by its nature can only be hinted at."[86]

These "strangers" offer not the witness of the prophets or apostles. Yet they call us to praise God, messengers of the Word of God in the nexus of human relations: "if we know the incarnation of the eternal Word and the glorification of humanity in Him, we cannot pass by any man, without being asked whether in his humanity he does not have this mission to us, he does not become to us this compassionate neighbor."[87]

This expansion and intensification of the neighbor is conveyed by the New Testament language of "brother," showing "nearness of our neighbor" and the impossibility of "trying to be the children of God alone and without him."[88] Barth writes, "Whether willingly or wittingly or not . . . my neighbor acquires for me a sacramental significance . . . a visible sign of invisible grace, a proof that I, too, am not left alone in this world, but am borne and directed by God."[89] The neighbor is not a second revelation or a second Christ. He cannot forgive sins. But the neighbor manifests divine forgiveness.

Despite this secular sacramental realism, Barth rejects what he terms the "religio-social" teaching that holds "true worship of God consists in our co-operation in the removal of these sufferings."[90] To preach a gospel of "world-amelioration would again mean Law (instead of Gospel first and then as such Law)."[91] This rejection, however, is not put in the service of a mystical flight under the banner of love to God. Barth identifies this contrast-

---

85. *CD* I/2, 425–26. Barth repeats this list in III/2, §68.3.

86. *CD* I/2, 426.

87. *CD* I/2, 426.

88. *CD* I/2, 426. David Clough points out that Barth is not consistent in his use of the terms "neighbor" and "brother," in Clough, "Eros and Agape," 198.

89. *CD* I/2, 436.

90. *CD* I/2, 427. For a related yet distinct treatment of sacramental realism, see Ronald F. Thiemann, *The Humble Sublime: Secularity and the Politics of Belief* (New York: I. B. Tauris, 2014).

91. *CD* I/2, 427.

ing turn as a medieval danger long past. His worry is the apparently noble efforts of liberal Protestantism which he thinks reduce love to God to love to neighbor. Indeed, Barth fears a "pronounced Puritanism has become the fashion in relation to love for God or for Jesus."[92] Becoming a slave to social justice betrays the rhythm of our twofold existence.

The sufferings of the world, its injustices and many needs, do not confront us with an ethical task as such. In IV/2, for example, Barth criticizes Kierkegaard's *Works of Love* for its "unlovely, inquisitorial, and terribly judicial character."[93] For Barth, this reflects the onerous demands of Kantian dutiful right uncorrected by the liberating gospel of the good news and gracious free response. The suffering neighbor does not confront us as a demand but as a gift. Indeed, "our fellow-man in his oppression, shame and torment confronts us with the poverty, the homelessness, the scars, the corpse, at the grave of Jesus Christ."[94] This analogy of the crucified Christ with the crucified neighbor certainly risks sentimentalism, paternalism, and voyeurism. But Barth doubles down by appeal to Matthew 25: "in recognizing my neighbor in my fellow-man, I am actually placed before Christ."[95] The sacramental neighbor, it seems, is both the Samaritan and the wounded man. To love and be loved by the neighbor who conceals and reveals Jesus is to enter our future with God. Fellowship in love with the neighbor is an eschatological enactment of the Kingdom of grace. In fact, remarkably for Barth, it is to "participate in the divine justification."[96] I find this a wonderful joining of Luke 10 and Matthew 25, gospel and law. The neighbor hides and reveals the hidden and revealing God, always opening to the God with us.

Of course, Barth admits, we typically prefer to see ourselves in the role of good Samaritans. We do so at our convenience. We are prone to self-deception and self-righteousness. We are tempted to become spiritual tourists through the needs of the world. Even our guilt can be self-gratifying pride. In a brief excursus worthy of contemporary postcolonial exegesis, Barth warns that the neighbor who evokes our pity and aid may simply confirm our superiority and our idolatry. This feeling blinds us to the gospel. The true neighbor "will cause me a really mortal headache . . . will seriously give me cause involuntarily to repudiate his existence and in that way to put

---

92. *CD* IV/2, 794. Barth whimsically suggests it is better to be with Zinzendorf and Novalis than Kant and Ritschl.
93. *CD* IV/2, 782.
94. *CD* I/2, 428.
95. *CD* I/2, 429. Barth emphasizes, "We repeat, actually."
96. *CD* I/2, 431.

myself in serious danger."⁹⁷ The true neighbor is the one we wish to deny rather than the one who excites sympathy.

Yet we always love in guilt and corruption as redeemed sinners. In exhaustion or pessimism, we are tempted to "seek refuge in the excuse that I am not God" or the plea that "because I am only a man, have I to choose between 'Am I my brother's keeper' and the way of the Law?"⁹⁸ The third way, the better way, is to be a witness of Jesus Christ trusting that he will use our service. This is the obedience of sinners with nothing left to hide or to merit. The truth of love for others is given to God as well. Such freedom from moral anxiety or existential paralysis is a mixture of courage and humility. It is the hope and joy of the Christian nourished by baptism, prayer, and the Lord's Supper. This is the gospel within the commandment that relies on the grace of God.⁹⁹

Humanitarianism Today

I conclude by drawing out some implications for Christian communities often at the forefront of humanitarian aid. This aid is increasingly met with suspicion by development economists who think it is counterproductive, anthropologists who believe it masks relations of power, and political theorists who are heirs of Enlightenment concern that a Christian politics of charity obscures the demands of justice.¹⁰⁰

Many identify a revolution of moral sentiment associated with the rise of humanitarianism and changes in attitudes toward human suffering. Charles Taylor, for example, argues that "never before have people been asked to stretch out so far, and so consistently, so systematically, so as a matter of

---

97. *CD* I/2, 431.

98. *CD* I/2, 440.

99. Gene Outka helpfully describes a similar account of Christology to ethics: "when we release our works from the weight of a final seriousness they cannot bear, we may be able to display a certain lightness in the way we comport ourselves, a lightness that resembles only superficially the frivolous or the complacent," in Gene Outka, "Following at a Distance: Ethics and the Identity of Jesus," in *Scriptural Authority and Narrative Interpretation*, ed. Garrett Green (Philadelphia: Fortress, 1987), 144–60, at 155.

100. See, for example, Michael Barnett and Thomas G. Weiss, *Humanitarianism in Question: Politics, Power, Ethics* (Ithaca, NY: Cornell University Press, 2008); Angus Deaton, *The Great Escape: Health, Wealth, and the Origins of Inequality* (Princeton: Princeton University Press, 2013); and Luke Bretherton, "Poverty, Politics, and Faithful Witness in the Age of Humanitarianism," *Interpretation* 69, no. 4 (2015): 447–59.

course, to the stranger outside the gates."[101] Taylor's own christological reading of the parable frames his entire book on a secular age. He expresses a Weberian lament about the character of these moral demands. For Taylor, they signify an insidious transformation of the event of Christian charity into a rigorous code in an immanent frame. He calls this "excarnation," a transfer of proximate "brother" to remote "other." Taylor's critique of modernity resonates with Barth's concerns about abstraction, altruism, and philanthropy.[102] At the same time, many secular moral philosophers (and many of my Christian undergraduates) characterize the current situation of extreme poverty as a preventable yet constant emergency. Despite diminished inequality between countries, global poverty solicits their moral anguish for complicity in systems of injustice thought to be no fault of their own and burdened by massive histories of unjust acts. Scholars of humanitarianism, in fact, characterize humanitarianism itself as a "material project of salvation."[103] The demand for solutions is manifest in the various entrepreneurial, managerial, and technocratic savvy brought to bear on this project.[104]

Barth's reading of the parable ends with discussion of three forms of witness: word, deed, and disposition. He develops each at greater length elsewhere in later sections of the *Dogmatics* on the ministry of the community. Like contemporary critics of humanitarianism, Barth knows the pathologies of love and the tricks of compassion. Christian love, he writes, can become "attempts at domination."[105] He admits that the ministry of the diaconate in caring for the sick, the feeble, the orphan, the prisoners, the refugees, and the stranded "can obviously never be more than drops in a bucket."[106] With Augustine, however, Barth's anti-Pelagianism invested these drops with a pathos of eternal significance, tangible bodies in time, bearing witness to the cosmic work of Christ in free obedience. Our response to the crucified neighbor is not liberal benevolence and altruism, but repentance and conversion.

---

101. Charles Taylor, *A Secular Age* (Cambridge, MA: Belknap, 2007), 695.

102. On Taylor and Barth, see Webster, *Barth's Ethics of Reconciliation*, 214–30. I suspect Barth would resist Taylor's notion of prolonging the Incarnation through works of mercy.

103. Peter Redfield, "Secular Humanitarianism and the Value of Life," in *What Matters? Ethnographies of Value in a Not So Secular Age*, ed. Courtney Bender and Ann Taves (New York: Columbia University Press, 2012), 144–78, at 169.

104. On the dangers of "solutions thinking," see Willis Jenkins, *The Future of Ethics: Sustainability, Social Justice, and Religious Creativity* (Washington, DC: Georgetown University Press, 2013).

105. *CD* IV/3.2, 891.

106. *CD* IV/3.2, 891.

Some might find Barth here insufficiently other-regarding, swallowing ethics into soteriology or lessening the ethical demand with flight to providence. Yet Barth clearly argues that the church must address systemic roots of social ill. He writes, "the diaconate and the Christian community become dumb dogs, and their service a serving of the ruling powers, if they are afraid to tackle at their social root the evils by which they are confronted in detail."[107] He recognized that the rise of the welfare state posed a challenge, one that continues today with efforts to reconcile institutional and interpersonal charity.

Critics of Barth's christological reading of the parable would be wise to attend to these praxis-oriented passages. By my lights, Barth was right to emphasize the relational aspect of ethics rather than juridical norms or utilitarian emphasis on maximizing states of affairs. The command to love others "does not float in empty space."[108] While proximity need not be geographical, love "presupposes that the one or the many who are loved stand in a certain proximity to the one who loves—a proximity in which others do not find themselves."[109] Contemporary Christian ethicists emphasize the moral and theological significance of proximity and vocation as part of the goodness of embodied finitude. Guided by providence, they structure our own creaturely and limited participation in the excellence of God's universal love. Secular ethics has a hard time interpreting these commitments as anything other than self-deception.

Love is neither measured nor calculated for Barth. It must be done "at the right time and in the right place: everything with the clear knowledge that we are unable even to give the sign, let alone to make it effective."[110] Is this cheap grace and moral evasion? I think Barth offers pastoral tonic for much of our contemporary paralysis in the face of the scale and complexity of global issues. Nigel Biggar rightly argues that "careful moral deliberation about, and discrimination between, different sets of empirical data—between different cases—was not [Barth's] forte."[111] Here I confess I am not sure what Barth might offer current discussions of global justice and its idiom of human rights. Barth's contributions to ethics appear unable to engage philosophical distinctions between perfect and imperfect duties or

---

107. *CD* IV/3.2, 893.
108. *CD* III/4, 488.
109. *CD* IV/2, 803.
110. *CD* I/2, 447.
111. Nigel Biggar, "Barth's Trinitarian Ethics," in *The Cambridge Companion to Karl Barth*, ed. John Webster (Cambridge: Cambridge University Press, 2000), 212–27, at 225.

the role of aggregation in assessing conflicting obligations or tradeoffs, let alone practical discussions of whether social egalitarianism leads to capital flight, whether Americans, given their history, have special obligations to our southern neighbors in Mexico or more responsibility to first address gaps between whites and blacks in this country.

No doubt there are Barthian stances relevant to current discussions, including Barth's emphasis on the special relationship of the church. While Barth is no nationalist, his claim that Switzerland had a divine mandate to defend its borders indicates other special loyalties as well. Barth's theology of nations in relation to ecclesiology strikes me as a relatively unexamined field for Christian cosmopolitanism, often constrained by exclusive attention to his own historical context. But the debate over global justice raises fundamental questions about the character of moral life in the world. This Barth does address.

Barth's equivocation on the identity of the neighbor, if we want to call it that, may be a salutary one. It is yet another consequence of his dialectical theology. Like Augustine, his strongly eschatological and christological determination of ethics tries to navigate between universal and communal bonds. Augustine found it difficult to reconcile his account of the order of natural loves and their eschatological consummation, leading him to appeal to a "divine lottery" that constitutes our neighborly relations. Much of contemporary Christian ethics rejects the view that human beings are responsible for the ultimate good of the world. But it is trying to find ways to affirm virtuous kinds of contingent particularity even as it rejects vicious ones.

Here ethicists again might have something to learn from, rather than rail against, in Barth's aversion to an ethical system that cranks out solutions. Ad hoc apologetics, prudential, particularist, and providentialist, may be the best we can muster in the face of exceedingly complex moral and political issues of the global scale.

Christian ethics and theology must always be written *after* revelation, *after* grace. Unlike most Christian ethicists, Barth, with devotional joy, showed rather than theorized the place of scriptural exegesis in the Christian life. Biblical language shapes moral experience but it also is the revelation that transforms lives in the shadow of God's freedom and condescension. This God bore the cross. This God did not cross to the other side.

Augustine wrote for a very different age, with different "either/ors" and "both/ands" at stake. He too suffers caricature. We can be misled by his own rhetoric and polemic in the image of the emotionally wrenched pessimist and sweaty Platonist. He gave Christianity a biblical spirituality for the long haul in the face of unjust domination and wicked powers. Revolutionary and prophetic critique is easy. Patient and confident love is hard. Barth is not Augustine, though his accent is also the remission of sin rather than perfection of virtue, an ethics for the *viator*. Yet, and some might consider this faint praise, I think Barth's fundamental contribution to global justice debates may be a pastoral one: learning to live a life of gratuity without denying the claims of solidarity in the veil of the Law, the Gospel within the commandment. Here this "child of the 19th century" might still help us in the twenty-first century.[112]

---

112. John Webster, "Introducing Barth," in *Cambridge Companion to Karl Barth*, 11. I thank David Henreckson for helpful comments on a previous draft of this essay.

4 A Rich Disciple?

Barth on the Rich Young Ruler

WILLIE JAMES JENNINGS

The rich you have always with you.

And what will the disciples of Jesus do about this fact? What will the disciples of Jesus do if *they* are the rich or they want to be rich? Karl Barth's reflection on the rich young man, more famously called the rich young ruler, captures an aspect of the dilemma of discipleship in the Western world. Barth reflects on this rich man throughout his life and his work, but I will limit my observations to the snapshot of his reflections that we find in the *Church Dogmatics* II/2, §37, titled "The Command as the Claim of God," under the section called "The Form of the Divine Claim."[1] Reflecting there on Mark 10:17–22, Barth does what he does so well. In a way that is unparalleled in modern theology, he performs a theological reading of the political and a political reading of the theological—never allowing his thought to escape the real-world implications of following Jesus.

Karl Barth in a World at War

The year is 1941, a difficult year in Barth's life. He had returned home, back to Switzerland, back to a place caught painfully between a world at war and a world at its door, both geographically and financially. Barth is now among the bankers. As we now know, Switzerland was at the epicenter of the flow of monies not only between Axis powers but the Allies as

---

1. *CD* II/2, 613–30.

well.² We also know that Swiss banks were the destination of so much of the treasures of Holocaust victims, both those who out of desperation placed their resources there for safekeeping and those who had their resources stolen by the Nazis and placed in those same banks.³ Switzerland was also the destination of refugees, especially Jewish refugees seeking to escape from genocide. These refugees made poor and destitute by the war and racial oppression were trying to enter a country permeated with Nazi sympathizers, Allies and Axis spies, and people concerned only with making a profit from war.⁴

Barth watched and protested the treatment of these refugees who were all too often turned away at the Swiss borders, especially if their only reason for seeking entry was to avoid death, the death of another Jew.⁵ At the border, Jewish lives did not matter. These elements, (1) a country profiting from war yet afraid of attack, and (2) lives that do not matter, especially at the border and most especially at the checkpoints, expose some of the social and political fabric that Barth rubs against in his reflections at this moment and that we should rub against in our own theological work. Our times and 1941 are both similar and different—different in who now waits at checkpoints, both in Israel and the US for example, but similar in that there are lives that seemingly continue not to matter. Barth was not in an easy space as he reflected on the rich young man. His son Matthias had been killed in a climbing accident. Barth preached the funeral sermon for his own son on the first half of 1 Corinthians 13:12, "For now we see in a mirror, dimly, but then we will see face to face" (1 Cor. 13:12 NRSV). A young man gone and a father in mourning—this is Karl Barth.⁶

This is also Karl Barth in his home country, a country increasingly

---

2. Gerhard L. Weinberg, "German Plans and Policies regarding Neutral Nations in World War II with Special Reference to Switzerland," *German Studies Review* 22, no. 1 (Feb. 1999): 99–103.

3. Alan Cowell, "Dispatch: Switzerland's Wartime Blood Money," *Foreign Policy* 107 (Summer 1997): 132–44. Also see *Switzerland, National Socialism, and the Second World War: Final Report* (Zürich: Pendo Verlag, 2002).

4. *Die Schweiz und die Flüchtlinge zur Zeit des Nationalsozialismus [Switzerland and Refugees in the Nazi Era]*, Publications of the ICE, vol. 17 (Zürich: Chronos Verlag, 2001).

5. Angelo M. Codevilla, *Between the Alps and a Hard Place: Switzerland in World War II and the Rewriting of History* (Washington, DC: Regnery, 2000). Also see Isabel Vincent, *Hitler's Silent Partners: Swiss Banks, Nazi Gold, and the Pursuit of Justice* (New York: W. Morrow, 1997).

6. Eberhard Busch, *Karl Barth: His Life from Letters and Autobiographical Texts* (Philadelphia: Fortress, 1976), 311.

hostile to him because he refused to be silent in this anxiety-filled time of war and in a space governed by facile neutrality. In his famed lecture, "In the Name of God the Almighty," delivered that same year on the occasion of the 650th anniversary celebrations of Switzerland, Barth spoke a truth those in power did not want to hear. He spoke of a government that was exploiting the economically disadvantaged; that was restricting the freedom of the press and of speech; that was undermining the right of sanctuary for refugees; and that was engaged in lively trade with the Axis powers.[7] Barth was performing in speech what he wanted to see in action—the Christians of Switzerland exercising their citizenship by resisting collaboration with Germany and by refusing to cooperate with policies that were hurting the poor and oppressed.

The German government demanded that Barth be dealt with, and the Swiss authorities had lost all patience with their famed son. Barth knew that this was about money and fear as well as about political alliances and theological allegiances. This was about the rich young man.

The rich young man appears in small print in Barth's exposition of how God claims us. This is part of Barth's extensive work in laying the foundations for his ethics through thinking out the command of God. The rich man comes alive through Barth's exegesis, marking his every gesture and word with significance and connection to us. This is Barth's way with a text. He pays attention to the flow of the story and he improvises inside the flow. His reflections on this story are also flowing inside a wider story that encompasses Switzerland, Germany, and the West. It is the story of the self-sufficient man as he would name him in his open letter to American Christians a year later in 1942.[8] There he would talk about the self-delusion of the West as nations had looked in admiration at Hitler at the beginning of his emergence. They imagined Hitler as the instantiation of this self-sufficient man, one who embodied the greatness of the civilized human. In this regard, Hitler illumined the fantasy of the great white man as the productive symbol of national consciousness, cultural and political agency, and civilization.

Barth never wrote about generic humanity. His human was precisely two—the human performed in self-sufficiency through the political, economic, cultural, military, and theological operations of the West, and the

---

7. Karl Barth, "Im Namen Gottes des Allmächtigen! 1291–1941," in *Eine Schweizer Stimme: 1938–1945* (Zollikon–Zürich: Evangelischer Verlag, 1945), 201–32.

8. Karl Barth, "The Churches of Europe in the Face of the War," in *The Church and the War* (Zürich: Theologischer Verlag, 1944, reprinted by Wipf & Stock), 4.

human performed in and through Jesus of Nazareth. Call it the old Adam and the new Adam, or the old human and the new human if you wish, but what Barth was brushing up against was the image, the fantasy, and the imaginary of the great white man and drawing him into comparison with Mary's son. Barth compared them in order to destroy the one and give witness to the other. A christological determination of the human—this is what Barth was driving toward in his improvisation. Much like the great Thelonious Monk who in his compositions aimed at an openness of form through which conventional jazz formulations would collide with a studied dissonance and thereby be stated ever afresh, so too Barth's exegesis aimed at an openness that would set the stage for the collision of the old human with the new human and present the possibility of a fresh hearing of the Spirit's voice.[9]

Barth's Exegesis of the Story of the Rich Young Man

So enter the young man of Mark 10. Let's remind ourselves of the story:

> [17] As he was setting out on a journey, a man ran up and knelt before him, and asked him, "Good Teacher, what must I do to inherit eternal life?" [18] Jesus said to him, "Why do you call me good? No one is good but God alone. [19] You know the commandments: 'You shall not murder; You shall not commit adultery; You shall not steal; You shall not bear false witness; You shall not defraud; Honor your father and mother.'" [20] He said to him, "Teacher, I have kept all these since my youth." [21] Jesus, looking at him, loved him and said, "You lack one thing; go, sell what you own, and give the money to the poor, and you will have treasure in heaven; then come, follow me." [22] When he heard this, he was shocked and went away grieving, for he had many possessions.
>
> [23] Then Jesus looked around and said to his disciples, "How hard it will be for those who have wealth to enter the kingdom of God!" [24] And the disciples were perplexed at these words. But Jesus said to them again, "Children, how hard it is to enter the kingdom of God! [25] It is easier for a camel to go through the eye of a needle than for someone who is rich to enter the kingdom of God." [26] They were greatly astounded and said to one

---

9. Gabriel Solis, *Thelonious Monk and Jazz History in the Making* (Berkeley: University of California Press, 2008). Robin D. G. Kelley, *Thelonious Monk: The Life and Times of an American Original* (New York: Free Press, 2009).

another, "Then who can be saved?" ²⁷ Jesus looked at them and said, "For mortals it is impossible, but not for God; for God all things are possible."

²⁸ Peter began to say to him, "Look, we have left everything and followed you." ²⁹ Jesus said, "Truly I tell you, there is no one who has left house or brothers or sisters or mother or father or children or fields, for my sake and for the sake of the good news, ³⁰ who will not receive a hundredfold now in this age—houses, brothers and sisters, mothers and children, and fields with persecutions—and in the age to come eternal life. ³¹ But many who are first will be last, and the last will be first." (Mark 10:17–31 NRSV)

The rich man is no generic man. He is inside Israel's reverberant story that sounds loudly inside the Christian story and inside the Western Christianity that Barth confronts with his reflections. It would be fair to call this man a properly formed religious subject, formed inside the faith of his people. He comes seeking Jesus and when he finds him, he falls on his knees in front of Jesus. According to Barth, this action is the right action. It is a proper seeking of the command of God by one who is displaying a body formed in ritualized obedience. This rich man asks the right question of Jesus. "Good teacher, what must I do to inherent eternal life?" (v. 17). Barth will push his question into crisis, turning the question back on the one asking. He does this by splitting the rich man's question into two new questions—*who are you* as you ask this of Jesus? and do you know *who you are addressing* when you ask Jesus a question?

Although the rich man does not know it, he has entered risk by asking his question of Jesus. Jesus signals that risk by his immediate response to the man, "Why do you call me good? No one is good but God alone" (v. 18). Barth reads this interaction as a holy one in which the rich man is talking to God and now cannot avoid this space of judgment. This is Barth's way of overcoming theologically abstract visions of the judgment of God by humanizing and normalizing that judgment inside the quotidian realities of those with power seeking self-justification. The text gives us Jesus at work weaving Israel's story into his own story. His words to the rich man signal that story, "You know the commandments" (v. 19) and then he recites part of the so-called second table. Jesus speaks of a shared knowledge between himself and this man. But it is a shared knowledge with deep social and political consequences because it points directly to the neighbor.

Do not kill, steal, bear false witness, commit adultery, defraud anyone, and so forth—these things point to, as Barth says, "the most concrete doing or not doing in dealing" with one's neighbor.[10] The response of the rich man to Jesus's recitation begins to expose the problem of a formation in the faith that thwarts faith. "I have observed these things since my youth" (v. 20)—these words of the rich man, Barth suggests, capture the state of self-sufficiency. Yet Barth has captured more than simply *this* man's state of self-sufficiency. I cannot help but hear in his exegesis of the rich man's voice the Western self-sufficient man, a form of masculine existence that glories in accomplishment, achievement, and most centrally mastery. It is a form of masculine existence flexible enough to cover women and even entire groups of peoples. The rich man speaks of a mastery of divine command that marks his past and that will characterize his future. Barth, however, imagines Jesus unmasking this mastery to reveal not a saint but a transgressor.

Barth's reflections on verses 21–22 interpret this unmasking. The verses read as follows:

> [21] Jesus, looking (*emblepō*) at him, loved (*agapaō*) him and said, "You lack one thing; *go, sell* what you own, and *give the money to the poor*, and you will have treasure in heaven; then *come, follow me*." [22] When he heard this, he was shocked and went away grieving, for he had many possessions.

The verbs in this passage reveal much to Barth. They show a God who challenges the attitudes and actions that constitute an imprisoned subjectivity. Jesus, however, does not respond to this man's self-sufficiency with condemnation. Instead, he responds with love: "looking at him, he loved him" (v. 21). Jesus does for this man what this man cannot do—look out to the world with love and act on that love. The rich man's captivity—a captivity concealed to him—is a familiar theme, but Barth reads that theme against the backdrop of the rich man's religious formation. Here Barth opens an interpretative horizon on which to see modern Western visions of mastery as likewise forms of captivity. It is exactly such mastery that has coalesced so beautifully with religious formation, especially Christian formation from the colonial moment forward.

Barth understood well how theological mastery could be synchronized with racial mastery. That is, he understood how a *Volk* theology could fantasize a growth in Christian faith that was coordinated with the accumulation of knowledge and the celebration of the national and artistic spirit of a people—all woven together to the glory of their civilization.

---

10. *CD* II/2, 616.

Barth did not, however, fully grasp the wider racial and colonial horizon of this synchronization and its deep penetration into the didactic modes of Christian formation. Nevertheless, his exegesis of this text in fact intervenes powerfully into that very synchronization. The rich man imagines that his practice, his liturgical practice (if you will), has brought him close to Jesus (he falls on his knees and says the right words). But as Barth says, in coming to Jesus, the rich man has really passed him by.[11] The rich man is engaged in a sick form of self-evaluation that endlessly turns on assessing his accomplishments in relation to his formation. This is why he has not really obeyed the commandments, and has failed to recognize that he is being evaluated by God at that very moment. God is bringing judgment against his self-evaluation.

Once again Barth has pushed up against a wider horizon in his exegesis—the rich man exposes white Christian masculine subjectivity in its synchronization of its formation with its political, social, cultural, military, and economic accomplishments. This kind of subjectivity forms as a life strategy that strives for significance. Confined in an endless evaluative cycle, it is a form of subjectivity that imagines what Dana Nelson calls national manhood, a fraternity of men who see primarily—and sometimes only—other men in a calculus of esteem and respect.[12] Such is the world that Barth theologized inside and against, and such is our world, especially the world of Christian theology where many are yet caught in this soul-killing optic and this life-diminishing calculus. The rich man cannot see with the eyes of love, although he is seen by Jesus with love. Jesus responds to the rich man not with hatred, but with an invitation. He invites him to covenant partnership.

Barth captures the intensity of divine judgment embodied in this interpretive move. Jesus identifies what the rich man lacks from within the optic of love. Jesus speaks to him of his lack through love. Here we find a response to those with wealth that does not condemn and yet provides a way out of their endless self-evaluation. His lack appears precisely at the site of his wealth. It is only now, as Barth says, that we learn in the story that this man is rich. Although we have called him a rich man, his wealth was the hidden but always present subtext of his interaction with Jesus. But now it is revealed and with it, the power of mammon. Barth at this point in his exegesis will press hard the actions Jesus demands of the rich man—*sell* what you own,

---

11. *CD* II/2, 617.
12. Dana D. Nelson, *National Manhood: Capitalist Citizenship and the Imagined Fraternity of White Men* (Durham, NC: Duke University Press, 1998).

give it to the poor, then *come and follow* me. These words, Barth says, are the "unmasking and the annihilating" of the rich man.[13]

Unmasking and annihilating are hallmarks of Barth's Christology, which always opens toward the new human found in discipleship. By calling the rich man to covenant partnership, Jesus has killed him. He has killed him by bringing him into his life, his obedience to God his Father, and his life in the Spirit. God confronts the rich man with a death that leads to life. If no one can see God and live, then the rich man is now looking at God who is asking him to die. I cannot help but imagine Barth's exegesis at this point against the background of Swiss neutrality and wealth in a world convulsed in war. The rich man's position mirrors Barth's own nation's wealth in its refusal to attend to the poor and disadvantaged, and its commitment to and collaboration with the self-serving banking interests. Swiss neutrality presented itself as a commitment to peace and justice, but its subtext was the securing of its leadership in the financial markets.

Barth's exegesis of this text theologizes at the nexus of religious formation and banking practices, working at the ways in which the former have been enfolded in the latter. The rich man, Barth says, already has a covenant partner which is mammon: "He is ruled by the life proper to his great possessions with their immanent urge to preservation, exploitation, and augmentation."[14] So the demands placed on the rich man by Jesus present a new way of seeing oneself that confronts mammon's lordship. Jesus situates discipleship and a path to an alternative subjectivity at the site of the market—go and sell what you have, give it to the poor, and then come and follow me.

The rich man's theological mastery is resourced by his financial mastery, and he is being asked by Jesus to exercise that mastery in offering up both to God and neighbor. The rich man's giving up is little in comparison to what the Son of God has given up, but the crucial matter for Barth is that the rich man's giving up is placed inside this self-giving of Jesus. The man through his giving will have treasure in heaven and thereby begin the reorientation of his life through an alternative financial calculus. That alternative financial calculus is aimed concretely (to use one of Barth's favorite words) at the poor as the new point of coordination of faith and possessions. Concrete solidarity with the poor and disadvantaged shows the love of one's neighbor and constitutes the material conditions for the transformation of the rich man. Yet what brings the first two demands of selling possessions and giving the

---

13. *CD* II/2, 619.
14. *CD* II/2, 620.

money to the poor into clear focus is the third demand: to follow Jesus. The new financial calculus is enfolded in Jesus's life.

Jesus is inviting the rich man into his own freedom, a freedom for God and neighbor. The demands of Jesus are, for Barth, mapped across financial terrain as the productive site of the new human and the site that situates discipleship. And if we read this invitation against the backdrop of a Switzerland whose borders had been reduced, as Barth said, to one border (with Germany and the Axis powers), and who imagined constraint on all sides, then we can begin to see the theological and political density of Barth's evolving notion of freedom. Freedom for Barth never simply redirects obligation. Freedom is reframed within the life of Jesus. Citizenship for a Christian, as Barth is urging his Swiss compatriots to see, must be performed in the freedom of God concretely for neighbor both at the border checkpoints and for those affected by the financial dealings of the Swiss banks.

The rich man's horror and deep sorrow over hearing the demands of God show not only his captivity to his financial arrangements but also the abyss between God and humanity. The rich man's shock is matched only by that of the disciples of Jesus. Barth now turns his exegetical focus to the interaction between Jesus and his disciples, and makes *this* interaction the heart of the matter. For Barth, the contrast between the rich man and the disciples of Jesus *is* the point. Just as Jesus looked at the rich man, he now looks at the disciples within the same optic of love. Jesus looks at the disciples as his own (Barth says), but this looking does not turn away from the rich man. He looks at the rich man through his disciples, watching the rich man separate himself from the disciples as he walks away. This angle of vision again shows Barth's deepest ecclesial (reformed) sensibility. The obedient and the disobedient are always confronted with the same divine word. As Barth says, "It remains a Word of judgment even to the obedient, and a Word of promise even to the disobedient."[15]

Jesus speaks to his disciples in the wake of the rich man's leaving, that is, in the wake of his unmasking. Barth believes that what is exposed at this moment is the struggle of obedience to God. Jesus's repetition of the phrase—"How hard it is for those who have wealth to enter the kingdom of God!" (vv. 23–25)—shows the abyss of disobedience that "yawns even at [his disciples'] feet."[16] Disobedience is always within reach of Jesus's disciples because the rich man is always what they are reaching toward. The rich man

15. *CD* II/2, 624.
16. *CD* II/2, 624.

in them has been unmasked. The disobedient inside the obedient, the sinner inside the saint, yes, but Barth is doing different work with this theological insight. The disciples' question to Jesus, "Who then can be saved?" shows for Barth their realization that they have been caught up in the aspirations of the rich man and are therefore in exactly the same position as he. *They want to be the rich man.*

Barth's Exegesis of the Story as Challenge to the Church Today

That aspiration illumines human powerlessness in the face of the command of God. That powerlessness, however, is less about human capacity, although Barth does work with the language of capacity, and much more about subjectivity. As Barth says, those who follow the command would have to be able to remake themselves and become something other than they are.[17] Barth's point becomes crucial for us once we read it against the backdrop of the identities enabled by modern financial markets. As his Swiss compatriots did, we also inhabit an economic anthropology that frames life options, organizes appetites, and presents agency within constrained conditions. The fullness of Jesus (as Barth describes it) stands over against this man, the one constituted in economic constraint. By using the term "man" I want to highlight the masculine character of this performativity and try to capture the contrast that Barth is working out in his corpus.

That contrast is between the Western masculine and Jesus of Nazareth. The condition of captivity is found in the former and freedom is found only in Jesus. As Barth says, the disciples "accepted Jesus's different existence as determinate for themselves."[18] Life beyond this economic anthropology emerges through faith in and with Jesus. As Barth says, the disciples become obedient in faith. So Jesus's exchange with his disciples opens up a new vista into his life, and especially what I call his vicarious financial existence. Peter says to Jesus, "we have left everything and followed you" (v. 28). Jesus responds by speaking of what will be gained back. No one who has left anyone or anything for his sake and the sake of the gospel will not gain back a hundredfold. Barth queries what does this gaining back mean? Did it simply mean that the disciples were due a return on their investment? And if so, when would that be? Was it ever going to happen

---

17. *CD* II/2, 625.
18. *CD* II/2, 626.

and was Peter then justified in his concern? So much pivots on how we read Peter's concern.

When read from within a Western masculine frame, Jesus gets aligned with banking interests and his ministry moves inside a wider religious formation and financial cultivation toward the rich man. In such a schema, Peter's concern frames the ministry of Jesus: Jesus lives inside the temporal expectations of Peter and the other disciples. Barth reads Peter's concern differently; he reads it within the anxiety of the rich man. Though Peter is not rich, he functions inside the rich man's anxiety. Jesus, however, is inviting everyone who would be his disciple to leave precisely this concern and this anxiety and enter his journey with its complicated expectations and joyous hope. Barth imagines a chasm between Peter's concern and Jesus's response, which is bridged only by the Holy Spirit. Jesus is not answering Peter's concern but killing it and drawing him to new life inside Jesus's own hope. Indeed, by following Jesus, Peter is moving forward in faith. However, in his concern for what he might get back for his effort, he shows he is also looking back in half regret. Barth in a remarkable phrase says that when a disciple truly hears the command of God they will regret their regret.[19]

Barth is here working out a very different fiduciary vision of the divine promise bound up with the command of God. It could help us think out the relation of money to divine promise in ways that might draw Christians toward the freedom of God and away from the anxiety of the rich man. Even more importantly, if we cast Barth's reflection on the rich man against the modern formation of life between banking interests and white masculine subjectivities, then it opens up the possibility of rethinking what the divine command of selling what we have, giving it to the poor, and following Jesus might mean for us at this moment.

At a minimum, I think the command of God invites us to unmask the banking interests at work not only in our world, but in us. It is time we begin asking ourselves how our formation as Christians is enfolded in banking interests, and how we might start to unravel those entanglements in the ways we understand our faith and our life. It also invites us to envision a covenant partnership with God that requires that we be open not only to selling what we have but also more importantly to rethinking who we are.

19. *CD* II/2, 630.

5 The Compassion of Jesus Christ

Barth on Matthew 9:36

PAUL T. NIMMO

This chapter offers some brief theological reflections upon Karl Barth's treatment of the compassion of Jesus Christ. The focus will be on Barth's engagement with the theme at a significant juncture in the *Church Dogmatics* by means of the text of Matthew 9:36, a verse in which the compassion of Jesus Christ is rendered explicit. In the NRSV—the Greek and the German will be considered later—this text reads:

> When [Jesus] saw the crowds, he had compassion for them, because they were harassed and helpless, like sheep without a shepherd.

Though referenced at various points in the *Church Dogmatics*,[1] this verse receives especially close attention in part-volume IV/2.[2] The purpose of this chapter, then, will be threefold: first, to outline the dogmatic context of this attention; second, to exposit its core material concerns; and third, to offer some broader reflections on three dogmatic matters that arise in relation to its content.

---

1. *KD* II/1, 439; III/2, 252; and IV/3, 885. All translations of *KD* are the author's own. For reference, the published English translation is *CD*, here citing II/1, 390; III/2, 211; and IV/3, 774. References to page numbers in the English translation will be given in parentheses following the reference in the original.

2. The pages in question are *KD* IV/2, 205–8 (184–87).

PAUL T. NIMMO

The Setting

Karl Barth's most detailed exposition of Matthew 9:36 takes place in the doctrine of reconciliation, in *Church Dogmatics* IV/2, that part-volume which seeks to explore the way in which Jesus Christ is "the true human being, that is, the human being who in all His humanity is exalted above it."[3] This exaltation is not an isolated individual event: in this particular human being, all of humanity is implicated and included.[4] This kingly work of Jesus Christ is explored in the opening paragraph of the part-volume, §64, titled "The Exaltation of the Son of Man."

The opening section of this paragraph, "The Homecoming of the Son of Man," treats of the person and the knowledge of the One who is exalted. It considers the basis of his exaltation in the divine act of election, the realization of his exaltation in the event of the incarnation, and the basis of the revelation of his exaltation in the events of the resurrection and the ascension.

The following section, "The Royal Man," seeks to build on these ontological and epistemological foundations. It thus develops in turn "the knowledge of Jesus Christ in so far as he, as the Son of God, is also the Son of Man—the human being Jesus of Nazareth."[5] Here, Jesus Christ as the true, new, exalted human being comes into view—and so too will Matthew 9:36.

Barth opens this section with a series of four formal observations about the human Jesus drawn from his overview of the Gospel texts. They concern the way Jesus was present among his contemporaries—as one who could not fail to be seen and heard, as one who demanded and effected a decision in respect of him, as one who was present in an unforgettable, and an irrevocable way.[6]

From such formal observations, Barth moves quickly to material considerations. He sets forth a thesis that will govern all that follows, stating: "the royal human being of the New Testament tradition is created 'according to God' (*kata theon*)." Barth offers the following elucidation:

> He exists as a human being analogously [*analog*] to the way of existence of God. His thinking and desiring, His acting and His attitude occur in correspondence [*Entsprechung*], form in the world of the creature a parallel [*eine Parallele*] to the plan and the intention, to the work and the

---

3. *KD* IV/1, 144 (131).
4. *KD* IV/1, 144 (131).
5. *KD* IV/2, 173 (154–55).
6. *KD* IV/2, 175–85 (156–66).

behaviour of God. He images God [*bildet Gott ab*]; He is as a human being [God's] εἰκών (Col. 1:15). . . . He does that which is demanded and expected of the human being in the covenant, corresponding [*entsprechend*] in a deed of [human] faithfulness to the faithfulness of God.[7]

In what follows, Barth details three specific ways in which this correspondence, this analogy or parallel, is evident. First, he observes that the royal human being—in common with God and the people of God—is "overlooked, forgotten, undervalued, despised"; second, he states that Jesus in a biased fashion preferred "the low, the small, the weak, [and] the poor to all those in the world who were high, great, mighty, [and] rich"; and third, he posits that Jesus evidenced a "markedly revolutionary character of relationship to the orders of value and life that were valid in His context."[8] These three material correspondences all serve, for Barth, to indicate how the life-act of Jesus Christ images the existence of God.

Yet precisely at this point, Barth indicates that the *decisive* material point has not yet been reached. Instead, Barth continues: "The word which is really the first and also the last word is undoubtedly that the man Jesus, like God, is not against but *for human beings*."[9] Indeed, Barth notes, "the royal human being Jesus reflects and images the divine 'Yes' to the human being and to their world."[10] The person of Jesus, his life and work, is thus a mirror in which there is revealed the "Yes" of God to humanity and to creation. Of course, the "Yes" of Jesus—like the "Yes" of God—is not without a "No": it is not a word of approval bereft of the power to divide, discover, and punish. Indeed, it is precisely in its affirmation that it encloses and accompanies its negation. Yet the note of affirmation is the first and the last and the dominant note throughout: if there is a dialectical relationship here, it is a supplementary or unbalanced rather than a complementary one. As such, it reflects similar dialectical conceptualities elsewhere in Barth's theology—that of Adam and Jesus, or of Law and Gospel. Of Jesus as the reflection and image of this inherently and deliberately imbalanced divine "Yes" and "No," Barth writes:

> The person of Jesus is the royal human being, in so far as He is not only *one* human being with other human beings, but *the* human being *for*

---

7. *KD* IV/2, 185–86 (166).
8. *KD* IV/2, 186–99 (167–79), with quotes taken from 186 (167), 188 (168), and 191 (171).
9. *KD* IV/2, 200 (180).
10. *KD* IV/2, 200 (180).

them: for them, just as God is for them—the human being, in whom the love, faithfulness, salvation and glory of God is directed to them in the concrete form of a historical relationship between two human beings.... He is as a human being the work and the revelation of the compassion of God [*des Erbarmens Gottes*], of God's Gospel, kingdom of peace, and reconciliation.... He is in this sense God's creaturely, earthly, human correspondence [*Entsprechung*].[11]

This, then, is the decisive point of the section, the apex of the argument that the human Jesus corresponds to God. Jesus is the perfect analogy, the perfect image, as he shows forth the compassion of God in the proclamation and realization of the kingdom of God and its attendant blessings of peace and reconciliation.

In the following small-print material, the reader is drawn into the heart of the exegetical support for this theological position, as Barth exposits in sequence four different sets of material from the New Testament. The *first* set of texts offers a record of the human reactions to encounter with the human Jesus, and Barth observes that any response of fear is opposed not only by the command not to fear, but also by the command to rejoice. The cause of such joy, Barth contends, is that "what encounters them in this human being is the clear, unambiguous, and *saving compassion* of God which speaks compellingly."[12] There is no abstract wrath of God, no "No" of God divorced from this encompassing "Yes." The *second* set of material is the *Magnificat* of Mary and the *Benedictus* of Simeon from Luke 1, both texts replete with citations of and allusions to the Old Testament, and both texts referring explicitly to the mercy and compassion of God. In view here, then, for Barth, is the "indirect identity" between "the merciful, saving visitation of God [to Israel] in faithfulness to Himself and to Israel" attested in these hymns, and "the life, words and deeds, and passion, death, and resurrection of Jesus of Nazareth" to which Luke's presentation is oriented.[13] The phrase "indirect identity" here serves to encompass what Barth has earlier described under the terms "image" and "analogy," and here again describes as "correspondence." The *fourth* and final set of material in view here comprises the list of beatitudes of the Gospels of Matthew and Luke. Barth considers these to be "synthetic statements," emanating not from human knowledge or wisdom,

---

11. *KD* IV/2, 201 (180).
12. *KD* IV/2, 203 (182).
13. *KD* IV/2, 205 (184).

and expressing not human endowments or virtues, but indicating "in human words the proclamation of a judgement *of God*."[14] The reason for the *Beati qui* of the beatitudes, the *makarioi hoi* of the makarisms, is that it is in the very person of the One proclaiming that the kingdom of God has drawn near and is now present, and that the message of this kingdom is revealed to be a message of salvation and life and joy.

But the important *third* set of material—where, in the course of four pages, Barth examines Matthew 9:36—has thus far been omitted, and it now demands attention.

The Exegesis

Of all the texts in the Gospels that might illustrate the divine compassion, Barth selects this one, describing it as "supremely instructive [*höchst lehrreich*]."[15] Particularly relevant is the opening clause: "When [Jesus] saw the crowds, he had *compassion* for them" (Matt. 9:36a). The noun "compassion" here—a form of the verb *erbarmen* is used in Barth's original German—renders the Greek term *esplanchnisthē*, from the middle verb *splanchnizomai*, meaning to have pity or to feel sympathy.[16] The verb is related to the Greek word *splanchnon*, usually found in the plural *splanchna*, which means one's entrails—one's bowels. As in the present world, so in the ancient world, "inner body parts serve [...] as referents for psychological aspects," and the bowels were perceived to be "the seat of the emotions."[17] The equivalent for us, then, of such visceral language, might be to speak of the "heart," as "the seat and source of love . . . sympathy, and mercy,"[18] although the colorful phrase "to vent one's spleen [*splanchna*]" still survives.

Barth begins his investigation by noting that this term *splanchna* appears in connection with the mercy *of God* in the text of the *Benedictus* which he explored immediately before, at Luke 1:78. There will be cause to recall this particular reference at the very end of this chapter. In Matthew 9:36, however, the same term is used, not of God per se, but of *"Jesus of Nazareth,*

---

14. *KD* IV/2, 209 (188).
15. *KD* IV/2, 205 (184).
16. W. Bauer, W. F. Arndt, F. W. Gingrich, and F. W. Danker, *A Greek-English Lexicon of the New Testament and Other Early Christian Literature* [hereafter BAGD], 3rd ed. (Chicago: University of Chicago Press, 2001), 938, s.v. *splanchnizomai*.
17. BAGD, 938, s.v. *splanchnon*.
18. BAGD, 938, s.v. *splanchnon*.

who walks through the cities and villages of Galilee, teaching, preaching, and healing."[19] The implication is clear: this same Jesus is the very image of God, indeed God himself, in these actions.

Barth moves immediately, however, to observe that this term is "untranslatably [*unübersetzbar*] strong ... the misery that was before Him not only affected Him, not only touched His heart—sympathy in our sense of the word would not be the word for it—but entered His heart, into His very being."[20] And the consequence was that "it was now completely His misery—no longer theirs, but completely His: He suffered it in their place."[21] Because Jesus had made the misery of the people his own, their own lament could in truth only be a lingering echo, a lament in a certain sense thus already obsolete and superfluous. And so Barth writes:

> To the compassion [*Erbarmen*] of God which saves radically, totally, and conclusively there corresponded the help which Jesus brought to humanity by way of His radical, total, and conclusive surrender [*Hingabe*]. In this surrender [*Hingabe*], in the fact that ... He had compassion [*es ihn erbarmte*] on seeing the people, He was on earth as God is in heaven.[22]

What moved Jesus was seeing the crowds—*tous ochlous*. This term "crowds," according to Barth, is all-encompassing and indiscriminating: "Strictly speaking, there is no one who does not belong to it."[23] Barth observes that precisely this holistic perception of the crowd runs counter to the universal human desire *not* to consider oneself to belong to "the crowd" but instead "to consider oneself as an exceptional case."[24] It is for this crowd that Jesus has compassion, a crowd that—in contrast to his treatment of the Pharisees, the scribes, and even his disciples—Jesus never accuses or berates. Instead, there is a "solidarity" with them, a "strong solidarity" even, "grounded in His compassion [*Erbarmen*]."[25] The strength of the connection between the crowds and Jesus and between Jesus and the crowds thus rests in his response to their plight, and only in that compassionate perception.

The plight of the crowds, Luke surmises, is their lack of a shepherd.

19. *KD* IV/2, 205 (184).
20. *KD* IV/2, 205 (184).
21. *KD* IV/2, 205 (184).
22. *KD* IV/2, 205 (184).
23. *KD* IV/2, 205 (185).
24. *KD* IV/2, 205 (185).
25. *KD* IV/2, 206 (185).

This explanation for the compassion of Jesus invokes Ezekiel 34:2–6, which describes how the sheep of Israel are scattered and lost on account of the selfishness, inattentiveness, and cruelty of their appointed shepherds. Jesus had compassion on the crowd, because they "were like these sheep, who had shepherds, and yet did *not* have shepherds, because the ones they had were not *true* shepherds."[26] Barth proceeds to outline—with reference to and paraphrase from the passage in Ezekiel—the respective characters of the good and the derelict shepherd. True shepherds, Barth writes, "would know themselves to be responsible for [the people] and thus completely *for* them"; this is in stark contrast to the pretend shepherds, who would be "not there for the people [*Volk*], but basically there for themselves."[27] There is thus a gap, a vacancy, for a good shepherd. And Barth observes that this gap "became clear and hurt even more, every time one of [the people] thought they should be the shepherd and [the people] thought that person could indeed be it."[28]

According to Barth, "the compassion of Jesus simply steps into this gap"—"It is precisely in this place that He Himself belongs."[29] And so Jesus is the good shepherd who comes among and for all people.[30] The crowds are suffering, though they realize neither that they are missing a good shepherd nor even that they are in misery; indeed they do not even recognize the good shepherd when he does arrive. Yet this lack of recognition, for Barth, does "not alter the actual deep and strong connectedness and solidarity of Jesus with this people, and of this people with Jesus."[31] It remains the case, Barth writes, that "[t]he visitation of God ... in ... this one person ... was earthly *history* in the form of the compassion [*des Erbarmens*] which Jesus had upon them; the 'great joy' intended and already prepared for all people was objective *event*."[32] Barth concludes with a reprisal of the key themes in view: the theme of divine visitation in the person of Jesus and the theme of the compassion of Jesus as the very image of God.

With this exploration—and the subsequent writing on the beatitudes—behind him, Barth moves in a third section of "The Royal Man" to discuss the inseparable connection between the person and the work of Jesus,[33] and

---

26. *KD* IV/2, 207 (186).
27. *KD* IV/2, 207 (186–87).
28. *KD* IV/2, 208 (187).
29. *KD* IV/2, 208 (187).
30. *KD* IV/2, 208 (187).
31. *KD* IV/2, 208 (187).
32. *KD* IV/2, 208 (187).
33. *KD* IV/2, 214 (193).

the arrival of the kingdom of God in the speech and activity of Jesus.[34] He concludes the section with a reflection upon the orientation of Jesus's life toward the cross,[35] but at this point it is helpful to return to consider in more detail Barth's treatment of Matthew 9:36.

The Analysis

In what follows, the relationship between Barth's exegesis of Matthew 9:36 and the principal loci of systematic theology is considered along three trajectories. The first two trajectories are explicit in the text itself, as within his exposition Barth expressly addresses issues in theological anthropology and atonement theory. Each of these will be considered in turn. The third trajectory, which will be treated by way of conclusion, pertains to the construal of the divine attributes. Though this trajectory is not explicit in Barth's writing on Matthew 9:36, it is thematically close to the text and seems implicit in its reflections; it also arises in other places in the *Church Dogmatics* where Barth considers the divine compassion in Scripture.

Insights for Theological Anthropology

Jesus's compassion has a particular object in Matthew's Gospel—the crowds. And so Barth reflects on precisely these crowds, and does so with reference to both the historical text and present reality. The result is that Barth suggests that all people are part of the "crowd"—without exception. The people of today are thus no different from the gathering of people whom Jesus saw in first-century Palestine.

There is a lovely pastoral insight here: Barth refers to the "tiresome desire" human beings share to think that it is only everyone else that belongs to the crowd, "but in precisely this way they show that they truly do belong [to it]."[36] Seeking to be individual and unique on the one hand, and to be separate and distinct from others on the other hand, renders the individual person more than ever part of the whole.

Yet belonging to the crowd is not just a function of shared createdness,

---

34. *KD* IV/2, 215–74 (194–247).
35. *KD* IV/2, 275–93 (249–64).
36. *KD* IV/2, 205 (185).

something that can be parsed through the basic denominator of common humanity. The deeper reality of this belonging lies in the fact that the reality of *this* particular crowd is an invidious thing. In the context of this particular crowd, names become indifferent and persons become characterless—"human beings," Barth writes, "are simply no longer human beings."[37] There is a fallenness to this humanity of the crowd, manifesting itself in something that might be considered a profound lostness—one might say even an *original* lostness, unavoidable and inescapable.

This material comes within touching distance of Barth's account of original sin, in which God sees, addresses, and treats humanity as a unity—as a "crowd," one might say—on account of a radical and universal disobedience. This verdict, Barth notes elsewhere, implies "a judgment on that which is human history apart from the will and word and work of God,"[38] such that "all of us [are] concluded in disobedience."[39]

And the lostness of the crowds is not simply something external to the people involved, something in which they are involved but over which they have no control. Rather it is something for which they are—at least in part—responsible. In their freedom and responsibility, they have in the past raised false shepherds from their midst, and in the present do not recognize the True Shepherd who stands before them. The same is true of today's readers of the text—their hearts are just as much a factory of false shepherds and of failure to recognize the True Shepherd.

Insights for Atonement Theory

The consequence of this fallenness of the crowd can only be misery. Yet misery is not the end of the story. Jesus desires nothing from the crowds—nothing "*apart from* their misery, to take it away from them and onto Himself."[40] And this is true, remarkably, despite the fact that the extent of the crowd is not coterminous either with the disciples or with the community, and indeed that the crowd "usually never believed."[41] Despite all this, it was the misery

---

37. *KD* IV/2, 206 (185).
38. *KD* IV/1, 563 (505).
39. *KD* IV/1, 570 (512). This is what original sin means for Barth: that the whole of human history, including both individual human beings and the crowds, stands before the divine judgment under the sign of Adam.
40. *KD* IV/2, 206 (185).
41. *KD* IV/2, 206 (185).

of this particular crowd that was precisely "that which Jesus saw, that which moved Him to compassion [*es ihn erbarmte*], that which He took from [the people] and onto Himself, and that on account of which the same people cried 'Crucify Him!'"[42] There is no member of the crowd upon whom Jesus did not, does not, have compassion—then or now.

This universal scope of the atonement of Jesus Christ resonates with an earlier dogmatic claim of Barth, linking Christology and theological anthropology: "[Jesus Christ] is the human being *for human beings*, for the other human being and other human beings, for His fellow human being and fellow human beings.... He is related to [other human beings] ... not just partly, not just incidentally, not just additionally, but originally, exclusively, and totally."[43] In light of this claim there can be understood in its full and majestic sweep Barth's language of the misery of the crowds not only affecting Jesus or touching his heart, but entering into his very being—constituting his very humanity.[44]

This absolute solidarity with the crowd has a twofold consequence. First, it leads Jesus into what Barth describes as the "greatest [possible] isolation over and against [the crowd]," in a way reminiscent of the solitude and separation of Gethsemane and Golgotha.[45] This isolation is a corollary of the *substitutional* nature of the atonement evidenced in the exegesis: Jesus's assumption of human misery becomes the primary mode of its being borne and then removed—in turn, it no longer belongs to the crowd but is completely his, suffered by him for them in their place.[46] Jesus alone, therefore, was not only *with* the crowds, but truly *for* them, and this as the very image of God. Barth writes of Jesus correspondingly as

> the true shepherd, who did not consider that the herd was there for Him, but that He was there for the herd, the truly royal human being, in whose human compassion the compassion of God was mirrored, the God who had sworn faithfulness to humanity and who was now in a final and complete way in the act of demonstrating it.[47]

Second, this absolute (and substitutional) solidarity with the crowd is *redemptive* for the crowd—in the Son's assuming of the burdens of the crowd,

---

42. *KD* IV/2, 207 (185).
43. *KD* III/2, 248 (208).
44. *KD* IV/2, 205 (184).
45. *KD* IV/2, 206 (185).
46. *KD* IV/2, 205 (184).
47. *KD* IV/2, 208 (187).

there takes place the liberation of humanity. And this in turn leads to the reconciliation of the crowd not only as individuals, but also as a collective or community of individuals. Barth writes that to the good shepherd described in Ezekiel, the people "would not be a nameless, inhuman mass, but a single group [*Volk*] of people: He would name and call each and every one, sustaining [*geweidet*] them, such that all would be together and yet everyone would have their own place."[48] In Jesus, the good shepherd, the individual is reconciled, not as an isolated or independent individual but rather as one individual in the crowd—the true crowd, the reconciled crowd. Similarly, the community is reconciled, not as an amorphous or impersonal collective but rather as a community of individuals—true individuals, reconciled individuals.

The Compassion of Jesus and the Compassion of God

One further area of dogmatic inquiry merits attention, and that is the relationship between the compassion of the human Jesus and the compassion of God, which the former images completely and perfectly. It was noted above that in one of the most compelling moments in his exegesis of the text, Barth refers to the use of the term *splanchna* in respect of Jesus as a predication that is "untranslatably [*unübersetzbar*] strong."[49] The import of this has already been registered in respect of the human Jesus. But given that it is God who in a second mode of being constitutes the personhood of the royal Jesus, a further question arises as to the extent to which this compassion touches the bowels—perhaps better, the heart—of God. There arise here a raft of germane questions on the relationship between the activity and disposition of God in the economy and the eternal divine being. There is vexed theological ground at stake here.

It is certainly true that in the exegesis under review there is no detailed treatment of the divine attributes. And yet the idea that the compassion of Jesus is "untranslatably strong" serves as an indicator of how profoundly it registers also in the being of God, for as already mentioned, it is God who in a second mode of being constitutes the personhood of the royal Jesus. Such a construal of the vivid and ineffable depth of the divine compassion is in turn clearly evident in Barth's treatment—prior to the doctrine of election, in

---

48. *KD* IV/2, 207 (186).
49. *KD* IV/2, 205 (184).

Church Dogmatics II/1—of the perfections of the divine loving, in particular the perfections of grace and mercy.

A brief reminder of some of the contours of Barth's position may be germane.

First, on grace, Barth explicitly opposes any position that considers that grace is "only a gift of God, which God might give or also not give, [or] only an attribute which can be accorded to God or not."[50] Instead, Barth emphasizes that "God is gracious . . . grace is itself really and essentially divine."[51] Barth continues: "Any . . . conception of God, in which God is not yet or is not yet fundamentally, decisively, and comprehensively recognized as gracious, is to think . . . of gods or idols of this world and not of the true, living God."[52] This grace, moreover, "is real in God Himself in a way which is other, hidden to us and incomprehensible."[53]

And second, on mercy [*Barmherzigkeit*], which German word derives from exactly the same etymological root as the word *Erbarmen* that has here throughout been translated as "compassion," Barth writes as follows: "God *is* merciful [*barmherzig*] . . . because and as God has pity [*es jammert ihn*] in eternity, because God only has to call to mind God's mercy!"[54] And Barth continues: "The freedom and power of God's mercy [*Barmherzigkeit*] is thus not first that of a 'disposition in the economy of salvation', but truly and rightly the freedom and power of God's eternal divinity."[55]

A truly charitable reading of Barth at this point might recognize not only the way in which, for Barth, mercy and grace pertain explicitly and essentially to the eternal being of God as well as to the divine work in the economy; it might also recognize the dogmatic significance and possible implications of this way of speaking about the divine being. Such statements may be striking and innovative, especially in comparison with the broad trajectory of the theological tradition. And such statements may indeed sit uneasily with, and even contradict, dogmatic statements that Barth advances elsewhere. However, statements such as these are far from isolated in the writing of Barth in the *Church Dogmatics* and beyond. To suggest that they are merely figures of speech or that they are simply trumped by other material elsewhere in Barth's corpus might in truth seem rather uncharitable.

50. *KD* II/1, 400 (356).
51. *KD* II/1, 400 (356).
52. *KD* II/1, 401 (357).
53. *KD* II/1, 402 (357).
54. *KD* II/1, 418 (372).
55. *KD* II/1, 418 (372).

The Compassion of Jesus Christ

In any event, precisely here, in the midst of the material on the divine mercy in *Church Dogmatics* II/1—where Barth is relating his innovation to the tradition, and to Polanus in particular—there is a striking echo of the visceral language of the *splanchna* of Matthew 9:36 on the divine compassion, and a striking indication of the radicality of Barth's position on the divine attributes. Referring to the *Benedictus* of Luke 1:78—which, as noted, is explored in *Church Dogmatics* IV/1 just before the treatment of Matthew 9:36—Barth concludes unequivocally (yet shockingly) that "[t]he compassion of God truly concerns His *splanchna* and thus no less than in the case of all God's other attributes His eternal and simple essence."[56]

In the innermost ineffable depths of the divine being, then, there is found grace and mercy—the divine compassion. It is this compassion of the eternal God, penetrating every moment of the essence of God, that is imaged in the compassion of the royal Jesus for the crowds. And it is this compassion that stands for Barth, and for the crowds, and for today's reader, at the very heart of the gospel.

---

56. *KD* II/1, 416–17 (371).

6 The Journey of God's Son

Barth and Balthasar on the Parable of the Lost Son

DANIEL L. MIGLIORE

Barth's striking interpretation of Jesus's parable of the lost son (Luke 15:11–32) is strategically located in his doctrine of reconciliation, and his reading merits careful study for a number of reasons. Barth is here vigorously engaged in interpreting Scripture, not merely formulating a doctrine of Scripture; he is employing analogy in his theological reflection, not just offering a theory of analogy; and he is using the parable of a risky leave-taking and a joyous homecoming to speak of God's free and costly gift to the world in Jesus Christ, instead of describing that event in formal, abstract concepts. What is perhaps most intriguing about Barth's reading of the parable, however, is that it offers an unexpected opportunity to revisit two much-debated issues in Barth's theology: whether it is necessary to ascribe "command" and "obedience" to the intra-trinitarian life of God as the basis of the obedience of the incarnate Son of God;[1] and whether Barth's all-encompassing christocentrism is finally "constrictive," as has been charged, because it fails to allow room for genuinely free human activity in the drama of creation, reconciliation, and redemption.

I begin with a review of Barth's earliest sermon on the parable of the lost son preached during his ministry in Safenwil. Then I analyze his striking analogical or "indirect christological" reading of the parable in *Church Dogmatics* IV/2. The core of the chapter is the third section, which examines the differences in Barth's and Hans Urs von Balthasar's analogical readings of the parable that reflect their distinctive trinitarian emphases. In a fourth

---

1. *CD* IV/1, 202.

The Journey of God's Son

section I comment on the divergent understandings of human freedom that inform Barth's and Balthasar's readings. In a brief final section I offer a few concluding reflections.

Barth's Earliest Sermon on the Parable

References to the parable of the lost son are found in notes for his confirmation classes during his pastorate in Safenwil. In one of the sessions of the class of 1915–1916, he instructs his youthful members on the meaning of the address "Our Father" in the Lord's Prayer, reminding them of the father in the parable of the lost son. "That is God as shown and brought to us by Jesus," Barth tells the class. "With him we are at home. He gives us freedom, he waits for us, he goes out to meet us, he welcomes us, and he is exceedingly joyful when we return to him."[2]

It was in 1917, however, that Barth first preached on the parable to his Safenwil congregation. The realities of World War I are the wider historical context of the sermon, although Barth makes only a few offhand references to the war. The sermon has three major themes. First, from the outset Barth draws attention to the words that come toward the end of the parable: "And they began to be joyful." Barth calls this "the kernel, the north star, the chief point" of its message. "This is the gospel, the message of the kingdom of God. It is called gospel because it is a message of joy. It proclaims this one and only thing: how joy begins."[3] Barth continues: Christ himself, in his very person, is the joyful message. He is the great divine miracle, or if one prefers, the great divine foolishness. He is Emmanuel, God with us, and if God is with us, then joy has begun. "Therefore in the story of the lost son, we have to do with gospel, Christ, God—we always say the same thing with these words: the source of joy, the power of joy, the creation of joy, that is for us, with us, and in us and our world, despite all else and victorious over all else that is now still in us and with us and in our world."[4] In this early sermon, Barth clearly gives priority to the message of joy in the parable. He goes immediately to the heart of its message, even though the unconditional love of the father for his son and the joyful celebration that ensues are described only at the

---

2. Karl Barth, *Konfirmandenunterricht 1909–1921*. Gesamtausgabe I:3 (Zürich: Theologischer Verlag, 1987), 138. See also 169, 323.

3. Karl Barth, *Predigten 1917*. Gesamtausgabe I:9 (Zürich: Theologischer Verlag, 1999), 306–7.

4. Barth, *Predigten 1917*, 308.

end of the story. Notable is the fact that the early Barth already places the proclamation of the gospel prior to consideration of the law and human sin.

Although one might describe Barth's first extended reading of the parable as proto-christocentric, it is nevertheless far removed from the full-throttled christocentrism of his later reading in the *Church Dogmatics*. Barth does not yet explain how or in what sense the parable bears witness to the atoning work of Christ. As we shall see, Barth's dissatisfaction with the dominant reading of the parable in nineteenth-century liberal Protestantism, with its almost exclusive focus on the love of the father, was one of the reasons he offered his strong christocentric interpretation in *CD* IV/2.

A second major theme of Barth's early sermon is that we are all one with the lost son, "really and truly all of us." He continues: "If we absolutely do not want to acknowledge ourselves as sinners, we can do this, but we thereby exclude ourselves also from the great joy."[5] Although none of us likes to be identified with this lost son, his experience is not only the experience of a wild, godless young man; it is, Barth says, the human experience of all of us, the deepest truth of our entire life. "We have all left the father's house and lost ourselves and our divine inheritance in a strange country and now must hunger and tend to the swine."[6] As already noted, Barth speaks of our being one with the lost son's self-endangerment only after he has called attention to the joy of the gospel. This order of the sermon clearly anticipates Barth's later explicit insistence that we discern the depth of human sin only in the light of the gospel of the grace of God in Jesus Christ. However, while calling his congregation to recognize themselves in the lost son and his way into the far country, Barth does not explicitly speak of Jesus Christ the Son of God who has preceded us on a journey into the far country and who leads us home to the Father.

In a third theme of the sermon, Barth speaks of God's gift of freedom to humanity and his refusal to employ coercion. "Look, here is the man who wants to be his own Lord, wants to live for himself. He can do it; no force holds him back; God has given freedom to his creature."[7] God does not violate his gift of freedom even when it is abused. The theme of human freedom and the divine refusal to coerce finds special prominence in Barth's description of the lost son's decision to return home. In his abysmal state, the lost son remembers the abundance of the life and love in the father's house. When this

---

5. Barth, *Predigten 1917*, 309.
6. Barth, *Predigten 1917*, 310.
7. Barth, *Predigten 1917*, 310.

recollection happens, it comes, Barth says, like a flash of lightning, and thereafter gives us no rest. Like the lost son, we remember that we belong to God, that our miserable and meaningless life is not our true existence. Meanwhile, God waits. He respects our freedom. There is in us, Barth insists, a voice that reminds us that we belong to God, a seed in us that carries the promise of the joy of the kingdom of God. "God is not the God of the brave, righteous, virtuous, and pious. God is the God of the useless, the unbeliever, the tax collector and sinner."[8] The one thing God expects from human beings is that in their alienation and misery, they seek God and dare to say, "I will [return to my father's house]." Just what is the catalyst of this recollection and what prompts the decision of the lost son to return to his father, Barth does not say.

In summary, while his initial sermon on the parable of the lost son shows the early Barth preaching with power and speaking in a manner that anticipates some of the emphases of his later work, it is far from being his last word on this text. So we turn to his provocative exposition of the parable in the *Church Dogmatics*.

Barth's Christocentric Reading of the Parable in *CD* IV/2

We should first note the strategic location Barth gives to his reading of the parable in his doctrine of reconciliation. Already in *CD* IV/1, §59.1, the theme of "The Way of the Son of God into the Far Country" is developed at length, even if it is not the parable of the lost son but John 1:1–14 and Paul's celebrated Christ hymn in Philippians 2:5–11 that provide the key New Testament texts.[9] According to Barth, the true divinity of God is actualized and revealed in Jesus Christ as a movement of self-emptying, self-humbling, and freely given obedience even to death on a cross. It is, however, in *CD* IV/2, §64.2, titled "The Homecoming of the Son of Man," that Barth offers his close reading of the parable as an analogy both of the self-humiliation of the Son of God for our salvation and of the return and exaltation of the Son of Man in his royal humanity to God the Father.[10] The motif of "the lost son" and thus indirect reference to Jesus's parable is found a number of times not only in Barth's doctrine of reconciliation but also in his doctrine of election.[11]

---

8. Barth, *Predigten 1917*, 312.
9. *CD* IV/1, 157–210.
10. *CD* IV/2, 21–25.
11. See *CD* IV/1, 11, 259, 481; IV/2, 23, 444; II/2, 157, 158, 173.

What Barth says in his prefaces to *CD* IV/1 and IV/2 sets these two volumes in the context of major theological controversies of the time. In the preface to IV/1, Barth tells us that in this volume he is engaged "in an intensive, although for the most part quiet, debate with Rudolf Bultmann."[12] Contrary to Bultmann's rule that we can speak rightly of God *only* by speaking of a particular human self-understanding, a central theme of IV/1 is that God in Christ "has revealed Himself and His nature, the essence of the divine."[13] In other words, in the light of God's self-revelation in Christ, Barth insists in IV/1 that we are able to speak of God's humility and self-expenditure as belonging to the very essence of his deity, even if this requires the most radical revisions of all our prior concepts of God.

In the preface to IV/2, Barth claims he now has a new dialogue partner and a new set of concerns. In this volume his aim is to offer an "Evangelical answer to the Marian dogma of Romanism — both old and new. I have nowhere mentioned this, let alone attacked it directly. But I have in fact shown that it is made superfluous by the 'Exaltation of the Son of Man' and its anthropological implications."[14] Here Barth summarizes his reply to the charge that his Christology is "constrictive." What God has done for us in the fully human life of Jesus Christ is inclusive rather than exclusive. The sufficiency of the new humanity of God in Jesus calls for our witness and participation but needs no supplementation to make up for what it supposedly lacks.

Turning now to Barth's exposition of the parable in *CD* IV/2, there is no avoiding the fact that for most readers what they meet here has the appearance at first glance — and maybe also at a second or third — of a highly strained and arbitrary interpretation, altogether reminiscent of lavish allegorical readings of biblical texts in the early church fathers and in the fourfold hermeneutic of medieval times. While Barth is in fact respectful of these earlier theological exegetes, it would be a mistake simply to dismiss his reading of the parable as allegory. Indeed, he readily agrees that a "direct Christological reference" of the parable would be a "strained" or "overinterpretation."[15] By a "direct Christological reference" he means the sort of allegorical interpretation that one finds in numerous patristic writers: for example, Augustine's description of the husks that the lost son has to eat in

---

12. *CD* IV/1, ix.

13. *CD* IV/1, 186.

14. *CD* IV/2, ix–x. Barth continues: "I can hardly expect that my Roman Catholic readers — to whom I turn more and more in the *Church Dogmatics* — will accept this, but I am confident that they will at least see that there is a positive reason for my Evangelical rejection."

15. *CD* IV/2, 21. The German is *Überinterpretation*.

The Journey of God's Son

his wretched condition as secular doctrines that fail to satisfy;[16] or Jerome's and Ambrose's discovery of a reference to the sacrificial death of Christ in the killing of the fatted calf;[17] or in the interpretation by many fathers of the robe, rings, and shoes given to the returning son by the joyful father as signifying rewards and pledges to the saints.

Having ruled out an allegorical or "direct" christological reading, Barth then considers several other ways of reading the parable. There is, first, the interpretation represented by much Protestant theology since the Enlightenment and perhaps paradigmatically by Barth's teacher, Adolf von Harnack. Here all the attention is given to the father of the parable. According to Harnack, only the father and his love belong to the gospel of Jesus. The parable contains neither direct nor indirect reference to the person and atoning work of the Christ enshrined in church dogma. It is this "unbalanced" reading of the text that Barth is determined to counter by reclaiming the role of the younger son as the "main figure" in the story.[18]

A second way of reading the parable focuses on what Barth calls its "direct" or explicit meaning. Here Barth readily acknowledges that the objections of the Pharisees and scribes to Jesus's welcoming and eating with publicans and sinners constitute the historical and literary context of Luke's inclusion of the parable in his Gospel immediately alongside the parables of the lost sheep and the lost coin. "The real message," Barth says, "is to be found in the story of the son who left his father but then returned and was received by him with joy and honor. And in this story it tells of the turning away and turning back of man in his relationship to God, in which there is not only no diminution but a supreme heightening and deepening of the fatherly mind and attitude of God towards him." More than this, Barth agrees, cannot be extracted from the parable in "*direct* exegesis."[19]

Third, there is what Barth calls an "indirect" interpretation of the parable. If we are to do justice to the text in its literary and historical contexts, Barth argues that we must not exclude "what is not expressly stated but implied in what is stated."[20] A clear example of the parable's "indirect" meaning is the controversy in the early church surrounding the extension of the

---

16. *Works of Saint Augustine: Sermons* III/5, 112A.3, trans. Edmund Hill, ed. John E. Rotelle (Brooklyn, NY: New City Press, 1990–).

17. See Stephen L. Wailes, *Medieval Allegories of Jesus' Parables* (Berkeley: University of California Press, 1987), 236–45.

18. *CD* IV/2, 22.

19. *CD* IV/2, 21.

20. *CD* IV/2, 22.

gospel to the Gentiles. We can safely assume this concern was on the mind of the evangelist Luke with his special interest in the missionary expansion of the church and the universal appeal of the gospel. In this reading, the younger son represents the Gentile sinners who are being received in the early Christian community while the older son represents Jewish Christians who resent the extension of God's grace to the Gentiles.

A precursor of Barth's christological interpretation is Helmut Gollwitzer's reading of the parable in his book *Die Freude Gottes*.[21] According to Gollwitzer, Jesus is present in "the running of the father to meet his son"; he is "hidden in the kiss which the father gives to his son"; and he is present in "the power of the son's recollection of his father and his home and in his father's readiness to forgive." "This is indirect exegesis," Barth says. "It is not allegorical but legitimate if there is to be an exposition of the parable in the context of the whole of the third Gospel and the whole New Testament message."[22]

While sympathetic to Gollwitzer's reading, Barth concludes that it is "not entirely satisfactory." "For," Barth says, "throwing all the emphasis upon the act of the father, and deriving the reference to Jesus Christ from this, Gollwitzer's reading destroys the essential balance of the parable and cannot effectively counter the more recent Protestant exegesis which is guilty of exactly the same error." Barth therefore moves boldly beyond Gollwitzer's christological intimations and reclaims the role of the younger son as the main figure in the story, in order "to demonstrate . . . the presence and action of the Son of God, and therefore of the atonement accomplished in him, in what takes place between God and man as indicated in the parable."[23]

As already noted, Barth concedes that a "direct Christological" reading of the parable cannot be demonstrated from the text and would be a "strained interpretation." The way of the lost son is not only far different from but a "sorry caricature"[24] of the way of the Son of God. Whereas the lost son severs his relationship with the father, the Son of God remains faithful and obedient to the Father. Whereas the lost son desires autonomy and wants to take possession of his share of the family wealth, the Son of God humbles himself and becomes poor for our sake, taking our sin and shame on himself. Yet for all the radical difference, Barth nevertheless discerns a "parallel," an

---

21. Helmut Gollwitzer, *Die Freude Gottes: Einführung in das Lukasevangelium* (Berlin: Burckhardthaus-Verlag, 1965), 168–77.

22. *CD* IV/2, 22. See Gollwitzer, *Freude*, 176–77.

23. *CD* IV/2, 22.

24. *CD* IV/2, 23.

"analogy" between "the going out and coming in of the lost son in his relationship with the father" and "the way trodden by Jesus Christ in the work of atonement, to his humiliation and exaltation." If we attend primarily to the son's movement from the heights to the depths, from home with the father to a far country, the way of the son of the parable is, despite the great differences, "analogous" to the way of Jesus Christ. "It is," Barth says, "similar for all its dissimilarity, like the being of Adam in relation to Jesus Christ."[25]

The same is true, Barth thinks, of the son's homecoming. While there can be no "simple equation" of the return and joyful welcome home of the lost son with the royal humanity of Jesus Christ and his crowning by the Father, nevertheless there is again a "feeble reflection," a "copy," an "analogy," a "type," of the exaltation of man as it has taken place in Jesus Christ. The way of the son of the parable, Barth says, "is not the original. It is only a copy. But it is the copy of this original, and therefore to be understood only in its relationship to it." The going from and returning to the father by the son in the parable "takes place on the horizon of the humiliation and exaltation of Jesus Christ and therefore of the atonement made in him. It has in this its higher law. It is illuminated by it."[26]

Not surprisingly, some New Testament scholars who are acquainted with Barth's reading are far from convinced. Kenneth E. Bailey, for example, says that Barth's christocentric exegesis does in fact "seem strained," and insists that the parable must be understood in its original historical setting of first-century Middle Eastern cultures and their prevailing assumptions about father-son relationships and the rules of inheritance.[27] However, there is no reason to think that Barth would disavow the insights of biblical scholars like Bailey. At the same time, his likely question would be: Is there only one valid method of biblical interpretation and does that privileged method exhaust all that can or must be said about biblical texts? Must we not ask what can and must be said about the parable when it is placed in its larger context in Luke's Gospel and when it illuminates and is illuminated by the New Testament message as a whole?

In Barth's reading of the parable, several features stand out. First, he does not dismiss literary-historical readings of the biblical text. He acknowledges their significance as legitimate aspects of biblical interpretation. His

---

25. *CD* IV/2, 23.
26. *CD* IV/3, 23.
27. Kenneth Bailey, *Poet and Peasant* and *Through Peasant Eyes: A Literary-Cultural Approach to the Parables of Luke*, Combined Edition Two Volumes in One (Grand Rapids: Eerdmans, 1976, 1980), 189.

own emphasis, however, is on intracanonical readings. Most important, whatever methods employed, Barth sees the primary goal of scriptural interpretation to be an encounter with the living Word of God whose center is God's self-revelation and reconciling activity in Jesus Christ.[28] To this end he takes seriously the christological and trinitarian creeds of the church as exemplary, although not infallible, guides in the reading of Scripture. It follows that Barth rejects the idea that the biblical interpreter must bracket all theological commitments in order to achieve a truly objective reading of the text. In this respect, Barth and Hans Urs von Balthasar have much in common as readers of Scripture, as I hope to show.

Second, Barth describes his exposition of the parable as "analogical" rather than allegorical. According to Barth, analogy means "similarity in difference," or more precisely, what is "similar only in the greatest dissimilarity."[29] This formal definition of analogy is stated explicitly or implicitly in the many uses of the term "analogy" in the *Church Dogmatics* under the names of *analogia fidei*, *analogia relationis*, or other "correspondences" and "likenesses" between divine and human activity. While Barth and Balthasar seem to share at least this formal definition of analogy, in his concrete use of the term Barth consistently emphasizes both the radical difference of the analogates, and equally important, the basis of the analogy strictly in the being and action of God in Christ. Hence Adam is to be understood in the light of Christ and not vice versa,[30] and the journey into the far country of the lost son of the parable has its hermeneutical "horizon" in the "original" journey of the Son of God crucified and raised for human salvation.[31] Concretely grounded in and normed by the revelation of God in Jesus Christ, analogy is a basic feature both of Barth's reading of Scripture and of his description of the relationship of God and humanity throughout the *Church Dogmatics*.

Third, Barth's analogical reading of the parable does not offer a moral code prescribing what we should do. Instead, it describes in parable form what God does in Jesus Christ as the source of new life and great joy in which we are called to participate. Just as the true identity of God is revealed in the history of reconciliation in Jesus Christ in whom God humbles Godself, so the true identity of human beings is made known in this same history in the

---

28. *CD* I/2, 720: "The Bible says all sorts of things, certainly; but in all this multiplicity and variety, it says in truth only one thing—just this: the name of Jesus Christ..."

29. *CD* IV/1, 636. This is the formula of the Fourth Lateran Council of 1215.

30. Karl Barth, *Christ and Adam: Man and Humanity in Romans 5* (New York: Harper, 1956).

31. *CD* IV/2, 23.

The Journey of God's Son

exaltation of humankind to fellowship and partnership with God. The parable of the lost son, interpreted analogically, points to this twofold history of God humbled and human life exalted in Jesus Christ. And for Barth all this has its eternal foundation in the electing grace of the triune God. As Barth states in his doctrine of election, "The Son of God determined to give Himself from all eternity. With the Father and the Holy Spirit He chose to unite Himself with the lost Son of Man."[32] If the electing grace of the triune God is for Barth the eternal basis of the work of reconciliation in Jesus Christ, it is also the ultimate point of reference, the "horizon" of Barth's reading of the parable of the lost son.

Differences in the Readings of the Parable by Barth and Balthasar

Does Barth's arresting reading of this parable contribute in any way to the wider theological debate about the use of analogy in theology? In particular, are there traces of the longstanding conversation between Balthasar and Barth in their respective readings of the parable of the lost son and in their different understandings and deployments of analogy in their interpretations? A recent article by Werner Loser raises this possibility, and while grateful for his initial excursion, I will pursue the topic in my own way.[33]

Loser rightly calls Barth's reading of this parable "nothing less than a short summary of his entire theology of reconciliation," and goes on to say that Balthasar's comments on the parable are also a kind of *Zusammenfassung* of the central motif of his remarkably rich theological work.[34] Loser's claim may seem shaky in view of the fact that to his and my knowledge Balthasar nowhere offers a fully developed reading of the parable comparable to Barth's.[35] Nevertheless, even if Balthasar's allusions to this parable are brief—amounting only to a few paragraphs—they are, as I will try to show, evocative of deep motifs in his theology of *Theo-drama*, thereby providing us with illuminating fragments for a comparison with Barth's exposition.

---

32. *CD* II/2, 158.

33. Werner Loser, "Karl Barths und Hans Urs von Balthasars Auslegung des Gleichnisses vom verlorenen und Wiedergefunden Sohn (Lk 15, 11–32)," in *Zusammenklang: Festschrift für Albert Raffelt*, ed. Michael Becht und Peter Walter (Freiburg: Herder, 2009), 322–36.

34. Loser, "Karl Barths und Hans Urs von Balthasars Auslegung," 330–31.

35. Brief references to the parable are, of course, to be found elsewhere in Balthasar's vast writings. See, for example, *Love Alone Is Credible* (San Francisco: Ignatius, 2004), 103.

Balthasar's most explicit comments on the parable are found in his essay "Why I Am Still a Christian."[36] Present in his reflections are two dominant themes, and each involves reasoning by analogy. I will focus on the first in the present section and the second in the next. The first theme of Balthasar's reading of the parable has to do with the distinctive Christian concept of God and especially with God's exercise of power both in relation to the world and in God's own being. According to Balthasar, the father of the parable offers an analogy of God the Father's way of being. In Balthasar's words, "The father, whose younger son asked him for his birthright in advance so that he could go to a foreign land, did not withhold anything that was asked."[37] I would contend that Balthasar's theological reading of the parable is condensed in this simple but pregnant statement. The action of the father of the parable reflects the being and action of the triune God both in the history of salvation and in all eternity. God is not a God of sheer power but a God who as the eternal Father gives himself freely and entirely to the eternal Son who gives himself freely and entirely to the Father in return. Balthasar calls this inner-trinitarian self-surrender of the Father to the Son and of the Son to the Father the "primal kenosis." This eternal kenosis makes possible "all the other kenotic movements of God in the world,"[38] including the self-limitation of God in creation, the gift of finite freedom to the human creature, and above all the act of redemption in which the Son of God freely gives himself on the cross and descends into hell for the sake of human salvation.

Even from this brief summary, it is clear that the doctrine of eternal divine processions does heavy lifting in Balthasar's theology. Like the father of the parable who gives his son his inheritance and his freedom, the eternal Father holds nothing back in his begetting of and love for the Son. In this free begetting of the Son by the Father and the Son's free "letting himself be begotten,"[39] there is both an infinite sharing of essence and an infinite otherness and distance between Father and Son wide enough to embrace all the events of the drama of the incarnation and crucifixion of the Son of God for human salvation.[40] To repeat: Balthasar reads the remarkable generosity

---

36. Hans Urs von Balthasar, "Why I Am Still a Christian," in *Two Say Why*, trans. John Griffiths (Chicago: Franciscan Herald Press, 1973), 9–64.

37. Balthasar, "Why I Am Still a Christian," 51.

38. Balthasar, *Theo-Drama, Theological Dramatic Theory* IV (San Francisco: Ignatius, 1988–98), 331.

39. Balthasar, *Theo-Drama* V, 87.

40. The "distance" between Father and Son in the eternal triune life is the possibility of "a distance that goes as far as the Son's abandonment on the cross." *Theo-Drama* V, 94.

of the father of the parable as a reflection, an analogy, of the Theo-drama played out in the decisive self-emptying (kenosis) of the incarnate Son of God in his passion and death on the cross. The redemptive self-emptying of the Son is eternally grounded in the mutual self-emptying and self-surrender of the begetting Father and the begotten Son in the eternal triune life. This is Balthasar's analogy of kenosis or what we may call his *analogia humilitatis*, and it rests on a particular understanding of the processions in the eternal triune life.

Let me be clear: I am not suggesting that Balthasar says all this explicitly in the limited comments he makes about the parable of the lost son. I am saying only that his marginal glosses on the parable in effect draw it into the orbit of a breathtaking trinitarian theology, a theology centered on the eternal processions of the triune persons. Readers of Balthasar's theology know that he does not hesitate to describe the inner-trinitarian life and relationships in considerable detail. So assured is he of our knowledge of the dynamics of the inner triune life centered in the primordial divine kenosis that he is able to inform us: that the Son "allows" the Father to beget him, that the Father is "thankful" to the Son for allowing himself to be begotten, and that the Father is "surprised" beyond his "wildest expectations" at the free and unlimited obedience exhibited by the incarnate Son in his mission of redemption. Karen Kilby, among others, poses sharp questions to Balthasar on these matters where he presumes to know more of the triune life than seems justified either on the basis of the scriptural witness or classical trinitarian doctrine.[41]

While the theologies of both Barth and Balthasar are deeply trinitarian and stand firmly in the Nicene tradition, they both aim to do more than merely repeat the terms of that tradition. Just as Balthasar offers a strikingly original interpretation of the doctrine of divine processions, Barth states that without "losing contact with the [Nicene] dogma," he endeavors "to go further," and acknowledges that he reaches conclusions that are "formally independent" of the dogma.[42] Furthermore, Barth and Balthasar also agree that our knowledge of God as Trinity is strictly rooted in the economy of salvation, and both contend that if God's activity on our behalf is truly revelatory, it must be "in continuity with," or "correspond to" God's own eternal life. Hence both hold that it is legitimate and necessary to reason back from

---

41. Karen Kilby, *Balthasar: A (Very) Critical Introduction* (Grand Rapids: Eerdmans, 2012), 94–122.

42. *CD* IV/1, 200.

the economy of salvation to its "background"[43] or "basis" or "condition of possibility" in God's inmost being. Only then does it become clear that the drama of salvation is a free and self-consistent act of the triune God rather than something self-contradictory, arbitrary, capricious, or accidental.

Nevertheless, Barth and Balthasar move in different directions in their analogical readings. Unlike Balthasar's reading, Barth's is not explicitly trinitarian. This is not to say, however, that his interpretation lacks an "inter-trinitarian background."[44] On the contrary, this background is explicitly stated or implicitly presupposed not only in his doctrine of reconciliation but in every doctrinal treatise of the *Church Dogmatics*. The difference is that whereas Balthasar's analogical reasoning moves from the parable and the drama of salvation to the triune processions as the "primal kenosis,"[45] Barth infers a basis in the eternal trinitarian relations for the Son of God's obedience in his journey into a far country, a journey markedly different from but faintly reflected in the parable of the lost son. We are, Barth argues, led to the "astounding deduction" (*erstaunliche Folgerung*) that the Son's obedience to the Father's command belongs to the eternal triune life.[46]

Thus Barth in his own way takes a step, no less daring than Balthasar's, beyond the language and conceptuality of traditional trinitarian doctrine. Like Balthasar's venture, it is not without its own difficulties. As Barth famously argues, especially in IV/1, §59.1,[47] the relationship of Father and Son both in history and in the eternal triune life has a particular order: "above and below," "first and second," "super- and sub-ordination," "command and obedience." This description of the relationship of Father and Son, and especially the word-pair "command and obedience," has become a kind of storm center among Barth's commentators.[48] Of note is the fact that Balthasar

---

43. *CD* IV/2, 94.
44. *CD* IV/2, 42, 333.
45. Balthasar, *Theo-Drama* V, 331.
46. "As we look at Jesus Christ, we cannot avoid the astounding conclusion of a divine obedience. Therefore we have to draw the no less astounding deduction that in equal Godhead the one God is . . . One who rules and commands in majesty and One who obeys in humility." *CD* IV/1, 202 (*KD* IV/1, 223).
47. *CD* IV/1, 195-210, esp. 195, 200-201.
48. Among recent essays: Paul Molnar, "The Obedience of the Son in the Theology of Karl Barth and of Thomas F. Torrance," *Scottish Journal of Theology* 67 (2014): 50-69, follows T. F. Torrance and thinks Barth's trinitarian reasoning is flawed on this point; Scott Swain and Michael Allen, "The Obedience of the Eternal Son," *International Journal of Systematic Theology* 15 (2013): 114-34, defend Barth's logic but think it must be clarified and amplified by drawing on Aquinas and the Reformed scholastic tradition in which a distinction is made be-

agrees with Barth's insistence that the Son's "form of obedience" in God is "the precondition for his acceptance of incarnation and the cross."[49] At the same time, Balthasar tellingly regrets that "Barth's reticence in the field of the divine processions within the Trinity will not allow him to go any further here."[50]

As I understand the current debate, it does not center on whether there is "order" (*taxis*) in the eternal triune life, but whether this order is best described by the word-pair "command and obedience." The issue is far too complex to be treated here in detail, but a few brief comments are necessary. At the very least, it must be said that Barth does not always adequately protect his deduction of "command and obedience," "super- and sub-ordination" in the eternal divine life from providing a dubious theological basis for hierarchical relationships in human life, gender relationships in particular. An unfortunate gesture in this direction by Barth is present when he argues that the super/subordinate relationship of Father and Son no more signifies inferiority than does such ordering in the relationship of husband and wife.[51]

There are, however, other biblical and doctrinal concerns. Barth's argument that a relationship of command and obedience belongs to the eternal life of God is clearly driven by the logic of revelation. He rightly insists that there is no gulf between God in relation to us (*pro nobis*) and God in Godself (*in se*) since nothing less than the truth of revelation and the reality of human salvation are at stake. In revelation and reconciliation God is self-consistent; God is faithful to Godself. Still we might ask: Does a command-obedience structure unambiguously capture the biblical depiction of the relationship of Father and Son in the work of salvation and in the eternal triune life?

---

tween divine attributes pertaining to God's triune essence and those designating distinctive properties of the three persons; also Paul Dafydd Jones, "Obedience, Trinity, and Election," in *Trinity and Election in Contemporary Theology* (Grand Rapids: Eerdmans, 2011), 138–61.

49. Balthasar includes the language of "primal obedience," which he defines as "willing cooperation and gratitude" in his description of the relationship of the Son to the Father (*Theo-Drama* V, 123), but his more frequent and overarching theme is the mutual "self-surrender" of the persons: "Self-surrender is ultimate; it is the ultimate in God the Father, in the Son, and in the Spirit; and it is ultimate in man too, when he has reached the end of his crazy path" (*Theo-Drama* V, 123).

50. Balthasar, *Theo-Drama* V, 239.

51. *CD* IV/1, 202. Happily, Barth nowhere speaks of the relationship of Father and Son in any way comparable to Balthasar's gendered description of the (super-) masculine Father's act of begetting and the (super-) feminine Son's receptive act of being begotten. See references and critique in Karen Kilby, *Balthasar*, 133–36.

Return for a moment to Barth's reading of the parable of the lost son. Has Barth given sufficient attention to the attitude and actions of the father of the parable in his relationship to his son? If the parable describes the father as humble and self-giving in relationship to his son, must not the "original" of this portrayal also have to do with the relationship, in all its singularity, of God the Father and God the Son both in the economy of salvation and in the eternal life of God? Here I confess that despite my previous questioning of the speculative range of Balthasar's trinitarian reading of the parable in contrast to Barth's relative restraint, I nevertheless think that Balthasar's attention to the father of the parable offers a valuable counterpart to Barth's decision to concentrate primarily on the son. In other words, if liberal Protestant exegesis was heavily tilted toward the father, does not Barth's interpretation run the danger of throwing off the "balance" in another direction by leaving dimensions of the figure of the father, if not unmentioned, at least underdeveloped?

More specifically, if the father of the parable quietly permits the son to go on his journey to the far country, does not this permission imply a cost to the father, does it not mean that the father suffers a loss, that he must now wait if he is not to be coercive, and that waiting is a form of suffering? In addition, does not the parable highlight the striking humility of the father who sets aside his paternal rights to expect the son to repent openly of his folly, and instead throws decorum and caution to the winds, runs out to embrace the son before he has had a chance to complete his confession, and on top of this arranges a great, and at least to the elder son, scandalous celebration? In my judgment, Barth's interpretation of the parable makes too little theologically of this astonishing humility and lowliness of the *father* of the parable and a fortiori, of the Father of Jesus Christ. If we take seriously the humility, suffering, and self-expenditure of the Father as well as the Son, will we not want to qualify the sense in which we might speak of the eternal life and electing grace of the triune God as ordered *decisively* in terms of command and obedience?

In Barth's defense, it must be said that in later passages he does speak of the Father's sharing in the humiliation and suffering of the Son. I have in mind above all the remarkable passage in IV/2 where Barth writes: "What is represented and reflected in the humiliation of God is the mercy of the Father in which He too is not merely exalted but lowly with His Son.... It is not at all the case that God has no part in the suffering of Jesus Christ *even in His mode of being as the Father*. No, there is a *particula veri* in the teaching of the early Patripassians. . . . primarily it is God the Father who suffers in the offering and sending of His Son, in His abasement."⁵² Unfortunately, Barth's point in this passage finds insufficient expression in his reading of the parable of the lost son.

If we follow Barth's line of thinking in the above passage, it must surely imply that no "person" or "mode of being" of the Trinity is insulated from the struggle, the suffering, and the cross of the incarnate Lord. As Barth often forcefully argues, we must not "evade the cross of Jesus Christ" as an event of God's self-identification, as do both modalism and subordinationism in their different ways.⁵³ He further rightly fights against every division of the person of Christ that would assign his suffering to his humanity while insulating it from his divinity. Consequently, he is fully consistent in insisting in the passage quoted above that we should not, in a final effort to evade the cross in our understanding of God, think that humility and suffering pertain to God qua Son but not to God qua Father. Do we not, however, come very close to inviting this conclusion if we *privilege* the language of command and obedience in describing the relationship of Father and Son over the many other ways Scripture speaks of this relationship, including mutual knowing (Matt. 11:27), mutual loving (Mark 1:11; John 10:17), mutual glorifying (John 17:4–5), the Father's giving the Son and the Son's self-giving (John 3:16; Gal. 2:20), the Father's giving of the cup to the Son and the Son's giving thanks to the Father (John 18:11; 6:11)? To do so would be, in my judgment, to endanger recognition of the real humility and lowliness of the Father as well as the Son in the Son's journey into the far country.

But, of course, as I have already suggested, everything depends on how the terms "command" and "obedience" are understood, and this is doubtless a major source of disagreement among interpreters of Barth. Notably, when Barth speaks of the eternal election of grace by the triune God, he carefully describes it as the concurrent free decision of Father, Son, and Holy Spirit.⁵⁴

---

52. *CD* IV/2, 357 (my emphasis); see also IV/3, 414: "With the eternal Son the eternal Father has also to bear what falls on the Son as He gives Himself to identity with the man Jesus of Nazareth. . . . In Jesus Christ God Himself, the God who is the one true God, the Father with the Son in the unity of the Spirit, has suffered what it befell this man to suffer to the bitter end."

53. "Both [subordinationist and modalist] . . . try to evade the cross of Jesus Christ." *CD* IV/1, 199.

54. *CD* II/2, 158: "The Son of God determined to give Himself from all eternity. With the Father and the Holy Spirit He chose to unite Himself with the lost Son of Man." There is no mention here of obedience to a command but simply a concurrent determination of Father, Son, and Holy Spirit.

It is the Father's free decision to graciously "give" his Son for our salvation; the Son's concurrent free decision to be "obedient to grace" of the Father; and the Holy Spirit's concurrent free resolve to maintain the unity of the Father and Son in love.[55] The triune decision from the beginning was "this offering of the Father and this self-offering of the Son" in the union of the Holy Spirit.[56] There is a distinctive trinitarian *taxis* here, but as Barth's own summary of the triune decision of election suggests, the *taxis* is at best ambiguously characterized in terms of a structure of command and obedience. Barth is surely right to insist that the triune life includes real difference, otherness, encounter, confrontation, even "antitheses." Precisely as such, however, it is a history of "the One who loves in his freedom and is free in his love,"[57] a love mutually given and received, in which majesty and humility, grace and gratitude, address and response, freedom from necessity and freedom for another, are shared. It is furthermore a history of self-giving love culminating in the uniting activity of the Holy Spirit, the often-neglected third party of the triune life. If there is majesty as well as humility in the Son's obedience and acceptance of the way of the cross, there is humility as well as majesty in the Father's offering and sending of the Son. The electing and faithful grace of the Father is met with the Son's free and faithful election of the Father's election. One might then fully agree with Barth that the relationship of Father and Son in the Son's journey into the far country "corresponds to" (*entspricht*)—that it is the "marvelously consistent final continuation" (*wunderbar konsequenter letzter Fortsetzung*)[58] of—the history in which God is God, but nevertheless ask why the concurrent and reciprocal love in freedom of Father and Son in the eternal triune life does not provide a real and sufficient "basis" for the relationship of Father and Son in the economy of salvation? Why must the Son's "obedience" to the Father's "command" rather than, say, the gracious humility and self-giving love of Father and Son in the Spirit be "the dominating moment (*beherrschende Moment*) in our conception of God"?[59]

I incline to think Barth would finally agree that the talk of command and obedience in God must ultimately be understood and redefined by the "one free love" of the triune God, Father, Son, and Spirit. Within a rich biblically funded context of speaking of the triune God *pro nobis* and *in se*, the terms "command" and "obedience"—which undeniably have a

---

55. *CD* II/2, 101.
56. *CD* II/2, 102.
57. *CD* IV/1, 203.
58. *CD* IV/1, 203 (*KD* IV/1, 223, my translation).
59. *CD* IV/1, 199 (*KD* IV/1, 218).

place in covenant history and in the Gospel narrative—acquire a singular meaning. Defined by the gospel in its fullness, the "command" of the Father is in the deepest sense the gift of freedom and the call to mission, and the "obedience" of the Son, rightly understood, is far more than acquiescence to the command of another; it is the free, joyful, thankful, and faithful act of wholehearted concurrence with, trust in, and gratitude to the Father and his unbounded goodness and gracious purpose.[60] Who better than Barth has taught us that the divine imperative is always enclosed in the indicative of God's grace, or that God's command is in the deepest sense a form of the gospel whose content is grace? Who better than Barth has taught us that the "obedience of faith," as the apostle Paul names it (Rom. 1:5), is not conformity to an abstract law or a mighty lawgiver but a life of faithfulness, freedom, and responsibility born of gratitude for the extravagant, fatherly love of God?[61]

Earlier I called the Holy Spirit the neglected third party of much reflection on the trinitarian relationship of Father and Son. Admittedly, there is no explicit reference to the Spirit in the parable of the lost son. Nevertheless, Barth alludes to the work of the Spirit in a later reference to the parable, and there is good reason to do so. If the parable offers a distant analogy of the relationship of Father and Son in the economy of salvation and in God's eternal triune life, it would also seem fitting to ask about the role of the Spirit. For it is in the Spirit of love that the Father graciously elects and sends the Son on his mission into the far country; it is in the Spirit of love that the Son elects the election of his gracious Father and freely gives himself in this mission; and it is by the Spirit of love that Father and Son are held in unity and the mission of God is brought to its completion in the reconciliation of the world to God. It is worth pondering whether the frequent omission of the Spirit in discussions of what Sarah Coakley calls the "privileged dyad of Father and Son" may bear some responsibility for such

---

60. See Jason A. Fout, *Fully Alive: The Glory of God and the Human Creature in Karl Barth, Hans Urs von Balthasar and Theological Exegesis of Scripture* (London: Bloomsbury, 2015), who argues against a tendency toward a "straight-line" understanding of obedience in both Barth and Balthasar and proposes instead an understanding of obedience that includes discernment, imagination, and faithful questioning.

61. According to Barth, the command of God "wills only that we make use of the given permission by the grace of God to be what we are," i.e., those who are free, "not in and by ourselves but in and by Jesus Christ." *CD* II/2, 588. See Gerald McKenny, *The Analogy of Grace* (Oxford: Oxford University Press, 2010), 178–200.

conundrums as are involved in the debate about command and obedience in the eternal triune life.[62]

In summary: With Barth and Balthasar I hold that the self-giving love of God embodied in Christ and manifest above all in his cross belongs to the very essence of God. There is no hidden God behind the God revealed in the crucified and risen Jesus Christ. When God in Christ humbles Godself even to the cross on our behalf, God does not enter into self-contradiction or self-alienation. On the contrary, God is faithful to Godself. God in history "corresponds" to God in eternity. My argument is simply that serious attention to the humility and self-giving love of the Father in relation to the Son, as well as the Son in relation to the Father, always together with and sustained by the Holy Spirit of love, may serve as the best antidote to suggestions of a problematic hierarchy in the life of the triune God and in human life that the abstracting or privileging of language of "command and obedience" may unintentionally encourage. We must never forget that the "order" (*taxis*) of the eternal triune life is singular; it certainly cannot be summarized without ado in the word-pair "command and obedience."[63] If it is to be illuminating rather than misleading, such language has to be parsed carefully with the aid of the multiplicity of scriptural depictions of the relationship of Father, Son, and Holy Spirit. As Barth himself emphasizes, all of our terms for the triune modes of being are "inadequate approximations."[64] It follows that in the context of the concrete history of Jesus Christ, conventional ways of understanding command and obedience are—to use Barth's own words with reference to the title of Son—"burst wide open." They "can be thought through to the end" only as we bring into them "meanings which they cannot have in any other use we make of them."[65] They must be "baptized," as it were, by the redescriptions they receive in the Gospel accounts of the incarnate Lord.

---

62. Sarah Coakley, *Sexuality, the Self, and the Trinity* (Cambridge: Cambridge University Press, 2013), 330.

63. "If we talk about an order or origin within the Trinity, we must underline its uniqueness and its incomparability when contrasted with any order or origin which is thought cosmologically." Jürgen Moltmann, *The Trinity and Kingdom: The Doctrine of God* (San Francisco: Harper & Row, 1981), 166.

64. *CD* IV/1, 205.

65. In the "one free love which is God Himself," the Son is no more divine and exalted than in his humiliation and faithfulness even to the cross, and the Father is no more majestic and glorious than in his giving of steadfast love for and paternal suffering with his Son. See *CD* IV/2, 357–58.

As for Balthasar's elaborate descriptions of the inner life of the triune God such that we are able to construct a metaphysics and even a psychology of the eternal intra-trinitarian persons, processions, and relationships, I am dazzled but even more mindful that our present knowledge is only partial (1 Cor. 13:12). God is triune, self-giving, communicative love both in relation to us and in the inner mystery of the triune life. The mutual love of Father and Son, perichoretically united by and overflowing in the Spirit of love, reaches out from the Father through the Son by the Spirit to all creation. That much, it seems to me, is warranted by the self-revelation and self-gift of God in Christ and the work of the Spirit as attested in Scripture. Beyond that, I am disposed to think that theology, and trinitarian theology in particular, in its justifiably relentless quest for understanding, must also have a place for reverent restraint. There is here indeed, as Balthasar says, a "knife edge"[66] that one walks in the doctrine of the Trinity: a knife edge between the way of apophatism, advocated by more than a few contemporary theologians,[67] and the way of precarious trinitarian speculation, which has always had a special attraction to some of the ablest theologians and philosophers and has, I believe, a brilliant modern theological representative in Hans Urs von Balthasar.

Human Freedom in Barth's and Balthasar's Readings of the Parable

The constraints of a single chapter allow only a much briefer treatment of the second theme in Balthasar's reading of the parable and how it differs from Barth's. In the freedom of the son to go his own way—a freedom given and respected by the father's noncoercive and self-expending love—Balthasar sees an analogy of the great Theo-drama from creation to eschaton. In complying with the request of the son of the parable, the father gives room to the son to exercise a real finite freedom. Balthasar contends that this gesture of the father corresponds to the attitude of the eternal Father. God is no all-powerful Caesar but a God who grants real freedom to his creatures. As Balthasar writes in his gloss on the parable, "Such a God of power—even if his power were that of grace—would never have dared, or been able, seri-

---

66. Balthasar, *Theo-Drama* IV, 324.
67. See Denys Turner and Oliver Davies, eds., *Silence and the Word: Negative Theology and Incarnation* (Cambridge: Cambridge University Press, 2002); Bruce Milem, "Four Theories of Negative Theology," *Heythrop Journal* 48 (2007): 187–204.

ously to give the gift of freedom to his creature."[68] According to Balthasar, God has given to the human creature a finite freedom to obey or disobey, to say Yes or No to God, and this finite freedom is respected by God even if God will also act, not necessarily but freely, to convert and renew the misuse of finite freedom by his creature. Here again it is evident that analogy plays an important role in Balthasar's reading of the parable.

Balthasar's insistence on God's respect of finite freedom does not imply that when the son of the parable "comes to himself" and resolves to return to his father, his decision is entirely independent of the grace of God. As he writes, "If the prodigal son had not believed that the father's love was always there waiting for him, he would not have been able to make the journey home."[69] Rather, Balthasar's contention is that the God of the Theo-drama, in his abiding love and readiness to welcome the sinner home, refuses to violate human freedom. This rejection of divine coercion is a recurrent theme of Balthasar's work.[70] His emphasis on the finite freedom of the son of the parable is fully in accord with his construal of the relationship of infinite and finite freedom in his *Theo-Drama* as a whole. God "has endowed man with a freedom that, in responding to the divine freedom, depends on nothing but itself . . . human freedom participates in the divine autonomy, *both when it says Yes and when it says No*."[71] Again: The creature has "an inherent freedom, its freedom to act within the covenant with God; its own groundlessness is not expropriated and stifled by the 'omnipotence' of divine goodness (as in Islam, for instance). Within the Trinity, God's all-powerful love is also powerlessness, not only giving the Son an equal, divine freedom but also giving the creature itself—the image of God—a genuine power of freedom and taking it utterly seriously."[72] The triune God is "above the necessity to dominate, let alone use violence." Given Balthasar's emphasis on humanity's freedom to say Yes or No to the grace of God, there is good reason for Loser to say that although the basic formal principle of Balthasar's theology is *analogia entis*, he increasingly expressed this concretely as *analogia libertatis*, the analogy of divine and human freedom.[73]

---

68. Balthasar, "Why I Am Still a Christian," 51.
69. Balthasar, *Love Alone Is Credible*, 103.
70. Balthasar, *Theo-Drama* II, 189-344. According to Balthasar, God is "latent" (i.e., present in hiddenness) in creation and even "more profoundly latent" in the incarnate Son of God. "God's 'latency' is his loving respect for human freedom." *Theo-Drama* II, 273, 276.
71. Balthasar, *Theo-Drama* IV, 328. My italics.
72. Balthasar, *Theo-Drama* IV, 330-31.
73. Loser, "Karl Barths und Hans Urs von Balthasars Auslegung," 334.

It would not be difficult to show that Barth too deploys an *analogia libertatis*. For Barth, the triune God "rules in and over a world of freedom."[74] From all eternity, God wills to have a free humanity as his partner. Barth's rejoinder to Balthasar, however, would likely be that in Christian theology the analogy of freedom must always be a consistent and unambiguous *analogia libertatis Christi*. That is to say, it is God's free act of self-giving love in Christ in which God has elected to be God with and for us that provides the ontological ground and the epistemic criterion of our true human freedom. God's exercise of freedom is the basis and norm of human freedom. For Barth, this relationship is irreversible. The decision of the son in the parable to leave his father is what is commonly called "freedom of choice" or *liberum arbitrium*. But freedom of choice is not for Barth an act of human freedom in the proper theological sense. Freedom of choice is for him, as for Luther, Calvin, and the Reformation tradition as a whole, what Barth calls in his reading of the parable, a "caricature" of genuine freedom. True freedom is grounded in and defined by the freedom of God from the foundation of the world to be God with and for us. We understand the true freedom of Adam in the light of the freedom of Christ and not vice versa.[75]

Barth's talk of the gift of true human freedom, however, prompts the question: How would he square his understanding of human freedom with the moment of the parable when the son "came to himself," arose, lifted himself up, and said "I will return to my father"? Does not this turning point of the parable buttress Balthasar's emphasis on the inalienable finite freedom of the human creature, the freedom to say Yes or No to God? Does it not support his charge that Barth's christocentrism is unnecessarily "narrowing" or "constrictive" (*Engführung*)?[76] Barth's answer to this question is found in his frequent rejection of the idea of human freedom as "Hercules at the crossroads." According to Barth, we "come to ourselves" and to our true freedom, as did the son of the parable, by an act of divine grace. When we

---

74. *CD* III/3, 93.

75. As Barth puts it: "The gift of freedom . . . involves more than being offered one option among several. It involves more than being asked a question, being presented with an opportunity, and having a possibility opened up. . . . It is true that man's God-given freedom is choice, decision, act. But it is genuine choice; it is genuine decision and act in the right direction. . . . Man becomes free and is free by choosing, deciding, and determining himself in accordance with the freedom of God." *The Humanity of God* (Richmond, VA: John Knox, 1960), 77.

76. Hans Urs von Balthasar, *The Theology of Karl Barth* (San Francisco: Ignatius, 1992), 242. See Barth's response to this charge in IV/1, 768.

own the reality that is already ours in Christ, when we have "the courage and resolution to reach out here and now for this reality," this has its *primary* source not in ourselves but in God. It is by a "particular power, distinct from all others," that we freely arise and go to our Father and thus correspond to "the liberation already accomplished in Jesus Christ."[77] According to Barth, the Holy Spirit is this particular resurrection power, uniting us to Christ and activating our new freedom in him.

For Balthasar, then, the freedom to say Yes or No to God is a God-given potentiality, an exercise of a capacity to act or not act in correspondence to, in analogy with, God's free grace for us in Christ. For Barth, by contrast, the freedom of God is no "free choice" any more than our true freedom is a matter of "free choice." From the foundation of the world God has elected to be our God and has elected us to be his people in Christ. Our true freedom is grounded and included in the freedom of Jesus Christ, the one who is truly free for God and for others. By virtue of God's electing grace from all eternity, by virtue of what God has done in Christ for us, and by virtue of the power of the resurrection of the crucified one we are liberated for freedom and new life. The power by which this takes place here and now is "the mystery of the life-giving Spirit."[78] True human freedom is a gift that is given according to the "law of divine action."[79] That is to say, it is an event that is "both wholly creaturely and wholly divine." Yet the "initial shock comes from God" through the living Christ in the power of the Holy Spirit. The freedom of the creature in this event is in no way excluded or impaired, and yet in it there is "the absolute primacy of the divine over the creaturely."[80]

The difference between Barth and Balthasar on the matter of divine and human freedom may be further illumined by considering the final scene of the parable. The father, we recall, encounters the elder brother's refusal to rejoice at the homecoming of his lost brother. Most commentators today understand this concluding scene to be an integral part of the parable as a

---

77. *CD* IV/2, 312.

78. *CD* IV/2, 529.

79. *CD* IV/2, 528, 556. This "law of divine action" is Barth's understanding of "theonomy" as distinct from both an abstract autonomy and an equally abstract heteronomy. I/2, 857.

80. *CD* IV/2, 557. See further IV/3.1, 447: "What is given [man] and required of him, is the freedom of one who belongs to the free God and is freed by Him." Freedom means "the courage and joy to make the only possible and meaningful use of it corresponding to its nature, i.e. the only use which can be considered in view of the fact that it is given and required by the free God. . . . It is a matter of the freedom to elect Him as elected by Him."

whole and even suggest that the story might be better named "the parable of the lost sons." In the marginal references to the parable I have cited from Balthasar, there is no mention of the elder brother. Barth, however, does devote a paragraph to him. For Barth, he is a figure of the man who protests God's lavish act of forgiveness in Jesus Christ in whom God is humbled and humanity exalted. Without pursuing the matter further, Barth simply advises his readers to keep their eyes on the final invitation of the father to the elder brother to join the celebration and rejoice at the return of "this son of mine" (Luke 15:24) and "this brother of yours" (15:32), designations that Barth suggests offer exegetical support for his indirect christological reading of the parable as a whole.

While neither Barth nor Balthasar proposes a connection between the father's encounter with the elder brother and questions of human freedom and universal salvation, these issues, I would argue, are not far beneath the surface of the parable's final scene. Does the ending of the parable with its vivid depiction of the encounter of the father and the elder son have any bearing on whether Christians may or should hope that in the end all will be saved? Put more sharply: If the elder son were to refuse to join the celebration, could the father who exercises such stunning love and forgiveness to the younger son and who refuses to employ coercion to achieve his purposes, do anything else but accept the elder son's refusal if that is his choice? Can God's astonishing grace finally be defeated?

On this issue, as elsewhere, Barth and Balthasar have substantial agreements. Both agree that we cannot offer guarantees one way or another. Both insist that there are warnings in Scripture that are not to be evaded, even as there are also scriptural grounds for affirming the final and all-embracing victory of God. Both call for Christians to hope and pray for the salvation of all.[81] But once again, side by side with their deep unity of faith in the holy and gracious triune God are their persistent differences in that faith. For Balthasar the question of universal salvation must remain open because the elder son is free. God has given human beings the inalienable freedom to say Yes or No to God, and that simply rules out any guarantee of universal salvation. For Barth, on the other hand, the question remains open because the grace of God is not reducible to a principle or idea that we can control, but is the ever-astonishing free gift of God in Jesus Christ. This difference in emphasis has deep roots in their respective theologies.

---

81. Hans Urs von Balthasar, *Dare We Hope "That All Men Be Saved"?* (San Francisco: Ignatius, 1988); Karl Barth, *The Humanity of God*, 59–62; see also *CD* IV/3.2, 477–78.

Clearly, for Barth, what is most important is that theology and church keep their gaze on the final words of the father to the elder son: "It is fitting that we rejoice," the father says. He does not threaten and he does not scold. Instead he invites, and the invitation remains open. "Son, you are always with me; and all that is mine is yours. But we had to celebrate and rejoice, because this brother of yours was dead and has come to life; he was lost and has been found" (Luke 15:31–32). These words contain no solution to the perennial question of universal salvation. They do, however, replace all resentment and presumption with a call to joy. They extend a clear, sincere, and open invitation that might be paraphrased: "Come join the festivities." For Barth the parable and its ending reiterate the gospel of God humbled and humanity exalted and its grounding in the eternal electing grace of God. What is properly awakened by the parable and the gospel can only be joy, pure joy.[82]

Concluding Comments

What general conclusions can we draw from this description and analysis of Barth's and Balthasar's readings of Jesus's parable of the lost son? I suggest three.

First, both Barth and Balthasar are masters of theological exegesis. As they pursue it, theological exegesis is not an enemy of critical-literary-historical readings of Scripture. Nor is it a method to be mechanically learned and artificially applied. Theological interpretation of Scripture is essentially a strong and imaginative reading, attentive to the density of scriptural texts and their intratextuality, attuned to the dramatic sweep of Scripture and its center in the person and work of Christ, informed and enriched by the treasury of the church's meditation on the message of Scripture over many centuries, and alert and open to the fresh possibilities of new light that Scripture and the Spirit of God shed on Christian life and the mission of the church in the present. The parables of Jesus, like the gospel proclamation of his life, death, and resurrection, are infinitely rich. No single interpretation can exhaust their meaning and relevance for a Christian understanding of God, of God's work of reconciliation in Christ, and of God's summons to us to bear witness to and thereby take part in this work.

---

82. See *CD* II/2, 174. The theme of joy runs like a red thread through Barth's theology. See Migliore, "Joy," in *The Westminster Handbook to Karl Barth*, ed. Richard Burnett (Louisville: Westminster John Knox, 2013), 125–27.

Second, the similarities and differences between Barth and Balthasar, as displayed in their readings of the parable of the lost son, are instructive for ecumenical conversations in the twenty-first century. It is significant that throughout their encounters their debate about the use of analogy in theological reflection was pursued in a mutually respectful rather than a mean-spirited manner. Balthasar obviously learned much from Barth, and Barth, without ever abandoning his own Reformed moorings, showed strong interest in the signs of a reforming Roman Catholic theology and church, wondering at times whether the Roman Catholic witness might one day "put us in the shade," i.e., might bear a more faithful Christian witness than some versions of modern Protestant theology.[83]

Third, at the heart of the differences between Barth and Balthasar—evident in their readings of the parable of the lost son and, one might venture to say, in their theologies generally—is their respective emphases on the eternal electing grace of the triune God (Barth) and the primal kenosis or self-surrendering love in the intra-trinitarian life (Balthasar). Interestingly, the proper understanding of the relationship of the doctrines of Trinity and election in Barth's theology has been vigorously debated in recent Barth scholarship. Study of the similarities and differences in the theologies of Barth and Balthasar—their bold and imaginative interpretations of Scripture, their distinctive deployments of analogy, and their respective renewal of trinitarian doctrine—may help illuminate that debate by setting it in a wider ecumenical context.

---

83. See Eberhard Busch, *Karl Barth: His Life from Letters and Autobiographical Texts* (Philadelphia: Fortress, 1976), 481.

7 Parabolic Retelling and Christological Discourse

Julian of Norwich and Karl Barth on the Parable of the Lost Son

KENDALL COX

Why does Karl Barth turn his attention to the parable of the lost or prodigal son at a pivotal moment in his account of reconciliation?[1] What could this parable have to do with Christology? His unusual interpretation of Luke 15:11–32 comes at a surprising, and telling, point in *Church Dogmatics IV: The Doctrine of Reconciliation*.[2] Here, on the cusp of IV/1 and IV/2, Barth draws an association between the younger son in the parable—who goes into a distant land and squanders his inheritance—and Jesus Christ. Such a reading has been considered unprecedented, even idiosyncratic. However, in *A Revelation of Love*, the fourteenth-century English anchorite and visionary writer Julian of Norwich tells a story that bears striking similarities to Barth's treatment of the Lukan text.[3] In her "Example of the Lord and Servant," which is an oblique gloss on the biblical parable, she too establishes

---

1. I will refer to this passage as "the parable of the prodigal son" as that is how it is best known in English. But the epithet is absent from the Greek and forces the story's meaning in a certain direction. Barth uses the German *"Der verlorene Sohn,"* which more clearly relates to the other two parables in Luke 15 (vv. 3–7, the lost sheep, and vv. 8–10, the lost coin) and draws attention to the parallelism "lost and found" so central to his christological reading.

2. *CD* IV/2, 21–25 (*KD* IV/2, 21–25).

3. Julian of Norwich, *The Writings of Julian of Norwich: A Vision Showed to a Devout Woman and A Revelation of Love*, ed. Nicholas Watson and Jacqueline Jenkins (University Park: Pennsylvania State University Press, 2006). Julian's writing consists of two texts, one earlier and shorter, another later and longer, referenced as: *A Vision* or the Short Text (ST) and *A Revelation* or the Long Text (LT). The "Example of the Lord and Servant" is found in *A Revelation*. All quotations will be from this text, in Watson and Jenkins's modernized version of the Middle English, cited by chapter and line.

an identity between the second person of the Trinity and a lost servant/son figure. If we set his exegesis and her narrative alongside one another, deep congruencies between them emerge, not only on an interpretive level, but also doctrinally.[4] What becomes clear is that Barth, like Julian, narrates Luke 15:11–32 not only as the parable of incarnation and atonement but also as the parable of election and, as such, the parable of God.

Barth's Exegesis of Luke 15:11–32 in His Doctrine of Reconciliation

As he turns from Chapter XIV, "Jesus Christ, the Lord as Servant," to Chapter XV, "Jesus Christ, the Servant as Lord," Barth evokes Luke 15:11–32, saying,

> we can hardly fail to think of the . . . passage which in every age . . . has always been valued by the Church (with all kinds of different interpretations) as central to the whole New Testament. . . . I refer to the so-called parable of the Prodigal Son, the son who was lost [*verlorenen*] and was found again [*wiedergefundenen*]. (Luke 15:11–32)[5]

Barth seems to think it is only fitting that he reflect on the parable at this juncture in his Christology. However, an obvious objection arises: Jesus Christ is nowhere to be found in the parable. Barth is fairly sensitive about this. He repeatedly denies the possibility of any "direct christological reference."[6] But he also thinks "more recent Protestant exegesis" of the parable is in danger of missing "what is not expressly stated but implied in . . . and therefore necessary to what is stated." Barth questions the tendency in modern theology to over-literalize the absence of Jesus in what takes place between the father and his sons. (He singles out Adolf von Harnack in particular who, on the basis of the parable of the prodigal son, concludes, "nothing extraneous can interpose itself between God and the soul," including Jesus Christ.[7]) Summoning sacramental language, Barth suggests there is an "in-

---

4. The subsequent comparison is based on a larger body of research in which Julian's text receives the equal attention it deserves. In this essay, however, my focus is on Barth, so I will have to pass over a great deal with respect to her work.

5. *CD* IV/2, 20.

6. *CD* IV/2, 21.

7. *CD* IV/2, 22. Barth is summarizing from von Harnack's lectures at the University of Berlin, *Das Wesen des Christentums* (1899–1900). See Adolf von Harnack, *What Is Christianity?* trans. Thomas Bailey Saunders (Eastford, CA: Martino Fine Books, 2011), 76.

direct" meaning given "in and with and under what is said directly."[8] This yields at least two levels of significance for him.

Barth begins his excursus by providing a preliminary reading of the parable that he calls "direct" (*direkt*). Assuming Luke 15:1-2 as the referential backdrop for the whole narrative picture, Barth rehearses a fairly common interpretation in which the father represents God, the younger son the "publicans and sinners" with whom Jesus socialized, and the older son "the scribes and Pharisees" who judge Jesus for the company he keeps. Significantly, Barth, like Julian, focuses on the story of the younger son as inclusive of all humanity, rather than emphasizing differences between the two brothers.[9] On this first level, the parable seems to be a generic account of grace. In Barth's words, it simply "tells of the turning away and turning back" of humankind in "relationship to God."

Barth admits that to force a "direct Christological interpretation" at this point would produce a "strained interpretation" or an "over-interpretation" (*Überinterpretation*).[10] Yet the fact that he has gone as far as he has in his first reading is a significant achievement for his subsequent interaction with the passage. In addition to claiming that the parable narrates divine love, he takes for granted that the three parables of Luke 15 cohere and are therefore inter-referential, that these are the parables *of Jesus*, that the parabolic referents stand outside the text, and that the life of Jesus echoes within his own speech. This takes Barth a long way toward an expansion of the story's meaning. As he goes on to claim, if we leave off at a direct reading we risk leaving the parable "under-interpreted."

So midway through his treatment of the passage, Barth commences a new exposition. (He prepares the way by surveying a range of typological and allegorical readings from the tradition.[11]) In a second, "indirect"

---

8. *CD* IV/2, 22.

9. Barth reads the passage as two parables—the story of the younger son's relationship with the father (vv. 12-24) and the story of the elder son's attitude toward the father and the younger son (vv. 25-32). But he claims the story of the younger son contains "the real message" of the parable (*CD* IV/2, 21). Julian simply leaves out any mention of a second servant/son.

10. *CD* IV/2, 21.

11. Barth mentions Augustine, among others, but he is particularly drawn to Helmut Gollwitzer's christological interpretation in *Die Freude Gottes: Einführung in das Lukasevangelium*, vol. 2, *Studienreihe der Jungen Gemeinde, Heft 27-29* (Berlin: Burckhardthaus-Verlag, 1941). Summarizing Gollwitzer's exegesis, Barth writes, "In the parable, then, Jesus is 'the running out of the father to meet his son.' Jesus is 'hidden in the kiss which the father gives his son.' Jesus is the power of the son's recollection of his father and home, and his father's

approach, he identifies "a most illuminating parallel" between "the way trodden by Jesus Christ in the work of atonement" and "the going out and coming in of the lost son in his relationship with the father." As a movement "from the heights to the depths, from home to a far country," the prodigal son's departure is "analogous" to the descent of the Son of God into "lost human existence."[12] Barth says, "The fatal journey of the lost son . . . is similar for all its dissimilarity, like the being of Adam in relation to that of Jesus Christ: the pattern of the one to come" (Rom. 5:14). In fact, it is not just analogous to it; it actually becomes his own way in that he "accepts identity and solidarity with this lost son . . . taking his place . . . his sin and shame, his transgression."[13]

This association Barth draws between the divine Son and the lost son is by no means a "simple equation." It is noteworthy that he shifts from the language of "parallel" to that of "horizon."[14] What takes place in the parable takes place on the horizon of the atonement made in Jesus Christ. The way of Jesus Christ is "like" that of the lost son only in the sense that it "is" the way of the lost son. It becomes it; it overtakes it, rewriting it from within. The fictional trajectory of the lost son, then, must be situated within Jesus's history, embedded in the encompassing trajectory of his life. According to Barth, this is signaled within the story by the parallel verses Luke 15:24 and 32, where the father says his son "was dead and is alive again, was lost and has been found." Barth concludes that a christological reading becomes "unavoidable" if we hear these words in the context of Luke and in light of "the whole New Testament message."[15] Hence the fact that Barth frames the par-

---

fatherliness and readiness to forgive" (*CD* IV/2, 22). Gollwitzer can render Jesus present in the story in this way because he interprets the passage, as Barth does, in light of its *Sitz im Leben* indicated in Luke 15:1–2.

12. The word "lost" is heavily freighted for Barth. Throughout *The Doctrine of Reconciliation*, he uses it to stand for "flesh" and fallenness. The word gathers together the whole history of humankind—wayward, alienated, perishing. Barth says "lost" sums up "the situation of Old Testament man," of exile, wilderness, and desertedness (Deuteronomy 32). In other words, it describes "a history of suffering" (IV/1, 173–74). All of this is evoked in the image of the younger son in an alien (Gentile) land, in the pit or pigsty.

13. *CD* IV/2, 23.

14. *CD* IV/2, 23–24. Barth says, "the going out and coming in of the lost son, and therefore the fall and blessing of [the human], takes place on the horizon of the humiliation and exaltation of Jesus Christ and therefore of the atonement made in Him. It has this as its higher law. It is illuminated by it." For Barth, there is no viable explanation for the homecoming of lost humanity apart from the "being and action and experience of the one Son of Man."

15. *CD* IV/2, 22–23.

able as an elaboration on the Gospel narrative condensed in the four words "the Word became flesh" (John 1:14).[16] Such an extension of meaning, he says, is not "read into" but is genuinely "invited by the text itself."[17]

While there is a great deal more to be said about Barth's exegesis, this very brief sketch will allow us to set his interpretation in conversation with Julian's.

Julian's "Example" as an Interpretation of the Parable of the Prodigal Son

Julian's "Example of the Lord and Servant" prefigures Barth's exegesis of the parable as well as its theological ramifications in a number of revealing ways. On my reading, this portion of Julian's text is a creative gloss on the parable of the prodigal son.[18] This is not immediately self-evident from the story, which she refers to as a "showing," but it becomes clearer once we understand the genre within which she works.[19] Julian retells the biblical parable as a medieval homiletic *exemplum*, an extended sermon illustration that loosely reanimates biblical narratives and theological themes in contemporary terms.[20]

---

16. Barth calls this verse "the whole of theology in a nutshell," in a letter to B. Gherardini, May 24, 1955. Eberhard Busch, *Karl Barth: His Life from Letters and Autobiographical Texts* (Philadelphia: Fortress, 1976), 380–81, n. 196.

17. *CD* IV/2, 22, 25.

18. For support for my reading of Julian's example, see: Denys Turner, *Julian of Norwich, Theologian* (New Haven: Yale University Press, 2011), 126; and, A. C. Spearing, "Introduction," *Revelations of Love* (New York: Penguin, 1998), xxviii. Elizabeth Spearing, one of Julian's modern translators, has confirmed in conversation that she also reads Julian's example as a gloss on the biblical parable.

19. More precisely, Julian refers to this as the "shewing of the example" (*A Revelation*, 51.52). She speaks of her visions altogether as a "showing"—a private revelation, vision, or visionary experience—"of love." It is beyond the scope of this essay to adequately treat this fascinating dimension of Julian's work. But I take for granted that there should be no sharp division between the contemplative or visionary quality of Julian's writing and its status as "spiritual interpretation" of Scripture, in Henri de Lubac's sense. I have had to limit myself to this portion of her text, which, regardless of its description as a "revelation," is written in the didactic genre of medieval homiletic *exempla* and is replete with scriptural allusions and doctrinal assertions.

20. This is the genre that Julian's contemporary Geoffrey Chaucer so famously satirizes. On the nature of this form see Larry Scanlon, *Narrative, Authority, and Power: The Medieval Exemplum and the Chaucerian Tradition* (Cambridge: Cambridge University Press, 2007).

Parabolic Retelling and Christological Discourse

In her example, Julian initially recasts the father and younger son from the biblical passage as a master and his servant. (Such a reassignment of identities is in keeping with treatments of this text by Bernard of Clairvaux, Anselm of Canterbury, and others.[21]) Her example is packed with graphic and symbolic details that she decodes over a period of many years. Retracing but the barest outline of her narrative: there is a kind lord who sends an eager servant out into his kingdom to do his will, namely to retrieve a precious treasure for him. But when the servant leaps up to go out, he immediately falls into a "slade." In his fallen state, the servant is blind to the nearness of his lord and this, for Julian, is the worst part of his condition. While she observes that one would expect the lord to blame the servant (as in Anselm's account), in her example, he expresses only "pitte" (compassion) and "good will" or "good pleasure" (language she uses as shorthand for predestination to grace).[22] She says, "continuantly his loveing lorde full tenderly beholdest him." In other words, the lord's gaze does not falter when the servant's steps do. In fact, the lord decides that, because of the suffering endured in his service, "his deerwurthy servant . . . shulde be hyely and blissefully rewarded withoute end, above that he shulde have be if he had not fallen."[23]

In her first retelling of the parable, Julian identifies the lord with God and the servant with Adam or, in her words, "alle manne." On this basic level, her story simply depicts human fallenness and divine grace, in much the same way as Barth's "direct" reading of the parable. The message is that God is not like a harsh and calculating master but a gracious and compassionate father. However, as she mulls over the narrative, Julian is troubled by certain aspects of the fallen servant's character. She says, "I sawe many diverse properteys that might by no manner be derecte [attributed] to singel Adam." In other words, the identity of the servant seems to exceed the

---

21. See Anselm, *Opera omnia*, ed. Francis Schmitt, OSB, 6 vols. (Edinburgh: Thomas Nelson & Sons, 1936–1961), 2:54; and, Bernard of Clairvaux, "The Story of the King's Son," in *The Parables & The Sentences*, trans. Michael Casey, OCSO, and Francis Swietek (Kalamazoo, MI: Cistercian Publications, 2000).

22. On the relationship between Julian's example and an Anselmian understanding of the atonement see Denise Baker, *Julian of Norwich's Showings: From Vision to Book* (Princeton: Princeton University Press, 1994), 100–101; Denys Turner, *Julian of Norwich*, 126; Edmund Colledge, *The Medieval Mystics of England* (New York: Charles Scribner's Sons, 1961), 21, 87; and Joan Nuth, "Two Medieval Soteriologies: Anselm of Canterbury and Julian of Norwich," *Theological Studies* 53 (1992): 611–45.

23. Julian, *A Revelation*, 51.29–49. Julian alludes here to the "how much more" of grace (Rom. 5:20). The asymmetry between fall and restoration is an important dimension in Barth's interpretation of the going out and coming in of the Son as well.

identity of Adam or Adamic humanity. This excess opens up another interpretive plane for her.

In a second retelling of the story, Julian lands on another set of referents for the two figures. She comes to see the lord as God the Father and the servant as the eternal Son. Julian begins to slip freely between the lord/servant and father/son pairings. Explaining that the fallen servant/son figure is "shown double," she writes, "In the servant is comprehended the seconde person of the trinite, and in the servant is comprehended Adam: that is to sey, all men" (lines 179–80). Outwardly, he is human, fallen, at a distance from God; inwardly, he is "the godhed," the "deerwurthy son . . . even with [equal to] the fader." In other words, the servant/son is very human and very God, consubstantial with the Father. Julian goes on to describe the two "kinds" (natures) manifest in the figure of the servant and appears to be playing with Chalcedonian Christology by renarrating her example on this deeper level.

Julian reinterprets the servant's "fall" as the Father sending the Son "to traveyle" in the world. His journey, his labor and travail, mirrors Adam's—except it is salvific.[24] Paraphrasing Philippians 2:6–7, Julian recounts the servant's mishap again: the Son "stode before his fader as a servant, wilfully taking upon him alle oure charge [burden] . . . full redely at the faders will, and anon he fell full lowe in the maidens wombe, having no regarde to himself."[25] In short, it becomes apparent that the example narrates the historical drama of creation, fall, and redemption as well as the Son's incarnation and passion.

Interestingly, Julian's account of the atonement also doubles as an account of predestination. She refers to both as an "endlesse oning" in which the Son is eternally "knit" (procreative language) and "bound" (nuptial language) to humankind.[26] Claiming that "God began never [never started] to love mankinde," Julian explains that, in Christ,

> the same mankind hath be . . . knowen and loved fro without beginning. . . . And by the endlesse entent and assent and the full acorde of all the

---

24. Alluding again to Romans 5, Julian writes, "by Adam I understand alle man. Adam fell fro life to deth: into the slade of this wreched worlde, and after that into hell. Goddes son fell with Adam into the slade of the maidens wombe, which was the fairest doughter of Adam—and that for to excuse Adam from blame in heven and in erth—and mightily he feched him out of hell" (*A Revelation*, 51.186–91).

25. Julian, *A Revelation*, 51.202–7, 244.

26. In Julian's words, predestination is the "rightful knitting and endlesse oning" in which God "knit us and oned us to himselfe" (*A Revelation*, 53.18; 58.5–6). Notably, "knitting" is also procreative language that she connects to the motherhood of God.

trinite, the mid person [second person] wolde be grounde and hed of this fair kinde [nature] out of whom we be all come, in whom we be alle enclosed, into whom we shall all wenden [go].[27]

She describes Christ's kenotic "fall," his assumption of the *forma servi*, as an intra-trinitarian occurrence predicated upon God's primordial love for and union with humankind in the second person of the Trinity.[28]

Shortly after recounting and analyzing the example, Julian commences her famous excursus on the motherhood of God in which the pairing father/son, which had supplanted lord/servant, gives way to mother/child.[29] It is precisely her retelling of the father's unwavering compassion for his lost son through the "Example of the Lord and Servant" that precipitates this development.[30] Closely related to her description of God as "moder" is her application of John 1:14—and what she refers to as the mutual "beclosure" (enclosure) and "wonning" (dwelling or indwelling) of God and

---

27. Julian, *A Revelation*, 53.21–27. She is evoking Colossians 1:15–17 and Romans 11:36 here. In a similar passage, Julian says, "God, the blissefull trinite, which is everlasting being, right as he is endless fro without beginning, righte so it was in his purpose endlesse to make mankind; which fair kind [human nature] furst was dight [assigned to] the second person. And when he [Christ] woulde [desired it], by full accorde of alle the trinite, he made us alle at ones [all in an instant, or all in one]. And in our making he knit us and oned us to himselfe" (58.1–5). On Julian's use of the word "kind," see Janet Soskice, *The Kindness of God: Metaphor, Gender, and Religious Language* (Oxford: Oxford University Press, 2007).

28. This is admittedly a rather Barthian reading of Julian, but one that I believe is faithful to her language and imagery. Julian's theological imagination is as relentlessly christological as Barth's. She insists that "the trinite is comprehended in Crist" (57.16–17)—and is not to be thought apart from him. For her, the descent of the servant/son is a portal into the intra-trinitarian love of God. In him, she "sees" humankind eternally "beclosed" (line 44) within the Trinity.

29. Julian proliferates kinship terms for God (father, mother, brother, spouse, friend, etc.). Significantly, she mentions divine motherhood for the first time in her analysis of the example (52.1–4). I read her subsequent reflection on the motherhood of the Trinity, in chapters 58–63, as an extended meditation on the homecoming of the lost child, where home is figured as the womb and bosom of God. Her later use of motherhood does not displace or exclude but expands and refines her earlier lordship/fatherhood imagery. On the non-opposition of gendered terms for God in medieval women writers, see Caroline Walker Bynum, *Fragmentation and Redemption: Essays on Gender and the Human Body in Medieval Religion* (New York: Zone Books, 1991).

30. I have not been able to address the central verb of the biblical parable: σπλαγχνίζομαι ("had compassion") (Luke 15:20). Julian's retelling captures the ambiguity of the term, which bears a visceral connection with motherhood in Hebrew (רחם gives us *raham*/compassion and *rahem*/womb).

humanity—which plays a presiding role in her reading of the parable, as in Barth's.

Prodigal Christ: Parable, Christology, and Election

To summarize, Julian and Barth both retell the parable of the prodigal son as the parable of Jesus Christ himself, the one who seeks and saves the lost (Luke 19:10) by being and becoming the original lost son. It is worth highlighting several of the more prominent points of intersection leading Julian and Barth to such a construal of the parable, on an interpretive level as well as with respect to the parable's theological import.

First, Julian and Barth use the language of the parable to speak about incarnation and atonement as a kind of "fall" or "journey" that both parallels and perpendicularly intersects the path of fallen humanity. As with Christ's life, the most prominent structural trait of the parable, as well as their retellings of it, is a double movement of *exitus* and *reditus*: departure and homecoming, descent and ascent, fall and restoration, humiliation and exaltation. At the center of the prodigal son's trajectory lies a certain topography—the pit or pigsty, *Sheol*, the grave. It is definitive of the geographical and figurative place: the far country (*regio longinque*), the region of unlikeness (*regio dissimilitudinis*), the land of wandering.[31] This distant land at the heart of the parable stands over against and constantly evokes the lost paradisiacal home, origin and *telos* of the narrative circle.

In other words, it is not primarily the conventional stock characters (father/son, master/servant) that give the story its force; rather, it is this double movement. If we can say, "Jesus Christ *is* the prodigal son," it is because his character is manifest and determined by traversing the same circuit—lost and found, dead and alive. His self-identity and his identity with the younger

---

31. *Regio dissimilitudinis* is a Plotinian phrase. Augustine uses it in *Confessions* I.18.28 and VII.10.16 to indicate the postlapsarian condition of having become "unlike" God. It is closely associated, especially in the later tradition (e.g., in Bernard and William of Saint-Thierry), with the *regio longinqua* of Luke 15. See Mette B. Bruun, *Parables: Bernard of Clairvaux's Mapping of Spiritual Topography*, vol. 148 of Brill's Studies in Intellectual History (Leiden: Brill, 2007), 188. This locus is both literal (in Genesis: outside of the garden; in the parable: the foreign land) and metaphorical (in both cases: the condition of sin, of having lost/diminished the image of God). Distance means dissimilitude. In contrast, the nearness of Christ (his going out) is initiated by and is effective because of his likeness to God as God.

son are indicated by the same narrative arc.³² The downward/upward and outward/homeward sequence gets transferred and redoubled—belonging specially to the human in Adam, belonging to both the human and God in Christ, and, on Julian's and Barth's readings, belonging eternally to God in God's second way of being.

Second, bringing Julian's work into dialogue with Barth's allows us to see that his christological reading is not naïvely or reductively typological, as might be argued on a strictly historical-critical basis. Given their different religious milieus, ecclesial traditions, and literary genres, the consonance of their innovative theological readings prompts us to consider whether they uncover an overlooked interpretive trajectory belonging to the text itself. In their recourse to a broader scriptural framework, Julian and Barth provide us with instances of deeply intrabiblical or intertextual reading.³³ As Barth maintains, to "do full justice to the passage" we must also attend to the relationship between the parable and the rest of the story.³⁴ Paul Ricoeur's

---

32. Hans Frei's understanding of narrative identity is certainly helpful here. See *The Identity of Jesus Christ: The Hermeneutical Bases of Dogmatic Theology* (Eugene, OR: Wipf & Stock, 2013). But at issue is not primarily the way Jesus is identified as himself—in Frei's words, how he "is what he does uniquely, the way no one else does it" (12)—but how he is identified *as another* (in traversing the identical course, differently).

33. My use of *inter*textuality is not to be confused with the "*intra*textual" understanding of Barth that McCormack rejects in his essay "Beyond Nonfoundational and Postmodern Readings of Barth." See Bruce McCormack, *Orthodox and Modern: Studies in the Theology of Karl Barth* (Grand Rapids: Baker, 2008). Based on Lindbeck's comments in "Barth and Textuality," McCormack defines "intratextual theology" as "without reference to God, the world, history, metaphysics—anything outside or beyond the text" (133). See George Lindbeck, "Barth and Textuality," *Theology Today* 43, no. 3 (Oct. 1986): 362. It is worth noting that Kathryn Greene-McCreight uses "intratextual" quite differently in reference to Barth's exegesis to indicate that "it is the text which governs the interpretive process rather than historical-critical reconstruction" (Greene-McCreight, *Ad Litteram: How Augustine, Calvin and Barth Read the "Plain Sense" of Genesis 1–3* (New York: Peter Lang, 1999), 202. The important point here is that an *inter*textual approach (*à la* Ricoeur) emphasizes the cross-pollination of meanings within texts without ruling out the extratextual reference that brings centripetal force to such meanings. The resulting "literary-*narratological*" quality of Barth's exegesis, to borrow George Hunsinger's descriptor, forms the hermeneutical assumption of my comparison of it to Julian's pre-historical-critical retelling of the parable.

34. *CD* IV/2, 22; cf. *KD* IV/2, 22. The English translators render Barth's "*Unterinterpretation*" in terms of not "doing justice" to the text, while "*Überinterpretation*" is translated "strained interpretation." Barth seems to be saying: between the "strained" or overeager interpretation and the "unjust" or meager interpretation, we must find the interpretation that listens to the indirect or analogical identity the text itself provokes.

account of parable and intertextuality proves helpful here.[35] Parable, as a "metaphorized narrative," is implicitly dialogical and polyvalent.[36] It always says what it says by speaking about something else at the same time. It amplifies its own meaning by resounding within the encompassing narrative.[37]

It is a very specific intertextual nexus of references that generates Julian's and Barth's christological renderings of the parable. Almost intuitively, without explicitly indicating as much, they each overlay the text with a certain set of biblical stories and figures: (1) the Genesis 2–3 account of creation and fall; (2) the narratives of Israel's captivity, exodus, and exile, and especially the "Suffering Servant" imagery of Isaiah 53; (3) the Gospel story in which "the Word became flesh" (John 1:14), even sin itself (2 Cor. 5:21); (4) the event of divine condescension (Phil. 2:6–11); and (5) the Pauline Adam-Christ identity (Rom. 5:14f., 1 Cor. 15:22).[38] The cogency of an association between the lost son and the eternal Son emerges when the parable is appropriately aligned along these referential correlates.

Third, Julian and Barth are not simply offering christological interpretations of the parable; they are actually doing Christology in the mode of parable. This is more evident in Julian's case, given the concise and highly condensed narrative form of *exempla*.[39] But it can be seen in Barth's case as well. While his modern exegetical reflection on Luke 15:11–32 is found in a discrete excursus in the small text of §64.2 (IV/2, 21–24), his suggestive applications of the parable range across *Church Dogmatics*, especially the fourth volume. Although Barth readily employs the technical language of

---

35. See Ricoeur, *Figuring the Sacred: Religion, Narrative, and Imagination* (Minneapolis: Fortress, 1995), and "Biblical Hermeneutics," *Semeia* 4 (1975): 29–148.

36. According to Ricoeur, parables are essentially "narratives within narratives." When a primary narrative (e.g., a parable) is embedded in a secondary narrative (e.g., the Gospel), it creates a "symbolic interference" that requires the "mutual interpretation" of both (Ricoeur, "Biblical Hermeneutics," 105). The "relation of intersignification" instituted between the smaller and larger narrative generates "a new signification" such that "isolated texts signify something *else*, something *more*" (Ricoeur, *Figuring the Sacred*, 161, 163). This is the process of "metaphorization" or "parabolization"—when "something passes from" one story to the other.

37. Ricoeur, *Figuring the Sacred*, 150.

38. While these are not the only shared biblical allusions, this set of intertexts is central to their interpretations of the parable and particularly the prodigal-Christ identity.

39. Of course, at this point in England, she would have been prohibited from explicitly "doing Christology" (promulgating and teaching doctrine), as well as paraphrasing and interpreting Scripture, by virtue of the fact that she was a layperson, woman, and vernacular writer.

the classical tradition, he also builds up his Christology in another way: by collecting and coordinating scriptural predicates. The language and narrative structure of the Lukan parable in particular provides a way of gathering together a number of christological categories. This is immediately evident from the titles of the complementary sections "The Way of the Son into the Far Country" and "The Homecoming of the Son of Man" (§59.1 and §64.2). These paragraphs are also strewn with allusive statements. For example, Barth writes, "The reconciliation of sinful and lost [humanity] has, above all, the character of a divine condescension, that it takes place as God goes into the far country"; and, similarly, "The event of atonement and the actuality of [humanity] reconciled with God can be described by those who know it only in the words of Luke 15:2: 'This man receiveth sinners, and eateth with them.'"[40]

In short, Barth sees the story of the lost or prodigal son as a thumbnail of all the doctrinal elements of reconciliation. It dramatizes what might otherwise be distilled in terms of the hypostatic union, justification, sanctification, the *status duplex*, the *munus triplex*, and so on. In fact, I think Alan Lewis is exactly right when he says we could view the whole of *The Doctrine of Reconciliation* as a "monumental and imaginative reconstruction of Christology upon the scaffold of the Prodigal Son narrative."[41] It is beyond the scope of this chapter to address this in detail, but Barth coordinates the structure and movement of the parable with classical doctrines as follows:

Structural Elements of the Parable:	Departure of the Lost Son	Homecoming of the Lost Son
Johannine Accent:	The Word became *Flesh*.	The *Word* became Flesh.
Standpoint and Direction:	Above to below	Below to above
Material Content of Reconciliation:	The Lord as *Servant* (IV/1)	The Servant as *Lord* (IV/2)
Ontological Emphasis:	Divinity of Jesus Christ	Humanity of Jesus Christ
Person:	Son of *God*	Son of *Man*, Jesus of Nazareth
Office:	Priest	King
State:	Humiliation (of God)	Exaltation (of the human)
Soteriological Emphasis:	Justification	Sanctification

40. *CD* IV/1, 83, 168.
41. Alan Lewis, *Between Cross and Resurrection: A Theology of Holy Saturday* (Grand Rapids: Eerdmans, 2003), 192.

Subject/Object:	Electing God (II/2)	Elected Human (II/2)
	Reconciling God (IV/1)	Reconciled Man (IV/1)
Scriptural Image:	Lamb of God	Lion of Judah

Finally, as I have already intimated, it is not simply the case that the parable of the prodigal son narrates atonement and reconciliation for Julian and Barth. It also narrates their doctrines of election and, concomitantly, their accounts of the Trinity. The lost son's story ultimately becomes the story of God. This is particularly evident in Barth's christologically grounded doctrine of election, which foreshadows his retelling of reconciliation through the Lukan parable.[42]

The language of the parable, as well as Barth's later interpretation of it, is present in II/2 (§32–33), where Barth asks, "Who is the Elect? He is always the one who 'was dead and is alive again,' who 'was lost and is found' (Lk. 15:24)."[43] He goes on to say,

> as the beginning of all things with God we find the decree that He Himself in person, in the person of His eternal Son, should give Himself to the son of man, the lost son of man, indeed that He Himself in the person of the eternal Son should *be* the lost Son of Man.[44]

The "lost son" becomes one of the primary images Barth uses for the divine decree, binding its content to that of reconciliation or atonement. According to him, God does not go into the "far country," with all that involves, as an afterthought or a response to creation gone awry. "It is not accidental," he says; "it could not be otherwise."[45] God wills from before time to be the lost son in and as the second person of the Trinity.

In other words, Barth's rendering of the parable, like Julian's, clearly exceeds soteriological parameters. To see Jesus Christ following after the prodigal son, in salvific solidarity with him, is not a strain once we situate the parable intertextually, as I have above. What is startling in Julian's and Barth's

---

42. *CD* II/2, 121. The connection between the parable of the prodigal son and Barth's refashioned doctrine of election is all the more remarkable in that the dynamic between two sons evokes the story of Jacob stealing Esau's birthright—a story that is commonly cited as evidence for the sort of Calvinist double predestination Barth specifically rejects ("Jacob I loved, but Esau I have hated," Mal. 1:2–3, Rom. 9:13).

43. *CD* II/2, 124.

44. *CD* II/2, 157.

45. *CD* IV/1, 176.

readings is not that the "fall" of Christ succeeds humanity's but that it is said to coincide with and, in some sense, even precede it. As Julian says, "when Adam felle, Goddes sonne fell" because of the "rightful oning [atonement] which was made in heven."[46] This pushes the way of the lost son back into the doctrine of God proper. His kenotic "far journey" and "homecoming" are eternally contained in the triune life. This, then, is what the parable finally recounts: the primordial prodigality of God in the "eternal covenant" (Barth), the "endlesse oning" (Julian) that *is* Jesus Christ.[47]

I will bracket a lengthy discussion of the ontological implications of this claim, an issue already addressed by a number of scholars.[48] But, needless to say, the suggestion is that Barth's later exegesis of the parable of the prodigal son should have some bearing on our understanding of his doctrine of election and what it means for his trinitarian ontology.[49]

---

46. Julian, *A Revelation*, 51.185. In Barth's analysis of the parable he says, Christ *"precedes all men as a King who draws them after Him"* (IV/2, 24).

47. *CD* III/1, 97; Julian, *A Revelation*, 53.18, 58.5-6.

48. What election and reconciliation mean for the Trinity "in se" is a much-debated topic in Barth scholarship. For one side of the debate see, for example, George Hunsinger, "Election and the Trinity: Twenty-five Theses on the Theology of Karl Barth," *Modern Theology* 48, no. 2 (2008): 179-98; Paul Molnar, *Divine Freedom and the Doctrine of the Immanent Trinity* (London: T&T Clark, 2002); and Molnar, "The Trinity, Election, and God's Ontological Freedom: A Response to Kevin Hector," *International Journal of Systematic Theology* 8, no. 3 (2006): 294-306. For loosely related positions on the other side, see, for example, Bruce McCormack, "Grace and Being: The Role of God's Gracious Election in Karl Barth's Theological Ontology," in *The Cambridge Companion to Karl Barth*, ed. John Webster (Cambridge: Cambridge University Press, 2000); Kevin Hector, "God's Triunity and Self-Determination," *International Journal of Systematic Theology* 7, no. 3 (2005): 246-61; Paul Nimmo, "Election and Evangelical Thinking," in *New Perspectives in Evangelical Theology: Engaging with God, Scripture, and the World*, ed. Tom Greggs (London: Routledge, 2010), 29-43; and Paul Jones, *The Humanity of Christ: Christology in Karl Barth's Church Dogmatics* (London: T&T Clark, 2008).

49. Speaking of Barth's divine ontology, Jüngel says, the "precedence of God in his primal decision shows that God's being not only 'proceeds' on the way into the far country but that God's being is *in movement* from eternity. God's being is moved being ... moved by God." See Eberhard Jüngel, *God's Being Is in Becoming: The Trinitarian Being of God in the Theology of Karl Barth. A Paraphrase*, trans. John Webster (London: T&T Clark, 2001), 14-15.

Parabolic Theology and Christological Discourse

The fact that Julian and Barth so comprehensively and compellingly inscribe their theologies in the mode of parable raises a certain possibility for christological discourse. Much attention has been given to the role of the categories "history," "narrative," and "event" for Barth's theological method and particularly for his actualist ontology.[50] What I would like to emphasize here is the connection between these categories and the centrality of the "name." A decisive reason for Barth's recourse to story or history (*Geschichte*) is that a name can only be narrated.[51] As he remarks in a letter to Berkouwer,

> My intention ... has been that all my systematic theology should be as exact a development as possible of the significance of this "name" ... and to that extent should be the telling of a story which develops through individual events.[52]

While Barth does not shy away from scholastic definitions, he insists that fixed propositions, an essence, or a set of attributes must not take the place of the narrativity of the name. Even "grace," he says, is only "the paraphrase of the name of Jesus."[53] This "narrative commitment" is particularly evident in Barth's attempt to redynamize the "static" metaphysical language of the tradition.[54] Calling for historical or storied thinking, he sidelines talk of

---

50. See, among many others: Hans Frei, *The Eclipse of Biblical Narrative: A Study in Eighteenth and Nineteenth Century Hermeneutics* (New Haven: Yale University Press, 1957); David Ford, *Barth and God's Story: Biblical Narrative and the Theological Method of Karl Barth in the "Church Dogmatics"* (Frankfurt am Main: Peter Lang, 1981); George Hunsinger, "Beyond Literalism and Expressivism: Karl Barth's Hermeneutical Realism," *Modern Theology* 3 (1987): 209-23; David H. Kelsey, *The Uses of Scripture in Recent Theology* (Philadelphia: Fortress, 1975); Ronald F. Thiemann, *Revelation and Theology: The Gospel as Narrated Promise* (Notre Dame: University of Notre Dame Press, 1985); Kathryn Tanner, "Theology and the Plain Sense," in *Scriptural Authority and Narrative Interpretation*, ed. Garrett Green (Philadelphia: Fortress, 1987); David Ford, "Narrative in Theology," *British Journal of Religious Education* 4, no. 3 (1982); and Stanley Hauerwas and L. Gregory Jones, eds., *Why Narrative? Readings in Narrative Theology* (Grand Rapids: Eerdmans, 1989).

51. According to Larry Bouchard, "Narrative ... is really an enlarged act of *naming* that answers the question, 'Who?'" See Bouchard, *Theater and Integrity: Emptying Selves in Drama, Ethics, and Religion* (Evanston, IL: Northwestern University Press, 2011), 32.

52. Letter to Berkouwer, Dec. 10, 1954, cited by Busch, *Karl Barth*, 381, n. 205.

53. *CD* II/2, 173.

54. "Narrative commitment" is Sarah Coakley's phrase. See Coakley, *Powers and Submissions: Spirituality, Philosophy and Gender* (Malden, MA: Blackwell, 2002), 24-25.

"two natures" in favor of phrases like "twofold history," "double movement," "two-sided participation," "common actualization," and, somewhat less pithily, "the event of the coordination of the two predicates."[55]

In light of the material I have presented, my contention is that it is parable in particular, and not simply narrative, that capacitates the sort of dynamic but unified retelling of the name that Barth is after. There are at least two reasons for this. First, parable, as a metaphorized narrative, allows us to speak of two things at once and as one. It sustains the narration of multiple histories, identities, and realities in one *concretum*. This is remarkably convenient when it comes to speaking of things like the hypostatic union. The form of parable frees us from trying to talk out of both sides of our mouths. This is a problem that seems to bother Barth earlier, in *Church Dogmatics* I/1, where he says,

> It is impossible to listen at one and the same time to the two statements that Jesus of Nazareth is the Son of God and that the Son of God is Jesus of Nazareth. One hears either the one or the other or one hears nothing. When the one is heard, the other can be heard only indirectly.[56]

I would suggest that Barth's later use of the parable form constitutes an indispensable methodological discovery that enables him to overcome, so far as possible, the "onesidedness" of theological propositions.[57]

Second, parable facilitates a bifocality befitting the subject matter. In the parabolic form, we have an apt parallel to the content of incarnation

---

55. *CD* IV/1, 113, 133; IV/2, 115. For a helpful reassessment of Chalcedon as "horizon," "boundary," or "pattern," see Coakley, "What Does Chalcedon Solve and What Does It Not?" in *The Incarnation: An Interdisciplinary Symposium on the Incarnation of the Son of God*, ed. Stephen T. Davis, Daniel Kendall SJ, and Gerald O'Collins SJ (Oxford: Oxford University Press, 2002), 160. A basic assumption of my reading is that, in his later work, Barth progressively moves away from the language of "one person in two *natures*," opting for more actualist language like "two sides or directions or forms of that which took place" (IV/2, 116). As Paul Jones argues, Barth "effectively discards the language of 'nature' in his 'mature' Christology" (*The Humanity of Christ*, 28). But although Barth dispenses with *physis*, he retains the tensive relationship established in the twofold history of Jesus Christ as indicated by the four Chalcedonian adjectives: *inconfuse, immutabiliter, inseparabiliter, indivise* (unconfused, unchanged, inseparable, indivisible).

56. *CD* I/1, 180.

57. *CD* I/1, 181. Barth later concludes that abstract or purely conceptual forms of theological reflection have an epexegetical status, calling classical categories mere "commentary" on the biblical narrative (IV/2, 66).

and atonement.⁵⁸ It corresponds to the ontologically irreducible doubleness of the person and work of Jesus Christ. This helps Barth retain the logic or pattern of Chalcedon, while shifting away from "one person, two natures" to something more like "one name, two histories" or, more accurately, "one name, one twofold history."⁵⁹ In his parabolic retelling of the name of Jesus Christ all the major doctrinal loci—from creation to covenant to election to reconciliation—converge and refract as nonidentical repetitions of the same story. It is the Lukan parable, and not simply narrative per se, that enables him to gather together these complexly interpenetrating doctrines and map onto them multiple scriptural predicates.

We may need to speak, then, not simply of "narrative theology" but more specifically of "parabolic theology."⁶⁰ This is what I think we encounter in Julian's and Barth's christological retellings of the parable. In reenacting both the form and content of the story, they keep before us Jesus's own history in its intrinsically parabolic character.⁶¹ If narrative theology allows us to say, "Jesus is his story,"⁶² parabolic theology stresses that in Jesus's story he is not *only* himself—he is himself *and* another.

58. As Ebeling claims, "The parable is the form of the language of Jesus which corresponds to the incarnation." See Gerhard Ebeling, *Evangelische Evangelienauslegung: Eine Untersuchung zu Luther's Hermeneutik*, 2nd ed. (Darmstadt: Wissenschaftliche Buchgesellschaft, 1962), 108.

59. While Barth insists that it is one history—the singular and unified history of Jesus Christ—at the same time, the one history of Jesus Christ gathers together (at least three) very divergent histories: the history of God the Son, the history of the man Jesus, and the whole history of humankind lost and perishing.

60. "Parabolic theology" is a phrase that has also been used by Sallie McFague, *Speaking in Parables: A Study in Metaphor and Theology* (Philadelphia: Fortress, 1975). I am *not* using this phrase in the same way as she does. While she too is concerned about the relationship between form and content, she uses "parabolic theology" to refer to an "intermediary theology"—a mode of theology that falls somewhere in between the poetic and the conceptual. But I am interested in the *irreducibility* of parabolic theology, rather than its intermediary status.

61. Eberhard Jüngel addresses the parabolic quality of Jesus as the self-communication of God in *God as the Mystery of the World: On the Foundation of the Theology of the Crucified One in the Dispute Between Theism and Atheism*, trans. Darrell Guder (Edinburgh: T&T Clark, 1983). He claims, "The *son* is the *personal parable of the father*" and that "one can and must say Jesus is *the parable [Gleichnis] of God*" (288–89).

62. Frei, *Theology and Narrative: Selected Essays*, ed. George Hunsinger and William C. Placher (Oxford: Oxford University Press, 1993), 42. Thus, in contrast to the notion of authenticity upon which defenses of the absolute singularity of Jesus's identity depend, parable forces us to consider not the question of being oneself (*autos*) but of not quite being oneself, of identifying oneself otherwise, of becoming another. I do not wish to deny the

Parabolic Retelling and Christological Discourse

As Barth explains in his exposition of Philippians 2:6–7 (in *CD* IV/1), it was not an "an inalienable necessity" for God

> only to be God, and therefore only to be different from the creature... He was not committed to any such "only."... He had this other possibility ... in taking it upon Himself to be Himself in a way quite other than that which corresponds and belongs to His form as God... He can also go into the far country and be there, with all that involves.[63]

God is God; but God is not *only* God.[64] This is why election is truly "the sum of the Gospel"—because, in Barth's words, in "a condescension inconceivably tender," God "makes the being of this other [God's] own being."[65] God is Godself—and another. To use Julian's remarkable turn of phrase, "Grace is God."[66] That, for Barth, is the good news of the parable of the lost son.

---

claim about Jesus's singularity but only to point out that parabolic theology might help us articulate something else, which is not included in the usual emphasis of narrative theology on unrepeatable personal identity. That is the paradox of the person of Christ: the unsubstitutable substitution.

63. *CD* IV/1, 180. This is a reflection on divine *kenōsis*, a term Barth tends to avoid because of its theological baggage. (For his view of modern kenoticism see, e.g., IV/1, 182–83.) He seems to rely on "condescension" and "obedience" as stand-ins for what might otherwise be translated as "self-emptying."

64. Or, as Barth says, "God alone is God. But God is not alone." Quoted by Busch, *Karl Barth*, 280, n. 85. See Barth's 1937–1938 Gifford Lectures, *The Knowledge of God and the Service of God* IV.1–2.

65. *CD* II/2, 3, 121. As a result, Barth tells us, theology can no longer be the "doctrine of God" only; it must always be "theanthropology," the doctrine of God and humanity together. See Barth, *The Humanity of God*, trans. John Newton Thomas and Thomas Wieser (Richmond, VA: John Knox, 1960), 9.

66. Julian, *A Revelation*, 63.8.

8 The Riddle of Gethsemane

Barth on Jesus's Agony in the Garden

PAUL DAFYDD JONES

At a key moment in §59 of the *Church Dogmatics*, Barth offers an "outline of the evangelical history" (IV/1, 224) that the Synoptic Gospels recount, and that Jesus enacts, undergoes, and declares.[1] The German word for "history," in this instance, is *Geschichte*: a loaded term, given the work of Martin Kähler, that identifies a narratable story, grounded in a delimited sequence of concrete events, that is received in faith and that bears witness to faith.[2] As Barth understands it, the history recorded in Matthew, Mark, and Luke comprises three discrete stages. In the first, Jesus is acclaimed as an active subject. Obedient to the Father, superior to and directive of the quotidian in which he exists, he exercises sovereignty in ways that show him to be the Son of God. He, and he alone, does what no mere mortal can do: he proclaims, inaugurates, and embodies the kingdom; he assures sinners that God's covenantal intentions are being realized.

The second stage of the synoptics' history, by contrast, presents Jesus as an object. There is a disconcerting reversal: Jesus no longer sets the terms for his existence; increasingly, he seems to be at the mercy of others. Proclamation and activity are replaced with "silence and ... suffering" (IV/1, 226) and Jesus is not so much active as acted upon. The kingdom, accordingly,

---

1. All in-text quotations are from the *CD*. "Rev." indicates my revised translation. Although I have restored many of the original emphases from the German, I have not indicated this in every instance.

2. I refer here to Martin Kähler, *Der sogennante historische Jesus und der geschichtliche, biblische Christus* (Leipzig: George Böhme, 1896). ET: *The So-called Historical Jesus and the Historic Biblical Christ*, trans. and ed. Carl E. Braaten (Mifflintown, PA: Sigler, 2002).

recedes into the background. In its place one finds a murderous combination of religious jealousy, political scheming, rank cowardice, and embittered groupthink. Remarkably, however, God is at work in all that transpires. As Jesus's contemporaries drive him toward his death, the Father asks that Jesus understand their actions as a vehicle of God's judgment against sin. The Father asks, to put it more strongly, that Jesus view his enemies' conduct as a means by which God achieves the salvation of the world—that Jesus understand the net of cruelty that surrounds him as a vehicle of God's reconciliatory activity. Jesus consents. And he consents in such a way that his status as an "object" is not a fate to which he has no choice but to submit, but a future that he embraces and intends. He treats the actions of his contemporaries as a divine command to be realized; freely and obediently, he leads himself, even as he is led, to death. More: in acting in this way, Jesus plays his part in the drama of salvation. When he dies on the cross, he freely takes on the full weight of our sin and the full force of God's judgment against it.

And then another shift, another reversal, which inaugurates the third stage of the "evangelical history": Jesus is raised from the dead. Once again, he lives as a superior and directive subject. No longer acted upon, he is active once more; no longer silent, he speaks anew, and does so with unfettered authority. But he does so in a new way. Loosed from his quotidian and unconstrained by temporal and spatial limitations, Jesus declares himself the Savior of humankind. He shows his followers that judgment is behind us and, with the Spirit, he mediates God's reconciling and redeeming love to the world. The risen Christ reveals to us, in short, what he was, is, and always will be: the history of God with humankind and the history of humankind with God.

The Connection between Exegesis and Dogmatics

Why does Barth sketch the synoptics' "evangelical history" at this juncture of IV/1? Why, specifically, does he interrupt the fast-paced centerpiece of §59 (section two, "The Judge Judged in Our Place") with an excursus that requires readers to attend to the "simple character" (IV/1, 224) of the gospel narratives?

There are two overlapping answers to these questions. On one level, Barth returns to a claim ventured in *Church Dogmatics* I: viz., that the synoptics and the Fourth Gospel provide complementary angles of vision on the incarnation, with each of Christ's two "natures" serving as a point of entry into a dogmatic description of Christ's person and work. The Fourth

Gospel shows that God in God's second way of being is the *human* identified as Jesus of Nazareth; the synoptics head in the other direction, and present the human identified as Jesus of Nazareth as the Son of *God*.[3] While Barth's doctrine of election lends this claim a slightly new charge (after II/2, Barth would say that John tells us about the electing God who is the elected human, while the synoptics tell us about the elected human who is the electing God), a rehearsal of the synoptic *Geschichte* in the middle of §59 therefore indicates how Barth goes about describing God in God's second way of being. To think rightly at this point, one must focus one's attention on "the man Christ Jesus" (1 Tim. 2:5 [KJV]), the principal witness to whom is the set of narratives forged by the authors of Matthew, Mark, and Luke. Retelling the synoptic *Geschichte*, still more specifically, indicates why Barth could not "avoid the astounding conclusion of a divine obedience" (IV/1, 202) in §59.1: because "obedience" is the best way to describe, summarily, how Jesus of Nazareth lives his life for and with God the Father. One cannot drive a wedge between the disposition, conduct, and identity of Christ qua human and the disposition, conduct, and identity of Christ as God in God's second way of being; one must understand that the "presence and action" of the Son "coincide with and are indeed identical with the existence of the humiliated and lowly and obedient man Jesus of Nazareth" (IV/1, 199). To acclaim Jesus as the "only begotten Son," one even might say, is dogmatically insufficient. The word "obedient" is a necessary complement. It completes the description of how the Son relates to the Father, in time and for all eternity, and identifies this relationship as the presupposition of God's reconciliatory action.

On another level, Barth's rehearsal of the "evangelical history" has a pedagogical function. It reasserts what Barth takes to be a basic connection between exegesis and dogmatics; it reminds Christians in general, and theologians in particular, that theological reflection must be grounded in and responsive to the narratives of the Bible. And who would suppose that he or she has no need of this reminder? Rather than letting the Gospels shape our thoughts, words, and actions, we tend to exploit them for our own purposes. Rather than letting exegesis determine the shape of doctrine, we fall victim to academicism of the worst kind, and let a commitment to theoretical or doctrinal "clarity" trump our faithful reception of the particulars of the text. Retelling the synoptic Geschichte, then, is Barth's attempt to help his readers pause, regroup, and recommit themselves to the most basic of theological

---

3. See, for example, I/1, 404, and I/2, 15–25.

tasks: encountering and responding to Scripture with as little presumption as possible, supported by the hope that God will render its words disclosive of God's ways and works, and will conform our (typically sinful) thoughts, words, and actions to the *ratio* to which it bears witness. It is an occasion, to draw on the second edition of Barth's *Romans*, in which we are encouraged to think of ourselves as sinners who exist on the "frontier of religion": the "place where we must *wait*, in order that God may confront us—on the other side of the frontier."[4]

A provocative remark, and one that raises a pressing question: How ought a theologian to "wait" when thinking about Christ's atoning work? What kind of dogmatic disposition does Barth encourage us to adopt, in view of Christ's trial, suffering, and death? A negative response: we ought not to rush ahead to Galilee; we ought not to suppose that we know, in advance, who it is that goes before us. (Presumption, one might say, is never a theological virtue.) Its positive corollary: if we are to have any hope of thinking well about reconciliation, we must endeavor to keep pace with the synoptic witness. We must strive to have its own rhythms and tempos determine the speed of thought; we must let ourselves be *led*, despite our conceited sense that we have the resources and expertise to find our own way. And as Barth's own excursus suggests, it is particularly important to reckon with those moments when the story of Jesus slows down, pauses, and heads in a new direction, for it is in those moments that theological reflection ought to slow down, pause, and head in a new direction.

All of this sets the scene for the interpretive claims of this chapter. Working mainly with remarks about Gethsemane advanced in §59, I hope to plumb the depths of Barth's account of the transition between the first and second parts of the "evangelical history": that moment of Jesus's life in which he teeters between two very different modes of being—being a subject and being an object, being active and being receptive—and then commits himself to bearing the judgment that secures our reconciliation. What does Barth make of this change of tempo, this pause—this stutter-step—in the synoptic witness?

---

4. Karl Barth, *The Epistle to the Romans*, trans. Edwyn Hoskyns (Oxford: Oxford University Press, 1968), 242. My emphasis.

PAUL DAFYDD JONES

Gethsemane in the Thought of Maximus, Calvin, and Schleiermacher

The treatment of Gethsemane in the Synoptic Gospels has, of course, long been a site of theological interest.[5] Perhaps the most important element of the patristic background is Maximus the Confessor's reading of Matthew 26:39 ("Father, if it is possible, let this cup pass from me; yet not what I want but what you want") as a decisive warrant for dyothelitism: the claim that the hypostatic union definitive of Christ's person includes the operations of *two* discrete wills—one divine, the other human. Maximus understood dyothelitism to be a legitimate and, in fact, necessary elaboration of the "Definition" of Chalcedon (451 CE). To suppose that Christ lacks a human will would amount to an abbreviation of his human nature; to say that Christ lacks a divine will would amount to a denial that "*God* was in Christ, reconciling the world unto himself" (2 Cor. 5:19 [KJV]). Or, to make the point more positively: while recognizing that Christ acts "uniquely, that is, as a single agent," one must also say that the actions of this single agent depend on and express the perfectly concurrent operations of "the natural energies of His two natures."[6] "Will" is as good a term as any to describe these "natural energies." It specifies those dimensions of Christ's divine and human natures in which discrete intentions are forged and from which discrete actions issue.

Could it be said, though, that the prayer in Gethsemane exposes a fracture in the hypostatic union, with Christ's humanity being at odds, if only momentarily, with Christ's divinity? Does the prospect of death occasion conflict between Christ's human and divine wills? Maximus answers these questions with a forceful *No*. Christian theology acclaims a hypostatic *union* because Christ's two wills are in perfect agreement at every stage of his life.

---

5. Matt. 26:36-46, Mark 14:32-42, and Luke 22:39-46. Many commentators find an echo of the Gethsemane tradition in John 12:27 ("Now my soul is troubled") and John 18:1. See for instance Raymond E. Brown, *The Gospel according to John (I-XII)* (New York: Doubleday, 1966), 475-76 (on John 12:27) and Brown, *The Gospel according to John (XIII-XXI)* (New York: Doubleday, 1970), 806-7 and 814-18 (on John 18:1); and Barnabas Lindars, *The Gospel of John* (London: Marshall, Morgan & Scott, 1972), 430-31 and 538-39.

6. These quotations are from *Ambiguum* 4 and *Ambiguum* 5. See Maximus the Confessor, *On Difficulties in the Church Fathers: The Ambigua*, vol. 1, ed. and trans. Nicholas Constas (Cambridge, MA: Harvard University Press, 2014), 28-29 and 42-43 respectively. Also important for understanding Maximus's position are *Opuscule* 6 and *Opuscule* 7. See here, respectively, *On the Cosmic Mystery of Jesus Christ: Selected Writings from St. Maximus the Confessor*, trans. Paul M. Blowers and Robert Louis Wilken (Crestwood, NY: St. Vladimir's Seminary Press, 2003), 173-76; and Andrew Louth, ed., *Maximus the Confessor* (London: Routledge, 1996), 180-91.

The Riddle of Gethsemane

The Gethsemane prayer simply shows that Christ's truly human will, deified though it may be, struggles to come to terms with the dreadful prospect of the cross. There is no temporary, sinful, lapse; there is only an understandable hesitation in view of suffering and death. Furthermore, and perhaps most interestingly, Jesus's prayer in Gethsemane shows that intentional human action is integral to his saving work. The hypostatic union is not simply a matter of both natures retaining their "constitutive elements."[7] One can say, also, that the "constitutive element" of Jesus's humanity that is the act of willing is ingredient to, and necessary for, the whole course of the incarnate Son's singular act of obedience to the Father. So when Christ says, "*Not what I will . . .*" he makes plain the "harmony between the human will of the Savior and the divine will shared by him and his Father."[8] And when Christ rises from prayer and begins the final stage of his journey, we see the working of "both of the natures from which, in which, and of which his person was"—a *unified* working in which Christ is "able both to will and to effect our salvation."[9]

The degree to which Barth was familiar with Maximus's writings is difficult to ascertain. While it would be surprising if Barth were unacquainted with his work, given the scholarly labors of Hans Urs von Balthasar, Maximus is not mentioned by name at any point in the *Dogmatics*.[10] Yet Barth is forthright in committing himself to thinking along lines laid down by Maximus and others during the "so-called monothelite controversy of the seventh century" (I/2, 158). To affirm Jesus as *vere homo* is to affirm that Jesus has a "true, human will, different from the will of God although never independent of it" (I/2, 158). Furthermore, Barth's decision to preserve a Reformed emphasis on the integrity and distinction of Christ's human nature—an emphasis that disallows any suggestion that Christ's humanity bears divine qualities such as omnipotence and omnipresence, and worries that Lutheran construals of the *communicatio idiomatum* drift in the direction of a questionable "divinization" of Christ's humanity—has as its corollary the

---

7. Maximus Confessor, *Ambiguum* 5 (42–43).

8. Maximus Confessor, *Opuscule* 6 (176).

9. Maximus Confessor, *Opuscule* 6 (176). I am here evading some difficult questions about Maximus's remarks about the different dimensions of Christ's humanity: e.g., about Christ's "gnomic will" as it relates to Christ's natural human will, and Christ's human passions. Such questions are of course important for an analysis of Maximus's thought: they bear on the issue of how Maximus understood human nature, and how consistent and radical his dyothelitism truly is. But they need not be tackled here.

10. See Hans Urs von Balthasar, *Cosmic Liturgy: The Universe according to Maximus Confessor*, trans. Brian E. Daley, SJ (San Francisco: Ignatius, 2003).

acceptance of an obligation to advance dogmatic claims about what it is, exactly, that Christ *does* as a human being, even granted that Christ's humanity is "inseparable from . . . and has no independent existence" apart from the divine Son.[11] To make the same point a bit differently: If it is truly the case that Christ's humanity, "despite its exaltation, is neither deified nor does it participate in the divine being and divine qualities," a Reformed theologian must find some way to talk about the manner in which Christ's human nature *actively* renders obedience to the Father.[12] If one demurs at this point, the charge of docetism lurks in the wings, for the suspicion arises that Jesus's humanity is a lifeless instrument wielded by the Son—precisely the claim that plays at the edges of the tradition of thought associated with Athanasius and Cyril of Alexandria, and precisely the claim that Maximus and the Sixth Ecumenical Council of 680–681 CE was wise to resist.

This brings us to Barth's conversation partners in the Reformed tradition. What did John Calvin and Friedrich Schleiermacher say about Jesus's agony in the garden of Gethsemane? How did they negotiate this passage in the synoptics and the attendant issue of dyothelitism?

Calvin's fullest treatment of Gethsemane is found in his commentary on the Synoptic Gospels.[13] Hard on the heels of the Last Supper, Calvin suggests, Jesus catches sight of the end that awaits him. That this sight proved horrifying is undeniable and understandable. Jesus faces a future worse than death. He faces a passion in which God takes stock of human sin, deems us utterly guilty, and then transfers the just and proper punishment that we deserve to Christ. To be sure, the faithful view Jesus's agony in the garden in light of the *beneficii Christi*. Exactly because "the force and curse of sin were slain in *his* flesh," Jesus's prayer does not prompt apprehension, but an overwhelming sense of gratitude: the Mediator's perfect obedience ensures our intimate relationship with God the Father.[14] Yet gratitude ought not to

---

11. Karl Barth, *The Theology of the Reformed Confessions, 1923*, trans. and annotated by Darrell L. Guder and Judith J. Guder (Louisville: Westminster John Knox, 2002), 183.

12. Barth, *Reformed Confessions*, 183.

13. John Calvin, *A Harmony of the Gospels: Matthew, Mark, and Luke*, 3 vols., trans. A. W. Morrison (vols. 1 and 3) and T. H. L. Parker (vol. 2), ed. David W. Torrance and Thomas F. Torrance, 3 vols. (Grand Rapids: Eerdmans, 1972). Calvin's principal remarks on Gethsemane come in vol. 3, 145–54. Per convention, subsequent references to the *Harmony* will note the relevant chapter and verse.

14. John Calvin, *Institutes of the Christian Religion*, ed. John T. McNeill, trans. Ford Lewis Battles, 2 vols. (Louisville: Westminster John Knox, 2006), III.4.27 (653). My emphasis.

be dissociated from the particulars of Jesus's mediatorial work, and the very fact that piety is textured by the scriptural witness obliges us to reckon, again and again, with the price at which salvation is bought. Calvin therefore takes pains to emphasize Jesus's terrified receipt of his future. As Jesus prays, the gracious countenance of the Father is replaced with a "dread tribunal" over which presides "the Judge Himself . . . armed with vengeance beyond understanding."[15] In contrast to those predestined to life, who await ever-greater participation in the triune *koinonia*, Jesus learns of a future in which he must endure the Father's righteous wrath.

Three more particular claims orbit this exegetical center. First, Calvin argues that Jesus's fear and suffering are especially pronounced in Gethsemane because Jesus's divinity temporarily "quiets" itself.[16] There is a divine withdrawal of sorts, and this withdrawal opens space for Jesus humanly to step forward and "fulfill the Redeemer's role of suffering."[17] While this is a fairly common move in Calvin's Christology, it is clearly questionable. Beyond the fact that it is difficult to imagine exactly what divine withdrawal entails, the synoptics do not suggest that Christ's divinity temporarily retreats, much less signal that the prayer in Gethsemane is especially associable with Jesus's humanity. It is also hard to reconcile talk of divine "quieting" with a straightforward affirmation of the unity of Christ's person as he undertakes his mediatorial work. (Is Christ not *always*, and unequivocally, the "Word become flesh"?) What seems to animate Calvin's thinking on this front is not the details of the Gospels, but two dogmatic desiderata: (a) a desire to hold Christ's divinity at a distance from an all-too-human instance of confusion and alarm; and (b) a concern to emphasize that Christ mediates salvation in his divine *and* human "natures."[18] Leaving point (a) to one side for the time

---

15. Calvin, *Comm. Matt.* 26:37.

16. Calvin, *Comm. Matt.* 26:37. The full quotation: "[T]he divine power of Christ is said to have reposed as it were in concealment for a time (*quasi abscondita ad tempus quievisse*) to allow Him to fulfill the Redeemer's role of suffering."

17. Calvin, *Comm. Matt.* 26:37.

18. This claim was forcefully expressed in Calvin's dispute with Francesco Stancaro. See Joseph Tylanda, "Christ the Mediator: Calvin versus Stancaro" and "The Controversy on Christ the Mediator: Calvin's Second Reply to Stancaro," in *Calvin Theological Journal* 7 and 8 (1972): 5–16 and 131–57, respectively. See also Stephen Edmondson, *Calvin's Christology* (Cambridge: Cambridge University Press, 2004), esp. 14–39. There is a slight irony here: while Calvin rejected Stancaro's claim that Christ is mediator only in his humanity and emphasizes frequently that Christ mediates our redemption concretely—and therefore in *both* of his "natures"—talk of the "quieting" of Christ's divinity risks lending support to Stancaro and his supporters.

being, point (b) has particular importance for my purposes: it marks one point of entry for dyothelite commitments to the Reformed tradition.[19] In Gethsemane Jesus reckons with the awful conclusion to the "whole course of his obedience," for the Father requires that he commit, divinely *and* humanly, to being obedient unto death.[20] And the fact that Jesus does so commit himself ensures that his mediatorial work encompasses, and is effected by, *both* of his natures.

Second, Calvin clarifies the extent to which Jesus is existentially undone when he prays. Against those who would confine Jesus's horror to the less rarefied regions of his soul, Calvin writes movingly about an "ordeal . . . of grief and sorrow." Christ "lies full on the earth as a Suppliant." There is "no rehearsed prayer"; rather, "the force and onset of grief wrung a cry from Him," and such "vehemence took from Him any present thoughts of the decree of heaven, so that for a moment He did not think how He was sent to be the Redeemer of the human race."[21] Remarks such as these are simultaneously a case study in plain-sense exegesis and a rhetorically powerful dramatization of Jesus's agony: a combination, so characteristic of Calvin, that pushes readers to encounter familiar texts in novel and spiritually formative ways.[22] Calvin aims to show readers, still more particularly, how it is that Jesus "*learns* obedience" (Heb. 5:8). In prayer, Jesus wrestles with, and struggles to accept, what God asks of him. He confronts—not for the first time, but in a new way—what it means to bear the punishment that lawbreakers deserve. Yet what Calvin gives with the one hand, he takes away with the other. Demurrals soon haunt his interpretation; initially bold exegetical lines are blurred and smudged. Having suggested that Christ is overwhelmed in Gethsemane, Calvin goes on to say that he entertained only "a certain kind of indirect dissent," and the "passion of grief and fear was such

---

19. Which is not to say that the language of "dyothelitism" was retained *simpliciter*. Many Reformed theologians opted to discuss the activity of Christ's humanity in terms of the *communicatio operationum* and *communicatio apotelesmatum*. See Heinrich Heppe, *Reformed Dogmatics: A Compendium of Reformed Theology*, rev. and ed. Ernst Bizer, trans. G. T. Thomson (London: Wakeman Great Reprints, n.d.), 445-46.

20. Calvin, *Institutes*, II.16.5 (507).

21. Calvin, *Comm. Matt.* 26:39.

22. Calvin's concern to shape the piety of his readers has been a particular concern in recent Anglophone scholarship. See here Serene Jones, *Calvin and the Rhetoric of Piety* (Louisville: Westminster John Knox, 1995); Julie Canlis, *Calvin's Ladder: A Spiritual Theology of Ascent and Ascension* (Grand Rapids: Eerdmans, 2010); and Mathew Myer Boulton, *Life in God: John Calvin, Practical Formation, and the Future of Protestant Theology* (Grand Rapids: Eerdmans, 2011).

that He held Himself in limits." Although his "fleshy sense was affected . . . His faith remained undamaged and unshaken."[23] Something of the medieval scholastics' wariness toward Gethsemane comes into view, albeit with earlier talk of "appetites" and "propassions" now described in terms of restraint, moderation, and self-control—motifs that bear witness to Calvin's negotiation of Stoic mores.[24]

But I want to hold fast to the horror that Christ experiences and expresses, for this dovetails with Calvin's third, and arguably most interesting, claim. In Gethsemane, Jesus comes to understand his death as an event whose negative force *exceeds* that of a lawful punishment for sin, exacted by the Father. The language of excess might strike some as misplaced, but it brings us to the heart of the matter. To be sure, Calvin often describes the "abyss of death" into which Jesus is cast in terms of a legal penalty.[25] The *Institutes* and the commentaries make ample use of the juridical language of both Testaments, and while Calvin's views on atonement ought not to be viewed in terms of a "theory" of penal substitution, the claim that Christ bears our punishment is one that Calvin often accentuates. However, while Jesus's anguish in Gethsemane is inclusive of his awareness that he will stand substitute for the guilty, it is not reducible to that. If one juxtaposes Calvin's reading of Gethsemane with key passages in his commentaries on the Hebrew Bible, the cross is also presented as the single moment of history, before the eschaton, in which God's patience, God's forbearance of sin, ceases. Prior to Calvary, God restrains Godself. God does not rush to rebuke sinners, so as to reorder a disordered covenant. God tempers God's punishment; God "accommodates" God's wrath to our capacity. That is why creation continues, and that is why ancient Israel survived for as long as it did—precisely because God does *not* execute judgment in a proportional way. With the cross, however, God expresses wrath without limit. There is, finally, neither mercy nor restraint. For a dreadful moment, there is nothing but a cursed death—a jealous (re)assertion of God's honor; a furious articulation of God's hatred of sin. Paul's letter to the Romans surely shaped Cal-

---

23. Calvin, *Comm. Matt.* 26:39.

24. On Calvin and stoicism see the valuable article by Kyle Fedler, "Calvin's Burning Heart: Calvin and the Stoics on Emotion," *Journal of the Society of Christian Ethics* 22 (2002): 133–62. Also useful is David Foxgrover, "The Humanity of Christ: Within Proper Limits," in *Calviniana: Ideas and Influence of Jean Calvin*, ed. Robert V. Schnucker (Kirksville, MO: Sixteenth Century Journal Publishers, 1988), 93–105.

25. Calvin, *Comm. Matt.* 26:39.

vin's reasoning: If "God, in his divine forbearance ... had passed over ... sins previously committed" (Rom. 3:25), God does not hold back on the cross.[26] God loses patience, once and for all. No wonder, then, that Jesus cried out. The Father discloses to him a future that is uniquely terrifying.[27]

What of Calvin's most illustrious descendant in nineteenth-century Europe? Does Schleiermacher develop these intriguing lines of reflection? No. Gethsemane is effectively a no-show in *The Christian Faith*. Insofar as redemption entails a communication of "unclouded blessedness," synoptic reports of Jesus's anguished prayer have incidental importance for dogmatic reflection.[28] Jesus's "soul-stirring exhibition of Himself," the material center of God's redemptive activity across time and space, is not inclusive of a dread anticipation of God-forsakenness.[29]

Schleiermacher's reasoning on this issue is relatively easy to track. As the Introduction to the *Glaubenslehre* makes plain, Schleiermacher believes that dogmatic claims should be derived from an analysis of the Christian community as it encounters God's saving action. God graciously gathers, sustains, and directs the church; and, as part of the body of Christ, the theologian trains her attention on its head. A central component of her intellectual task, more specifically, is to work up a cogent account of the one through whom God's wise and loving activity is routed. A simple but profound dogmatic rule then comes into play: the majestic quality of Jesus's work must be partnered with a proportionately majestic account of his person. There must be no mismatch: the creation-redeeming force of Christ's life demands a Christology able to bear its weight. And *that*, for Schleiermacher, requires that Christ be described in terms of the "imperturbable blessedness" in which believers are given a share.[30] The condition of possibility of an unimpeded and triumphant communication of grace is

---

26. Calvin's commentary on the verse: "that this remission was through the *forbearance of God*, means simply gentleness. This has restrained the judgment of God, and has prevented it from being inflamed for our destruction, until He received us at last into His favour." See *The Epistle of Paul the Apostle to the Romans and to the Thessalonians*, trans. Ross MacKenzie, ed. David W. Torrance and Thomas F. Torrance (Grand Rapids: Eerdmans, 1973), 77.

27. For my fuller interpretation of Calvin on the atonement, see Paul Dafydd Jones, "The Fury of Love: Calvin on the Atonement," in *T&T Clark Companion to the Atonement*, ed. Adam Johnson (London: T&T Clark, forthcoming).

28. Friedrich Schleiermacher, *The Christian Faith*, ed. H. R. Mackintosh and J. S. Stewart (London: T&T Clark, 1999), 431.

29. Schleiermacher, *Christian Faith*, 484.

30. Schleiermacher, *Christian Faith*, 436.

a Redeemer who, as God himself, suffers no "inner conflict" whatsoever.[31] Or, to switch the angle: precisely because Jesus's person is *wholly* defined by the "existence of God in him"—God's being and activity being "the innermost fundamental power ... from which *every* activity proceeds and which holds every element together"—so it is that God delivers God's blessings to the church, and believers' lives are defined by a peace "which surpasses all understanding" (Phil. 4:7).[32]

While it is useful to ponder the continuities between the Christologies of the *Institutes* and *The Christian Faith*,[33] it must be said that there is a curious cramping of thought, on Schleiermacher's part, when it comes to Gethsemane. The reason for this cramping can be stated simply: Jesus's humanity is interesting to Schleiermacher only insofar as it serves as a conduit through which God's grace enters into the world. It is frequently described as little more than a vehicle for divine activity: an instance of "vital receptivity" and "lively susceptibility," to be sure, but also, and most basically, an *instrument* of the "creative divine causality" that dominates and defines Christ's person.[34] To those who suppose that Schleiermacher espouses a "low" Christology, the *Glaubenslehre* is its own best defense: the technical apparatus of the Chalcedonian "Definition" may be sidelined, but its leading claim—that Christ is God incarnate—is advanced with impressive vigor.[35] Precisely because God's being is a matter of "pure activity," Christ's God-consciousness is the being-in-act of God as such, a "perfect indwelling of the Supreme Being

---

31. Schleiermacher, *Christian Faith*, 382. While Schleiermacher writes here about Jesus's "development," the claim applies also to Gethsemane. The full quotation: "His development must be thought of as wholly free from everything which we have to conceive as conflict. For it is not possible that, where an inner conflict has ever at any time taken place, the traces of it should ever disappear completely."

32. Schleiermacher, *Christian Faith*, 387.

33. Dawn DeVries has done some important preliminary work on this front: see *Jesus Christ in the Preaching of Calvin and Schleiermacher* (Louisville: Westminster John Knox, 1996).

34. Schleiermacher, *Christian Faith*, 365, 495, and 367.

35. That Schleiermacher embraces the intent of Chalcedon, while eschewing its technical terminology, is recognized by his more astute interpreters. See, *inter alia*, Martin Redeker, *Schleiermacher: Life and Thought*, trans. John Wallhausser (Philadelphia: Fortress, 1973), 136; Richard Muller, "The Christological Problem as Addressed by Friedrich Schleiermacher," in *Perspectives on Christology: Essays in Honor of Paul K. Jewett*, ed. M. Shuster and R. Muller (Grand Rapids: Zondervan, 1991), 141–62; Lori Pearson, "Schleiermacher and the Christologies Behind Chalcedon," *Harvard Theological Review* 96, no. 3 (2003): 349–67; and Kevin Hector, "Actualism and Incarnation: The High Christology of Friedrich Schleiermacher," *International Journal of Systematic Theology* 8, no. 3 (2006): 307–22.

as His peculiar being and His inmost self."³⁶ Yet Schleiermacher does not pair a vivid sense of Christ's divinity with a nuanced account of what Christ *does* as a human being. He holds fast to the claim that Christ is fully divine; he does not move much beyond it.

Let me explain in more detail. To begin with a qualification: It is obviously not the case that Schleiermacher has nothing to say about Christ's humanity. D. F. Strauss was wrong to view the end-result as no more than "an unreal mental construct, a lifeless ideal drawn according to a stencil."³⁷ At key points in the *Glaubenslehre*, attention is paid to the "perfectly natural historicity" of the Redeemer: Jesus lived in a particular sociohistorical context; Jesus had a certain "racial" identity; Jesus develops physically and intellectually; Jesus feels pleasure and pain. Schleiermacher's remarks about the "vital receptivity" and "lively susceptibility" of Jesus's humanity also mark a line of reflection that could have opened out into something quite astonishing. One finds here the building blocks for an "actualistic" account of the incarnation, with the union of divine and human understood in terms of a two-sided "uniting," the sole purpose of which is the redemption of humankind.³⁸ Yet none of this overcomes the basic problem. Schleiermacher's insistence on God's activity is something close to overpowering, and it is elucidated in such a way that little is meaningfully said about Christ's human comportment and action. So while Schleiermacher can certainly declare that "during the state of the union every activity was a common activity of both

---

36. Schleiermacher, *Christian Faith*, 388.

37. David Friedrich Strauss, *The Christ of Faith and the Jesus of History: A Critique of Schleiermacher's The Life of Jesus*, trans. Leander E. Keck (Philadelphia: Fortress, 1977), 32. Strauss offers this remark in view of Schleiermacher's handling of Luke 2:52 and Heb. 4:15, but it stands as a fair estimation of Strauss's attitude toward the Christology of the *Glaubenslehre* and *The Life of Jesus*.

38. This is a key element of Kevin Hector's essay, "Actualism and Incarnation: The High Christology of Friedrich Schleiermacher." Thus page 313: "The state of the union between Christ's divinity and humanity is a continuous *uniting*—the pure act of God's being is continually united with and reproduced in Christ's life." My worry is that the language of "reproduction," which Hector uses to describe the concretization of divine activity in the incarnation, obscures the meagerness of Schleiermacher's account of Christ's humanity. It is not impossible to say that, for Schleiermacher, "[e]very moment of Christ's life perfectly instantiates God's pure activity, because at every moment Christ apprehends and reproduces that activity" (313). That captures something of the manner in which the (single) divine decree is realized in time and space. Yet it also ascribes more intent, activity, and significance to Christ's humanity than the *Glaubenslehre* seems to allow. Schleiermacher's Christology, to my mind, lacks the *balance* that Hector discerns.

natures"[39]—a statement that shows sensitivity to the import of the dyothelite tradition, even granted wariness about the ascription of two "wills" to Christ—the way that he substantiates this statement is severely lopsided. On one hand, Christ's sinless perfection is understood in terms of a maximally efficacious and unwavering God-consciousness, which means nothing less than the "veritable existence of God in Him." (Again: for those with ears to hear, there is a ringing endorsement of Chalcedon's claim that Christ is truly divine, truly God with us.) On the other hand, Christ's human "nature" receives scant attention, and Schleiermacher struggles to mitigate the idea that Christ's humanity is little more than a creaturely medium for God's redemptive action. Schleiermacher's handling of Luke 2:52 ("Jesus increased in wisdom"), for instance, is awkward; and when Schleiermacher writes of Jesus's adult life, Jesus's humanity is typically described in terms of a *passive receipt* of divine activity.[40] There is no sustained interest in the way in which Christ humanly ascertains, accepts, and enacts his identity as Redeemer; there are only scattered and fairly cursory attempts to assure readers that "passivity" ought not to be understood in terms of lifelessness or inactivity.[41] Indeed, at key moments, Schleiermacher's rhetoric bears striking similarities with that of Athanasius and Cyril's less cautious followers. A telling example, with an almost-Apollinarian gloss on the intelligence/body analogy for the hypostatic union: "the existence of God in the Redeemer is posited as the fundamental power within Him, from which *every* activity proceeds and which holds *every* element together . . . everything human in Him *forms only the organism* for this fundamental power, and is related to it as the system which both receives and represents it, just as in us all other powers are related to the intelligence."[42] Given remarks like this, it is unsurprising that

---

39. Schleiermacher, *Christian Faith*, 398.

40. On this point see Pearson, "Schleiermacher and the Christologies Behind Chalcedon," 363–64.

41. Schleiermacher's contention that Christ stands in "sympathy with the condition of [fallen and sinful] men" (407), and that Christ shows "persistence in redemptive activity" (463) might seem to complicate the argument I am making: in both instances, Christ's divine and human "natures" are presented as *conjointly* enacting a specific history. However, all too often, Schleiermacher resorts to presenting passivity as the basic quality of Christ's humanity. For instance, on 407 Schleiermacher writes that "in *everything* which proceeded from this [passive and sympathetic condition] we shall most distinctly recognize the impulse of the reconciling being of God in Christ" (my emphasis). Then, to underscore the point, he writes that "in this interrelation [of Christ's two 'natures'], every original activity belongs *solely* to the divine, and everything passive *solely* to the human" (407–8, my emphases).

42. Schleiermacher, *Christian Faith*, 397 (my emphases).

Schleiermacher passes over Jesus's agony in Gethsemane. The basic moves of his Christology, controlled by the insistence that the Redeemer not undergo any "spiritual conflict," ensure that this synoptic episode falls from view.

I offer this analysis rather reluctantly. I sometimes tell students and colleagues that Schleiermacher is my second-favorite theologian—and then add, a bit more fiercely, that it is a close-run thing. Certainly I do not wish to join hands with those whose affection for Barth has, as its corollary, a snarling antipathy toward misguided, wayward Friedrich; the authors being two poles in a spectrum that runs from a noble iteration of "orthodoxy" to an erroneous and enfeebled instance of "modernism" or "liberalism." And certainly, to anticipate a possible expansion of this critique of the *Glaubenslehre*, it is not the case that Schleiermacher's neglect of Gethsemane is but another example of his defection from the principle of *sola scriptura*. Recent work has shown clearly that the brevity (and the location) of Schleiermacher's remarks on the Bible do not bespeak any desire to marginalize its role in dogmatic work.[43] The loss of a vital dyothelitism is the upshot of a combination of different factors: an outsized reliance on the Fourth Gospel, matched with a neglect of the synoptics; a construal of divine activity no longer normed by a covenantal outlook, with the result that the distinction between primary and secondary causation falls into abeyance; and, most problematically, a curious form of Platonism, such that Christ's "ideality," as the precondition of the believer's reception of a stabilized and redemptive God-consciousness, is presumed to involve an immobile, blissed-out communion with God *qua* Father. One might also speculate that Schleiermacher's disdain for the gloomier dimensions of the Reformed tradition, matched with a strong commitment to foregrounding God's sovereign activity, led to an exaggerated acclamation of the *beneficii Christi*. At any rate, and whatever the reasons for Schleiermacher's misstep, the upshot is plain to see. When it comes to Gethsemane, Schleiermacher is a disappointment.[44] The dyothelite perspec-

---

43. See Paul T. Nimmo, "Schleiermacher on Scripture and the Work of Jesus Christ," *Modern Theology* 31, no. 1 (2015): 59–90.

44. Schleiermacher's failings with respect to Gethsemane may, unfortunately, extend beyond the *Glaubenslehre*. In a sermon on Matt. 26:36–46, "The Power of Prayer in Relation to Outward Circumstances," he again struggles to make sense of Jesus's anguish. The particulars of the biblical witness do elicit a concession: Schleiermacher acknowledges that Jesus suffers some degree of "agitation" in the garden. But Schleiermacher also says that Jesus's prayer was not prompted "by fear of anything that might occur ... but the need of His heart to give Himself up to devout meditation, and to the undisturbed enjoyment of communion with His Father, without a definite wish or special request." See *Selected Sermons of Schlei-*

tive championed by Calvin, which established the "grammar" of much of post-Reformation Reformed theology, meets an unhappy end.

All of this brings us, finally, to the *Dogmatics*. As will become clear, Barth breaks with Schleiermacher. Something of Calvin's appreciation for the synoptics is restored; Jesus's prayer is understood to be of decisive importance, and deserving of careful reflection. At the same time, it is not the case that Barth simply works along lines set down by Calvin. Barth's treatment of Gethsemane blazes its own trail, and it leads us to some of the most innovative dimensions of Barth's account of Christ's person and work.

Gethsemane in *Church Dogmatics* IV/1

A fundamental point with which to begin: For Barth, Jesus's transition from judging subject (that is, someone superior to and directive of the quotidian in which he exists) to judged object (that is, someone whose history is, to a significant degree, shaped by the actions of others) is not a transition from activity to passivity, but a shift in the way Jesus comports himself. Jesus's becoming and being an object, in other words, should not be understood in terms of impassivity, a resignation to fate, or a lack of power to influence his context. Jesus's becoming and being an object is something he *does*, even granted that this action is also a licensing of others to do with him what they will. Thus: "Without ceasing to be action, as action in the strongest sense of the word, as the work of God on earth attaining its goal, His action becomes *passion*. . . . He fulfilled the will of God . . . because He did what had to be done . . . taking upon Him their sin and in that way taking it away from them. . . . [T]his action is the meaning of His passion" (IV/1, 238–39). The fact that the Gethsemane prayer amounts to a narrative "seam" that connects two parts of the synoptics' "evangelical history," then, is a function of an alteration in the *way* that Jesus obeys the Father.[45] In prayer, Jesus ascertains, endorses, and begins to apply the Father's demand that he invert himself, so as to open "space" for others to determine the course of his life. From this point forward, he exchanges a mode of activity in which he bears his own identity and sets the terms for the lives of others for a mode of activity

---

ermacher, trans. Mary F. Wilson (New York: Funk & Wagnalls, n.d.), 38–51 (quotation from 49). Thanks to Christophe Chalamet, University of Geneva, who alerted me to this sermon.

45. I borrow the language of "seam" from Ashleigh Elser's in-progress dissertation at the University of Virginia: "*Felix culpa*: A Theology of Hermeneutical Frictions in Biblical Literature."

in which his identity is at the mercy of others, and in which others set the terms for his life.

In contrast to Maximus and Calvin, Barth does not mark this shift in Jesus's comportment with a reminder that Christ has two "wills." The conceptual apparatus of classical dyothelitism does not feature in Barth's treatment of Gethsemane, and is in fact rarely employed in the *Dogmatics* as such. The principal reason for this is Barth's distinctive brand of actualism, which is just as pivotal for his Christology as it is for other aspects of his theology.[46] Because being and act are thought together, and because one cannot think about who Jesus is in isolation from what Jesus does, talk about Christ's wills is unnecessary. Christ's acts are not external to his divine and human "natures," for what these two natures *are*, they are in the concrete history that Jesus lives out before God. Isn't the marginalization of an established category like "will," though, problematic? Doesn't Barth miss the opportunity to connect his Christology with the broader Christian tradition? Such questions rather miss the point. On one level, it is a mistake to suppose that Barth reflexively aims to make common cause with the broader Christian tradition. He will certainly draw attention to contrasts and continuities between himself and past thinkers, but he does so for illustrative purposes—and *not* with an eye to consolidating a historic doctrinal consensus. (Put in terms of a rule: dogmatic work succeeds when it makes sense of God's self-revelation, to which Scripture is the principal witness; agreement with past and present thinkers has only incidental importance.) On another level, Barth's concern to think actualistically about Christ's person goes hand in hand with fierce determination to rivet attention on the utterly concrete life that Jesus lives. This particularism doesn't disallow dogmatic efforts to clarify the manner in which Christ's divinity and humanity relate to one another, but it does ensure that such clarifications have only a supporting, and never a starring, role in dogmatic reflection.[47] So while it is not improper to

---

46. I use this term as it has been defined by George Hunsinger, to signal that Barth "thinks primarily in terms of events and relationships rather than monadic or self-contained substances." So *How to Read Karl Barth: The Shape of His Theology* (New York: Oxford University Press, 1991), 30. For Barth's own description of his christological actualism see, e.g., IV/2, 113–16 (on the *communicatio operationum* as a matter of the "common actualisation" [113] of Christ's human and divine "essences") and IV/3, 40 (on the incarnation as a matter of "spontaneous actualization.... As Jesus Christ lives, there takes place in Him both the creative actualisation of being, yet also in and with it creaturely actualisation").

47. The fact that Barth writes about the *communicatio idiomatum*, the *communicatio naturarum*, the *communicatio gratiarum*, and the *communicatio operationum* in §64.2 of IV/2

talk about Barth's Christology as somewhat continuous with the dyothelite tradition (just as it is not improper to identify Barth's Christology as somewhat continuous with the "Definition" of Chalcedon), Barth is not going to invest heavily in talk about "wills." It is better simply to foreground the claim that while Jesus's history is single, this singularity is a function of the perfect concurrence of Christ's divine and human activity. There is no dimension of Jesus's humanity that is not always actively intending, enacting, and realizing the concrete history of Jesus Christ; there is no dimension of Jesus's divinity that is not always actively intending, enacting, and realizing the concrete history of Jesus Christ.[48]

In part because Barth eschews talk about wills, he gains the opportunity to tackle what he considers truly interesting about Gethsemane: how Jesus prayerfully *moves himself* from being a superior and directive subject to an acted-upon (but not passive!) object. Given that the accounts of Jesus's prayer in Matthew, Mark, and Luke are something of a shared narrative "seam," illustrative of the moment in which Jesus discerns anew and commits himself to the Father's command that he be obedient-unto-death, Barth seeks to describe this seam in terms of *Jesus's personal act*—and in so doing draws attention to dimensions of the atonement that might otherwise be overlooked.

On this front, four overlapping points merit close attention.

First: when he begins to pray, Jesus does not know exactly what the Father requires of him. He truly wonders if there might be another way for him to fulfill his mission. On this reckoning, while Jesus's remark about the "cup" (which alludes primarily to the "cup of wrath" mentioned in Isa. 51:17) shows some awareness of what is to come—of that there is no doubt—it also comprises a *request*, for Jesus implores God to tell him where he must go next, and to clarify what precisely it is that he must do. Of course, up to this point, Jesus has willingly stood in full solidarity with those who are "flesh" and live under the reign of sin. Jesus's decision to be baptized marks the onset of his particular venture of obedience, rendered to the

---

supports this point. At this juncture in the doctrine of reconciliation, the main moves of Barth's Christology are already in play. Barth's treatment of "scholastic" distinctions is not a matter of his introducing new dogmatic claims; his concern here is to foreclose possible misunderstandings and to add texture to an already-established position.

48. Bruce McCormack makes a comparable point when he writes that the "'exaltation' of the human Jesus consists in this: that he actively conforms himself to the history of God's Self-humiliation and, in doing so, *is made the vehicle of it*." See *Orthodox and Modern: Studies in the Theology of Karl Barth* (Grand Rapids: Baker, 2008), 226 (emphasis in original).

Father for our sake. It betokens a purposeful embrace of humanity's fragile, wayward, and death-directed condition, and it sets Jesus on a path that will obviously culminate in suffering: "He goes to the Jordan as . . . ready, according to the almost unbearably harsh expression in 2 Cor. 5:21, to be made sin by God, to be identified with it, to become a curse according to Gal. 3:13" (IV/4, 60). Furthermore, temptation by Satan, conflicts with the elites of his day, and the increasing incomprehension of the disciples surely gave Jesus an even-clearer sense of what solidarity with sinners involved. Death was not a prospect for which he was unprepared; it was an end that he expected. Yet when he enters the garden, Jesus is not *fully* cognizant of what it is that the future holds—for how could anyone truly human know, in advance, what historical form God's rejection of sin will take?—and he raises again the question of how, exactly, he ought to render obedience to the Father. Even as Jesus's prayer sounds a plaintive and resigned note, and even as Jesus does not seem seriously to anticipate anything other than an ignominious end, he sincerely asks for guidance. There is no posturing. There is only a simple and unimaginably fraught question. "Does all this have to happen? In this solemn moment, quite understandably but wholly unexpectedly and disruptively in view of all that has gone before, there is a *pause*. Jesus himself, in prayer to God, once more puts everything into question" (IV/1, 264 rev.).

Now for some theologians, the mere suggestion of nescience on Jesus's part is an embarrassment, a *pudendum* to be covered by artful feints and parries. Hilary of Poitiers, for instance, suggests that Jesus is not praying for himself, but for others.[49] Appealing to Ambrose, Augustine, and Hilary, Aquinas thinks similarly: Jesus prays "for our instruction," and not because of any kind of epistemological deficiency.[50] Recall, too, the medieval differentiation of Jesus's "infused" and "acquired" knowledge, and the attempt to confine suggestions of anguish to the more rarefied regions of Jesus's soul—sleights of hand that allowed the Gethsemane prayer to be characterized as an occasion in which Jesus's "half-passions" (*propassiones*) were engaged, yet not in such a way that his "mind's understanding is as a consequence re-

---

49. Hilary of Poitiers, *De Trinitate* 10.37–40. See *St. Hilary of Poitiers: Select Works*, ed. W. Sanday, trans. E. W. Watson, L. Pullan, and others, in *Nicene and Post-Nicene Fathers*, second series, vol. 9, *St. Hilary of Poitiers, John of Damascus* (Peabody, MA: Hendrickson, 1994), 191–92.

50. Thomas Aquinas, *Summa Theologiae* 3a.21.1. See *St. Thomas Aquinas: Summa Theologica*, vol. 4, trans. Fathers of the English Dominican Province (Notre Dame, IN: Ave Maria, 1981), 2050–51.

moved from righteousness or the contemplation of God."[51] In each instance, the gospel witness to Jesus's apparent fear and lack of knowledge becomes theologically uninteresting. The Gethsemane prayer, along with other seemingly "difficult" scriptural passages, does not *really* suggest fear, or ignorance, or anything unbefitting the Savior. It is a matter of Jesus teaching others. Or, at a pinch, it reports a form of disquiet that affects only a limited dimension of Jesus's human nature. Calvin's claim that the divine Son "withdraws" is a more daring and more interesting gloss on the Gethsemane passage, and one that usefully draws attention to Jesus's human embrace of the passion. But it also comes at an unacceptable price. The Reformer's desire to hold Christ's divinity at a distance from the anguish of prayer leads to strained exegesis and raises some acute christological difficulties.

Barth, however, handles Jesus's prayer in a refreshingly artless way. Because he frames his account of incarnation in terms of God's self-determination—the divine Son eternally electing, before the Father, to live and die as Jesus of Nazareth under the conditions of time and space and in the context of human sin—the challenge of balancing an infinite, serene, and maximally knowledgeable divine nature with a finite, scared, and non-omniscient human nature effectively disappears. The Son truly makes our situation his own. And given that the Son's realization of God's love for humanity takes *this* concrete form, there is no need to sidestep or downplay Jesus's epistemological limitations and fear. Barth can acknowledge frankly that Jesus does not know the future and cannot anticipate the exact nature of God's command.[52] Indeed, Barth seems almost eager to amplify Jesus's ignorance and disquiet about what it is, precisely, that the Father asks him to do. In §59, the somewhat tempered report of Jesus's agony in the garden provided by the Gospel of Luke receives only passing attention; Barth trains our attention on the more disquieting accounts found in Matthew and Mark.[53] Does all

---

51. For an excellent treatment of the distinction between "infused" and "acquired" knowledge, which was developed in part to make sense of diverse patristic opinions regarding Luke 2:52, see Kevin Madigan, *The Passions of Christ in High Medieval Thought: An Essay on Christological Development* (New York: Oxford University Press, 2007), 22-38. The statement about propassions is from Peter Lombard, *Sentences: Book 3, On the Incarnation of the Word*, trans. Giulio Silano (Toronto: Pontifical Institutes of Medieval Studies, 2008), 62 (*Sentences* 3.xv.2, point 2).

52. Thus IV/2, 95: "If the Word became flesh, if God became man, He necessarily existed as a man in a human history, and trod a human way, and on this way had human wants, was subjected to human temptations and influences, shared only a relative knowledge and capacity, and learned and suffered and died as a man."

53. I say "somewhat tempered" for good reason. Kevin Madigan's claim that, in Luke's

this *really* have to happen? Must salvation be accomplished in *this* way? And with the reality of Jesus's question in place, there is no need to downplay the wracking quality of his prayer. "It now broke over him: what it involved and carried with it, what he had given himself to, the power of the unbreakable *law* . . . the overwhelming *retribution* that must come upon him. . . . It was one thing to set out and continue on this way; it was another to tread it to the end—and in this world to its necessarily bitter end" (IV/1, 266 rev.).

The second dimension of Barth's account of Gethsemane that I would emphasize pertains to the answer Jesus receives from the Father. Or, rather, it pertains to the *non*-answer Jesus receives, for the Father's "command," in Gethsemane, is that Jesus accede to "the language of facts" (IV/1, 267) and endure the actions of those who seek his death. A key passage: "The will of God was done as the will of Satan was done. The answer (*Antwort*) of God was identical with the answer (*Tatwort*) of Satan. That was the horrible thing. The coincidence of the divine and satanic will, work, and word was the problem of this hour—was the darkness in which Jesus addressed God in Gethsemane" (IV/1, 268 rev.).

To understand what Barth is saying here, it is useful to back up a bit. At the beginning of the Gethsemane excursus, Barth considers the temptation narratives in Matthew and Luke. These narratives, Barth suggests, depict Jesus purposefully seeking out Satan and actively wrestling with what it means to exist in the "far country" of sinfulness: a realm in which God's commands are treated as inconsequential, impractical, and susceptible to seemingly pious redefinition. Barth then engages in a creative bit of demythologizing, albeit without anything of Bultmann's interest in the "existential" import of the synoptic texts.[54] Satan should not be dismissed as a quirk of a premod-

---

Gospel, "the grieving and fearful Jesus is transformed into a Socratic figure of equanimity and poise in face of death, one whose soul not even the most appalling suffering can vex" (*Passions*, 65) seems overstated. Jesus does, after all, sweat clots of blood (Luke 22:44), and I share the judgment of François Bovon that Luke 22:43 and 44 are original to the Gospel, not later interpolations (see François Bovon, *Luke 3: A Commentary on the Gospel of Luke 19:28–24:53*, trans. James Crouch, ed. Helmut Koester [Minneapolis: Fortress, 2012], 197-99). Yet it cannot be denied that Luke shies away from the bolder claims of Mark and Matthew. As Bovon points out, "by choosing his own source" for the Gethsemane prayer, Luke "avoided taking over Mark's two disquieting verbs: 'greatly frightened' (*ekthambeisthai*) and 'distressed' (*adēmonein*). . . . Luke is cautious, stressing that Jesus did not want anything opposed to God's will" (196).

54. Rudolf Bultmann's lapidary formulation is useful to recall at this juncture: Insofar as exegesis involves demythologizing, its "criticism of the biblical writing lies not in eliminating mythological statements but in interpreting them; it is not a process of subtraction

ern worldview; his appearance in the temptation narratives is a way for the gospel writers to make plain Jesus's struggle with "worldly wisdom." He represents the possibility that Jesus might evade the command of the Father, and reject the path of obedience in favor of a respectable life, unencumbered by conflict, suffering, and death. When Jesus casts out Satan, then, he renounces "religion." He demonstrates his readiness to proclaim and to be the kingdom that stands in *total* contrast to the reign of sin. And such readiness endures throughout Jesus's entire ministry. It is the basis on which he obeys the Father in everything that he says and does.

In Gethsemane, however, Satan is conspicuous in his absence. Jesus is denied even the (dubious) comfort of an identifiable enemy. He is truly alone—for when Barth does refer to Satan, he does so simply to draw attention to the wickedness of Jesus's enemies. And the fact that the devil is *not* a "third party" in this drama is quite apt. In order that he become and be the "object" of rejection, Jesus is asked by God to endorse a state of affairs in which the Father's will intersects, without remainder, with the plans of those who seek to kill him. Thus:

> One can describe the Gethsemane prayer as a "conversation" with God only with reservations. Nowhere in the texts is there mention of a divine answer taking up and corresponding to the address of Jesus.... Actually, Jesus receives *no* answer, *no* sign from God. Or, rather, he receives "the sign of the prophet Jonah" (Mt. 12:39f) who was three days and three nights in the belly of the whale. For Jesus, as for the whole of this evil and adulterous generation, the *only* sign will be the actual event of his death. (IV/1, 268 rev.)

In response to Jesus's prayer, then, "the answer of God will be given only in the language of facts" (IV/1, 267)—that slow, relentless walk to Calvary, animated by the collusion of religious elites and imperial functionaries.

One can engage these remarks from two angles. On one level, the horror

---

but a hermeneutical method." So *New Testament and Mythology and Other Basic Writings*, ed. and trans. Schubert Ogden (Philadelphia: Fortress, 1984), 99. This remark is taken from Bultmann's important essay of 1952, "On the Problem of Demythologizing." Unfortunately, Bultmann offers nothing comparable to Barth's reading of Gethsemane. He simply declares that the "Temptation story ... which involves reflection about what kind of messiah Jesus was or what kind of messiah the Christian believes in, is legend," and leaves it at that. See *Theology of the New Testament*, 2 vols., trans. Kendrick Grobel (Waco, TX: Baylor University Press, 2007), 1:27.

of Gethsemane is the horror of a wholly demythologized future. From this point onwards, Jesus's battle with sin is no longer connected to "religious" mores, and does not bear comparison with any dimension of human life. Still worse: Jesus's work is no longer fringed with the possibility that his peers might actually "repent and believe" (Mark 1:15) in the good news that he brings and is. Insofar as Jesus "grows in wisdom" (Luke 2:52) and learns obedience (Heb. 5:7–9), the final stage of this educative process is the realization that sinful human beings, when given the opportunity, can and will become demonic, and can and will presume to attack God himself. If Jesus did not truly know this in the desert, he knows it truly in Gethsemane.

On another level, the horror of Gethsemane is the horror of a future in which human sin runs alongside, and ultimately is united with, the activity of God the Father. As Jesus moves closer and closer to his death, a macabre counterpoint to the unity-in-distinction of the hypostatic union comes into view. Paralleling the dynamic and perfect union (but not confusion) of divinity and humanity that comprises Jesus's person, there is a dynamic and perfect union (but not confusion) of the Father's providential activity and the murderous schemes of Jesus's enemies. Still more: in prayer, Jesus learns that he himself must play a part in effecting the convergence of these two unities-in-distinction, and must do so in such a way that ensures that he dies as the one who is not only truly divine and truly human but also, at the same time, the one who bears our sin in himself and endures God's rejection of the same. Jesus is required, one might say, to *sustain* the "riddle" (*Rätsel*) that "confronts him with all the horror that it evokes ... the impending unity between the will of *God* ... and the power of *evil* which He had withstood" (IV/1, 270)—"sustain" in the sense that Jesus must let this riddle play itself out, and must do so in such a way that his total estrangement from God coincides with his being the person that he is: the Son of God incarnate. To be sure, these unities-in-distinction are marked by obvious differences. God's providential activity is not the being and presence of God as such; the operations of sinfulness lack a reality comparable with that of the human creature. Yet the idea that the unity of Christ's divine-human person must and will be crossed with the unity of God's providential action and human wrongdoing, so as to enable God's decisive rejection of sin, is one that Barth emphasizes to great effect. During the passion, and especially on the cross, the Chalcedonian adjectives—*inconfuse, immutabiliter, inseparabiliter, indivise*—no longer apply only to Jesus. They apply also to the work of God and the work of sinners.

Does this amount to a reprisal of Calvin's reading of Gethsemane? Yes and no. As is already clear, both Barth and Calvin stand at a distance from Schleiermacher's description of Jesus's untroubled God-consciousness. Further, Calvin's questionable claims about Christ's divinity "quieting" itself notwithstanding, both authors draw attention to the manner in which the concrete person of Jesus Christ, divinely *and* humanly, assents to the course of events that culminate in a death that cannot be summarily described as an instance of penal substitution. Yet it is also here that Calvin and Barth part ways. For Calvin, it is in Gethsemane that Jesus realizes that he must ready himself to absorb a punishment that is an expression of unfettered, unmoderated, divine fury. Barth's perspective is more complex. Jesus must accept a gruesome convergence of divine action and human sin, so as to enable a concrete actualization of God's eternal rejection of sin. And Jesus must himself "do his part," so to speak, to bring about this convergence. In that God asks Jesus to become and be an "object," and to accede to the "language of facts," Jesus is commanded to coordinate his actions with those of God the Father and those of wayward sinners in such a way that ensures he is expelled from his quotidian *and* dies as the "lamb slain from the foundation of the world" (Rev. 13:8). Inasmuch as Jesus does this, his loss is our gain. In the same moment that he draws the full weight of sin upon himself, he establishes and fulfills a covenant in which humankind and God exist in active and joyous partnership.

This brings us to a third dimension of Barth's reading of Gethsemane, and a crucial moment in Barth's understanding of atonement. In his prayer to the Father, Jesus freely decides to open himself to sin and to God's rejection of sin. He freely commits himself to receiving and absorbing, once and for all, both the worst that we can do *and* the worst that God can (and will ever) do. This act of "opening," on Jesus's part, is of course a divine act. But it is not only that. Reconciliation is not achieved over our heads; it includes, and in some ways depends on, a single and unrepeatable exercise of human obedience.

Important here is a bundle of sentences near the end of the Gethsemane excursus:

> In the power of this prayer Jesus received—that is, renewed, confirmed, and applied—his *freedom* to complete his *work*, to execute the judgment of God, which he himself underwent so that the sin of the world might be punished, which he took upon himself, in order that in his person, in his death, it might be taken away from the world. . . . This was the will of God in the horrible thing that Jesus saw coming: in the union of God's will,

work, and word with evil. The power of evil had to break upon Jesus, its deadly work had to be completed upon him, in order that, inasmuch as it happened to him, it might be done once and for all times, for all human beings, for the liberation of all. This happened when Jesus took the cup of wrath and drank it to the last drops. (IV/1, 271–72 rev.)

Much here is now familiar. Jesus accepts that God's "answer" to his prayer is a hideous echo of the hypostatic union: the Father's providential guidance of history uniting with the sinful machinations of human beings. Yet this answer does not occasion paralysis on Jesus's part; it is taken as a divine command that requires a discrete course of action. And when Jesus rises from prayer, he does so having committed himself to being the one who will endure the "power of evil" in its sharpest form. The "power of evil"? This phrase signals, once again, that Barth does not share Calvin's understanding of God's anger in face of humanity's disregard for the Law. It is not that Barth has no interest in the Law, of course; it is rather that his understanding of it is embedded within a distinct brand of supralapsarianism, wherein the cross is viewed as a historical and covenantal reiteration of God's primordial decision for salvation. "For the sake of the best, the *worst* had to happen to sinful humanity—*not* out of any desire for retribution and vengeance, but rather because of the radicality of divine *love*, which could 'satisfy' itself only in the full outworking of its wrath against sinful humanity, only by *killing* it, extinguishing it, removing it" (IV/1, 254 rev.). When Jesus drinks the cup to its dregs, then, he commits to becoming and, in death, *being* the total fact of sin that opposes God. He commits to fulfilling "voluntarily that which is resolved concerning Him" (IV/2, 259), and thereby supplies the temporal counterpoint to an eternal divine decision—for what is now rejected is not just an *impossible*-possibility for the divine life, but the impossible-*possibility* that has overtaken and corrupted human life. Jesus accepts, in other words, what Barth takes to be the "almost unbearably severe" (IV/1, 165) claim of 2 Corinthians 5:21: "For our sake he made him to be sin who knew no sin, so that in him we might become the righteousness of God." This is a kind of "vital receptivity" that Schleiermacher never imagined: Jesus drawing upon and into himself the full force of humanity's hatred for God, and doing so in such a way that God, in act of jealous love, is afforded the opportunity to "kill off" sin, once and for all, and to fulfill the covenant of grace.

Barth, then, does not shy away from identifying Jesus's decision in Gethsemane as pivotal—more: as *indispensable*—for our salvation. Inasmuch as Jesus "put this cup to His lips . . . He accepted this answer of God as valid,

The Riddle of Gethsemane

holy, just, and gracious and went towards what was to come, *thus enabling it to happen*" (IV/1, 271 rev., my emphasis). Can we go a step farther, and describe more precisely what this "enabling" involves? I think so. In Gethsemane, Jesus begins to dispose himself as an object defined by vulnerability and permeability. Vulnerability: because Jesus decides that he will not interfere with the sinful intentions and actions of those who drive him to the cross, and will not resist God's making and treating him as the sin that God rejects. Permeability: because, in light of his prayer, Jesus begins to empty himself of the Kingdom and, concomitantly, allows the whole scope of human sin to "fill up" his person — and does so to ensure that his own person, at the very end, just *is* the sin that God abhors, the sin that must be burned up in the fire of God's holy love. Inasmuch as Jesus's prayer is a genuine struggle, then, it is a struggle of self-determination and self-definition, undertaken before the Father and for the sake of all humankind. The nature of the prayer is nearly unthinkable; likewise, the act of self-determination coextensive with it. But the result is the basis upon which salvation is wrought. Because Jesus renders himself vulnerable and permeable to sin and judgment, when he rises from prayer, he does so in a way that allows human wrongdoing and God's unsparing rejection of sin to coincide in his person.

Given the interpretive tropes on which I am leaning, an interesting question starts to press: Was Barth right to have juridical language dominate his exposition of the atonement? I am not sure. While there is an intriguing excursus on sacrifice at the end of §59.2, and while Barth, like Calvin, adeptly combines sacrificial, juridical, and military imagery, the standard Reformed idiom does not obviously draw attention to Barth's most interesting claims. It also risks obscuring Barth's massive debt to Luther, given that the elucidation of the "judge judged in our place" connects often with Luther's understanding of *die fröhliche Wechsel*: Christ becoming "the greatest thief, adulterer, robber, desecrator, blasphemer, etc., there has ever been anywhere in the world."[55] Still, granted that Barth did opt to foreground juridical imagery, the pairing of permeability and vulnerability serves to clarify the distinctive "spin" that Barth puts on the tradition of which he is a part. In a late essay, Hans Urs von Balthasar wrote about the cross as an occasion in which Jesus "opens up his embodied Spirit as a space in which he passively lets human sin work out the whole unimaginable brutality of its antidivine fury."[56] That

---

55. Martin Luther, *Lectures on Galatians, 1535: Chapters 1-4*, ed. Jaroslav Pelikan (St. Louis: Concordia, 1963), 277. Luther is commenting on Gal. 3:13.

56. Hans Urs von Balthasar, *Explorations in Theology V: Man Is Created*, trans. Adrian

captures something of what Jesus realizes, in prayer, must happen. But Barth would add a qualification. As Jesus moves toward the cross, he does not only render himself vulnerable and permeable to *human* wrongdoing, but also vulnerable and permeable to *God's* rejection of sin. Jesus allows the union of divinity and humanity definitive of his person to become inclusive of another union—the union of human sin and God's crushing, annihilative "No" to the same. In the moment that Jesus prayerfully drinks the cup to its dregs, he accepts that the time and space of his own person will become the sin that God rejects. On the cross, he will not epitomize and announce the kingdom. He will be the concentrated reality of everything that stands against it: everything, that is, that God must and will destroy.

The fourth dimension of Barth's discussion of Gethsemane pertains to the consequences of Jesus's prayer. On one level, Barth suggests that Jesus's struggle with the future has an impact on God's own life, with there being a "pause ... not only on earth and in time, not only in the soul of Jesus ... but also, so to speak, in heaven, in the bosom of God himself. In the relationship between the Father and the Son there is a pause and delay in which the question of another possibility arises" (IV/1, 265 rev.). It is not too much to say, I think, that God *shudders* in view of what it takes for salvation to be accomplished—this shudder being the consequence of God's decision to bear within Godself Jesus's own, concrete history. On another level, this is a struggle that Jesus clearly *wins*. He does not simply assent to the command of the Father; he endorses it, embraces it, and realizes it. And precisely because Jesus's life is *not* a matter of "imperturbable blessedness," when Jesus heads toward the cross, he does so "with what we might almost call a supreme pride" (IV/1, 270) that accompanies a wholehearted response to God's command. Granted that the reference to pride (*Stolz*) nicely anticipates Barth's later treatment of sin in IV/1 (§60 being titled "The Pride and Fall of Man"), the more basic claim here is that Jesus exercises *freedom*. Eberhard Jüngel makes the point in a typically striking way: "It requires freedom from sin and guilt to be able to suffer the death that is the wages of sin in its God forsaken depths, and yet to be able to undertake one's life as a being towards *this* death."[57] That is exactly Barth's point. Precisely because Jesus obeys the Father's concrete command, and does so without equivocation, he is truly

---

Walker (San Francisco: Ignatius, 2014), 231. The essay in question is "Death Is Swallowed Up by Life" (230–38).

57. Eberhard Jüngel, *Theological Essays II*, trans. Arnold Neufeldt-Fast and J. B. Webster (London: Bloomsbury, 1995), 160. Emphasis in the original.

The Riddle of Gethsemane

free—even as his exercise of freedom culminates in the abyss of estrangement from God, the epitome of *un*freedom.

Given that Jesus's prayer commits him to a path whose terminus is his own death, it is valuable to ask: What does Jesus *know*, at the beginning of the passion, about the rest of his life? Upon leaving the garden, does Jesus envisage the second stage of the evangelical history as a "middle" to be followed by a glorious end—or is he unable to see beyond Calvary? Is a consequence of the prayer in Gethsemane a kind of ignorance that Hilary, Aquinas, Calvin, and Schleiermacher did not even begin to reckon with?

Such questions are not easy to answer. Barth is relatively uninterested in the issue of Jesus's so-called "inner life," and does not attempt to elucidate Jesus's experience during the passion and at the point of death. Given Barth's reticence on this front, the empty space between section 2 ("The Judge Judged in our Place") and section 3 ("The Verdict of the Father") of §59 speaks volumes. It conveys Barth's sense that the state of God-forsakenness to which Jesus is subjected, and to which Jesus subjects himself, is shockingly indescribable: a moment in history that utterly beggars reflection. Now for *us*—and here Simone Weil is eminently quotable—the cross is "a balance . . . a lever. A going down, the condition of a rising up. Heaven coming down to earth raises earth to heaven."[58] A grace of amazing, joy-inducing proportions, as Calvin well knew. For Jesus, however, the cross is quite different. It is not even a "going down," but an encounter with the nonplace and nontime of sin, death, and divine rejection; a null-point, a nothingness, in which there is no movement, no breath, no life. Necessarily, words fail. Just as God's primordial No to that which opposes God stands at the edge of what is theologically imaginable, the reiteration of God's No, in the context of time and space, pushes thought to its utmost limit.

But the question remains: Given Jesus's relative knowledge, must an implication of God's (non)answer to Jesus's prayer be that Jesus cannot envisage life *after* the cross? Might it be, to make the point very bluntly, that Jesus heads toward Calvary without knowledge or expectation of a vindicatory resurrection? Barth comes close to suggesting as much, if only in passing. He writes, for instance, about how "the purpose of God . . . was concealed from [Jesus] as from all men" (IV/1, 459). He will also suggest that the force and nature of Jesus's end is such that he is wholly overcome by his vicarious identification with sinners. Thus:

---

58. Simone Weil, *Gravity and Grace*, trans. Emma Crawford and Mario von der Ruhr (London: Routledge, 2002), 92.

> Taking our place, bearing the judgment of our sin, undertaking our case, he gave himself to the depth of the most utter *helplessness* in which he could not and would not dispose even of the help of God, the depth in which he had nothing but nothingness under, behind, and beside him, and nothing but God before and above him—nothingness in its unsearchableness and power, and God as the One into whose hands he was delivered up without reservation and without claim. (IV/1, 458 rev.)

The wages of sin, united to God's abyssal *No*, add up to a death beyond death, a terminus from which Jesus has no exit, no escape. Given Barth's vivid sense of Jesus's finitude and limited knowledge, do not statements of this kind signal that Jesus commits to a death that he knows will effect the reconciliation of God and sinners, but does so without any hope, and any expectation, of resurrection? Does it not seem that Jesus imagines his end to be *the* end?

It is important to tread carefully here. Obviously we have no models for thinking about the knowledge or foresight of God incarnate. There is also no situation analogous to the passion that might provide a basis from which to reason. Further complicating the matter is the fact that the synoptics sometimes suggest that Jesus anticipated some kind of vindication. Historical critics might well deem verses such as Mark 8:31 ("he began to teach them that the Son of Man must undergo great suffering, and be rejected by the elders, the chief priests, and the scribes, and be killed, and after three days rise again") to be stylized interpolations, ascribed to Jesus after the fact, but Barth rightly warns against using redaction history to settle debate.[59] Examinations of the processes through which the canonical Gospels gained their final form will not yield criteria that help to adjudicate dogmatic questions; at the end of the day, the theologian will still be confronted with the basic task of reading the canonical Gospels as witnesses to the history of God with us, and our history with God. Perhaps one way, then, to respond to the questions raised above is as follows: Whatever premonitions Jesus may

---

59. Barth makes the point explicitly in IV/2. "Those who investigate the origin of those texts [that is, "the three most comprehensive predictions of His suffering" in the synoptics], and the actual words used by the 'historical Jesus,' will be naturally inclined to find their original setting and form in this final version . . . being regarded as later transpositions and expansions and therefore dismissed as of no consequence. But however illuminating this procedure may seem to be, it involves a destruction of the way in which the Gospels actually saw and wished to see the passion. The passion of Christ is not for them a catastrophe which burst unexpectedly into His life. It is the necessary result of it. It is thus essential that it should be announced in it" (IV/2, 253).

or may not have had about his future, the Gethsemane prayer amounts to a decision that leads him to a time and place in which he beholds, *and is defined by*, nothing other than God's crushing judgment upon sin. Divinely and humanly, Jesus prays to accept this future—and moves, proudly, toward and into this future—even though it is no future at all. And when Jesus finally, terribly, reaches the point of death, there is no past with which he can reckon, no present beyond the yawning abyss of human sin and God's rejection of it, and no hereafter to console or fortify him. His sight is narrowed to a single point of devastation, and the *only* thing that he can manage to say (and even that is a miracle) is: "My God, my God, why have you forsaken me?" (Matt. 27:46 and par.). At this moment, which is no moment at all, there is no "next." There is only the crushing reality of God's annihilative rejection of the sin that Jesus has become.

Beyond Solitariness

"To love makes one solitary"—a line from Virginia Woolf's *Mrs. Dalloway* which, in its original setting, is wholly devoid of theological resonance.[60] Yet it is also a line that cuts to the heart of Barth's reading of Gethsemane. It underscores the motive behind Jesus's prayer: a love for his fellows, and indeed for the world, expressed in his willingness to obey the Father's command, no matter what form it may take. It tells us, too, something about what Jesus must do and suffer as he enacts God's command. That Jesus is alone in Gethsemane is an indication of what he will endure on the cross—a death in which there is no prayer, only an absorption of human sin and the receipt of God's unequivocal *No* to the same. And this is a solitariness, once again, that stands at the absolute edge of what is theologically imaginable.

At the absolute edge ... but *that*, to turn back to my opening remarks, is not a place that we need to stay permanently. Granted that Barth shows us how to read in ways that keep pace with the scriptural narratives—to slow down, to pause, and to wonder when those narratives slow down, pause, and wonder; and to tarry, more particularly, with that moment of Jesus's history when he confronts the grimmest of ends—we also know that the agony of Gethsemane does not last. Precisely because Jesus perfectly conforms himself to the will of the Father, there is now the basic fact of atonement, the basic fact that all human beings have been reconciled to God. There arises

---

60. Virginia Woolf, *Mrs. Dalloway* (London: Harcourt, 2005), 22.

the hope, too, that those who live "in Christ" might, by the grace of God, also attend and respond to the divine command, and in so doing live into the time and space of his resurrection. While I have sought to linger with Barth, then, as Barth lingers with Jesus in the garden, this is but "a fleeting, passing moment" (IV/1, 265 rev.). A "fleeting and passing" moment that is not the last word, even granted these words must now bring this chapter to a close.

9 The Passion of God Himself

Barth on Jesus's Cry of Dereliction

BRUCE L. MCCORMACK

Attempts to reconstruct the life of Jesus in a way deemed more historically accurate than that found in the Gospels are, by now, a dime a dozen. No one reconstruction has proven to be so thoroughly convincing as to bring an end to the quest itself, and so it continues on its merry way. We are accustomed to this, perhaps even weary of it. Most of the time, these things do not interest me all that much. But recently, I read one that did hold my interest—precisely because it did not present itself as "history."

The Challenge of José Saramago

José Saramago did not pretend to be a biblical scholar. He was a Portuguese novelist, well known through Europe and much of Latin America. Not so much here in the States (at least among Christian theologians), in spite of having been awarded the Nobel Prize in Literature in 1998! But, then, he was a controversial figure: a member of the Communist Party of Portugal for a time, a skeptic in matters of religion. In 1992, the Portuguese government under Prime Minister Anibal Cavaco Silva ordered his book *The Gospel according to Jesus Christ* (the book in which my interest lies) to be removed from the short-list for the prestigious Aristeion Prize on the grounds that it was offensive to religious faith. The book was, perhaps, all the more offen-

---

Note on the title: the phrase "the passion of God himself" is taken from Karl Barth, *Church Dogmatics* IV/1, 245.

sive in that it was more a "psychological portrait"[1] than a historical reconstruction. What Saramago did with great power in this work was to pose questions with regard to the morality of elements found in the Gospels' narratives. It is the goodness of the Christian God which he doubted; he needed only to tell the story his way to make the reader ask herself whether she does not share his doubts as well. This was protest atheism in a most poignant mode of presentation.

The pivotal moment in the novel comes at the point at which Joseph, who has obtained work in the Temple while Mary is recovering from the birth of Jesus in Bethlehem, happens to overhear members of the King's guard being informed by their captain that they are commanded to go to Bethlehem to murder all boys two years of age and younger. Filled with fear for his son, Joseph hurries to Bethlehem some minutes ahead of Herod's soldiers. He rushes immediately to the cave and tells Mary they need to leave quickly. But they are too late. The soldiers arrive. The screams of parents can be heard throughout the village as the slaughter of the innocents unfolds. Then quiet.

Joseph leaves the cave in the night to see whether the soldiers have left. While he is away, Mary is visited by an "angel" who informs her that Joseph has committed a horrible crime. He failed to warn any of the other villagers that their sons were in danger. There had been time, the "angel" insists, for the villagers to flee—to Egypt, perhaps.

The first night after this disaster, Joseph has a dream. He is with the soldiers, coming in search of his son to kill him. He has this dream every night thereafter until the day he dies—crucified at age thirty-three as a result of having been mistaken for being a rebel—at which point Jesus begins to have the same identical dream, albeit in reverse. In his version of the dream, the father whom he had loved is coming with soldiers to kill him. The dream itself is, of course, a sign of Joseph's guilt. He comes with the soldiers because his silence made him an accomplice to their crime.

Jesus is greatly troubled by this dream when it begins to come to him, night after night. He wants to understand it. Why is this happening to him? He learns from his mother that his father had the same dream. He presses her to tell him whether something had happened to cause this dream to come first to his father, and now to him. And finally, she does. Mother and

---

1. José Saramago, *The Gospel according to Jesus Christ*, trans. Giovanni Pontiero (New York: Harcourt, 1994). The phrase is lifted from the publisher's description on the back of this edition.

son walk into the desert, at some distance from Nazareth, to be alone. There she tells him the truth. Jesus is horrified. He tells his mother that she too is guilty (though she is not) and that he no longer wants to be called her son. She leaves, utterly disconsolate, and he is left alone to contemplate his fate. "When Mary disappeared from sight into the grey depths of the valley, Jesus fell to his knees and called out, his entire body burning as if he were sweating blood, Father, Father, why have you forsaken me, because that is how the poor boy felt, forsaken, lost in the infinite solitude of another wilderness, without father, mother, brothers or sisters, and already following a path of death."[2]

The cry of dereliction has been relocated by Saramago, quite obviously, and given a new significance by its new location. But that in itself should occasion no great consternation. It is what "life of Jesus" researchers often do. And the Evangelists themselves have artfully constructed a narrative arc that holds together sayings and events—which do not always agree with each other and clearly serve different purposes—which provides researchers with a needed rationale for reimagining the story, each in her own way. And so: it is not the fact that Saramago's narrative arc differs from that of any canonical Gospel which captured the attention of this reader. It is rather the moral scrutiny to which he is subjecting the principal agent at work in the drama itself, viz. God. How could God have allowed the slaughter of the innocents? How could he have effected the redemption of the world through the deliverance of one family from that horrific event, when he could have delivered all? A question that could be raised, and to be sure, has been raised with respect to many horrific events in human history; but raised, in this particular case, with respect to a detail in the canonical story we often pass over without pausing to think about it.

Bent low by his burden of remorse and shame, Jesus leaves home at the tender age of thirteen and makes the dangerous trip to Jerusalem on foot, there to question the scribes and authoritative teachers of the Law. He listens patiently as a scribe tells a questioner that human beings are granted freedom by God only in order that they may be punished when they inevitably use it for sinful purposes—an ominous answer, to be sure. Jesus then poses the question that now burdens his soul. Can it be right for a person to feel guilty for a crime he did not himself commit? He says to the scribe: "The Lord said that parents will not die for their children or children for their parents and that each man will be judged for his own crime." The scribe tells him that this

---

2. Saramago, *The Gospel*, 152–53.

was a precept for ancient times, "when an entire family, however innocent, paid for the crime of any one of its members." The precept cited, the scribe says, constituted a challenge to that code; perhaps, its overturning. But Jesus presses his question anew. "If the word of the Lord is forever, then one is right to believe that the father's guilt, even after his punishment, does not cease but is passed on to his children, just as all of us who are alive today have inherited the guilt of Adam and Eve, our first parents."[3] The scribe doesn't like the direction this conversation has taken, but finally is forced to agree. "Guilt," he says, "is a wolf that eats her cub after devouring its father." Jesus answers, "The wolf of which you speak has already devoured my father." And the scribe concludes: "Then it will soon be your turn."[4]

Four years pass, which Jesus spends herding sheep in the employ of a most unusual man who asks to be called "Pastor" but who turns out to be the devil. The devil is a curiously sympathetic figure in this novel; his motives are rarely clear and probably mixed. Jesus's time in the wilderness comes to an unexpected conclusion when God appears to him in the desert in a column of smoke, and promises him power and glory in exchange for his life. Jesus, no doubt feeling that he deserves whatever fate God should bring his way, agrees. God requires that he should offer a sheep in sacrifice to seal their covenant, and gives an audible groan of pleasure when the throat of the sheep has been slit. Jesus returns to "Pastor" to tell him that he has met God. "Pastor" already knows this, and banishes him from his service with the words, "You've learned nothing, begone with you." A fascinating reversal of the temptation of Christ in the wilderness in Matthew 4, to be sure!

Jesus begins to roam the countryside. He quickly learns that he has been endowed by God with miraculous powers. He can tell fishermen where to cast their nets, when their nets are full to breaking, etc. He gathers about him a following of disciples. But he is only waiting. He knows his life is forfeit; that it is only a matter of time until God requires his life of him. But he doesn't know why, and that begins to bother him. Finally, the day comes when God reappears to him. Sensing that this was the day he had been waiting for, Jesus rows a boat out onto the Sea of Galilee into a heavy mist. Suddenly he is joined by God who now takes the form of a wrinkled old man, resting in the stern of the boat. And before God has had a chance to answer Jesus's question, they are joined by "Pastor," who has swum to their boat and climbs aboard, expressing a desire to take part in the conversation.

3. Saramago, *The Gospel*, 173.
4. Saramago, *The Gospel*, 175.

The Passion of God Himself

Jesus's question of questions is: Why must I die? God explains that he has grown "dissatisfied." "Dissatisfaction," he says, has been written into the hearts of men and women with their creation and, indeed, belongs to the "image of God" which they bear because God too can become dissatisfied. He is dissatisfied with being the God of the Jews only. He longs to become the Ruler of the whole world, to supplant the gods of other portions of the earth. How will this happen? By ceasing to be the God of the Jews only and becoming "the God of the Catholics," whose "church" will spread throughout the earth.[5] To obtain this end, Jesus must die a martyr's death in order that men and women will be drawn to him and together worship his God. Jesus says he wants nothing more to do with the covenant. God tells him: sorry, you are in my power; you will fulfill the covenant.

Jesus says, "Then do with me as You will"—"On one condition."[6] There are no conditions, God says, but go ahead and name yours. Jesus says, "Tell me: what will the future bring after my death, what will it contain that it would not had I refused to sacrifice myself to Your dissatisfaction and desire to reign far and wide?"[7] Will those who believe in me in the future be rewarded for following me? Will they be happier? In the next world, God says; not this one. What will happen to them in this world? Jesus insists on knowing. And because God cannot lie, he tells him. First, with regard to the fate of his own friends. Then, covering page upon page, the names of those who would be martyred and the horrific deaths they would die; those who would practice a severe penitence; the victims of inquisitions; those killed in religious wars. And you feel no remorse for any of this? Jesus asks. God says No: "God, being God, feels no remorse." Jesus responds bitterly: "Well, since I am already having to bear this burden of dying for You, I can also endure the remorse which ought to be Yours."[8]

It is at this point in the dialogue that the protest atheism given such eloquent expression in this novel reaches a provisional climax. The devil intrudes himself into the conversation and makes God an offer. He says that he will acknowledge God's rule and repent of the evil he has done and return to God as his obedient servant: "Then evil will cease, Your son will not have to die, and Your kingdom will extend beyond the land of the Hebrews to embrace the whole globe, good will prevail everywhere, and I shall stand

---

5. Saramago, *The Gospel*, 311.
6. Saramago, *The Gospel*, 317.
7. Saramago, *The Gospel*, 317.
8. Saramago, *The Gospel*, 329.

among the lowliest of the angels who have remained faithful."[9] But God tells him No. Why? the devil asks. "Because the good I represent cannot exist without the evil you represent, if you were to end, so would I, unless the devil is the devil, God cannot be God."[10] And with that said, both the devil and God depart from Jesus.

I will not spoil the ending of this novel for you by telling you how Jesus tries to thwart God's plans for the future. There is much more to this story than I have been able to relate here. But what I have related will be enough.

Reading Saramago's brilliant portrait of Jesus of Nazareth, I was left with at least two questions. What do you say to a sensitive and brilliant critic who finds the God worshiped by Christians through the centuries to be morally repulsive? And, even more significantly, what do you say when the very elements in the Gospels that provide the building blocks of the traditional version of the story can quite reasonably be understood in a different light? When the eternal plan of God is not seen as the answer to the questions posed in a theodicy but rather as *their source*? What do you say? You could, of course, try to pick apart Saramago's gospel on historical-critical grounds, but it is historical research that makes it to be at least a possibility. That answer won't do in the long run. And, I would add, pointing to the power of the God depicted by concepts like aseity, simplicity, and impassibility most certainly will not do. It is precisely the God who cannot feel remorse, who remains aloof and unmoved by the pain of the world whose moral character Saramago has called into question. To respond to his challenge by insisting upon this God-concept for the umpteenth time would be no answer at all; it would amount simply to a refusal to entertain the questions of this deeply moral critic.

With the help of Karl Barth, I would like to give a different answer. My answer will not completely satisfy you; it does not *completely* satisfy me either. But I will say this: it is better than the alternatives, so far as I am able to tell. And if I could not tell the Christian story in the way I am about to tell it, I am not sure I could still tell it.

The Cry of Dereliction in Barth's Theology

The so-called "cry of dereliction" ("My God, my God, why have you forsaken me?") is embedded in the narrative presentation of the passion and

---

9. Saramago, *The Gospel*, 329.
10. Saramago, *The Gospel*, 331.

The Passion of God Himself

death of Christ in Mark 14:35 and Matthew 27:46. And here, immediately, we are confronted by at least two problems. First, the texts in question do not reflect on metaphysical or even only upon ontological questions. The cry is recorded; that is all. And that already places a limit on what exegesis can achieve. Exegesis is always constrained by the givenness of a text. Exegetes can argue about whether the cry is to be taken as the expression of real questioning, possibly doubt, on the part of the one who utters it or whether it is instead an expression of sympathy for others, an acknowledgment of what they would have experienced had they been in his place. They can debate whether Psalm 22 is "referenced" in it as a whole or whether its first verse alone should be considered in our efforts to understand the significance of the cry. But as soon as we begin to reflect upon the question of whether God truly has abandoned his Son, we pass beyond the limits of this text alone and begin to seek its meaning by reading across a range of texts, synthetically, in an effort to understand who the subject of this cry is, what the nature of the God to whom this cry is addressed might be, what this text might imply for the relation of the two, etc. We pass from exegesis into the realm of a theology that finds *its basis* in exegesis but is no longer simply exegesis. That much has to be said of every position taken on the questions raised with respect to this text by the tradition. All of that is on the one side.

On the other side is the fact that Barth nowhere engages directly the kinds of questions exegetes customarily put to this text. To be sure, he makes appeal to this text with fair regularity. Fifty uses of it can be found in his dogmatic writings, in sermons, etc. But in none of them is he doing exegesis in a straightforward fashion as he often does in relation to other passages—in the small-print sections of the *Church Dogmatics* especially. What he has to say with respect to this text is the consequence of his reading of other significant passages like John 1, Ephesians 1, Colossians 1, and Hebrews 1[11] on questions surrounding the identity of Jesus Christ. Also relevant is his provision of the building blocks of a theological ontology that itself stays remarkably close to the narrated history of the man from whose throat the cry of dereliction was wrenched. And with that, we shall have to be content. How then does Barth "use" the cry?

The first and most important observation to be made here has to do

---

11. See Bruce L. McCormack, "The Identity of the Son: Karl Barth's Exegesis of Hebrews 1:1–4 (and Similar Passages)," in *Christology, Hermeneutics and Hebrews: Profiles from the History of Interpretation*, ed. Jon C. Laansma and Daniel J. Treier (London: T&T Clark, 2012), 155–72.

with the subject of the cry. Who is it that cries out in such desperation and sorrow? Barth's answer is bound up with his conviction that God's history "is played out as world-history and therefore under the affliction and peril of all world-history."[12] The history in which God has his being is not a separate history, a history that remains "meta-" (above) the history we know and experience; it is our history. Or, to be more exact, God makes himself to be, through an act of self-humiliation, a participant in the history of the one man Jesus of Nazareth. And God does so as one who suffers this man's suffering—not merely empathetically, certainly not as a mere witness to it, but as the agent who himself is acted upon in that this man is acted upon.

> The Self-humiliation of God in His Son is genuine and real, and therefore there is no reservation with respect to His solidarity with us. He did become... the brother of men and women, threatened with them, harassed and assaulted with them, with them in the stream which hurries downwards to the abyss, hastening with them to death, to the dissolution of his being, to nothingness. With them He cries—knowing far better than any other how much reason there is to cry: "My God, my God, why have you forsaken me?" (Mk. 15:34).[13]

Seen in the light of this passage, the one who cries out here is the self-humiliated Son of God. With Jesus, he cries. In and through Jesus, the Son of God cries. But it is he who cries.

Barth confirms this understanding of the subject in passages too numerous to collect in a single essay. The passion of Jesus, he says, is "the passion of God Himself."[14] And again:

> The mystery of this passion... is to be found in the person and mission of the One who suffered there and was crucified and died. His person: it is the eternal God who has given Himself in His Son to be man.... He gives Himself to be the humanly acting and suffering person in this occurrence. ... It is not simply the humiliation and dishonoring of a creature, of a noble and relatively innocent man that we find here.... It is a matter of the humiliation and dishonoring of God Himself.[15]

12. *CD* IV/1, 215.
13. *CD* IV/1, 215.
14. *CD* IV/1, 245.
15. *CD* IV/1, 246.

The Passion of God Himself

Barth is well aware that there have been other men and women who suffered more and longer than did Jesus.[16] The physical side of his sufferings is not what makes his suffering unique . . . and uniquely redemptive. What makes his suffering unique and uniquely redemptive is the fact that these sufferings are taken up into God's own life. "We are not dealing merely with any suffering but with the suffering of God and this man."[17]

A second observation: the death that God suffers and dies in the man Jesus is not just any death. It is "eternal death," the sentence that hung over the entire human race and toward which it was rushing headlong. "We are dealing with the painful confrontation of God and this man not merely with any evil, not merely with death, but with eternal death, with the power of that which is not."[18] Again: "the concept of death in the New Testament means not only the dying of man but the destruction which qualifies or rather disqualifies it, eternal death, death as the invincibly threatening force of dissolution."[19] Why this emphasis upon "God . . . and this man"? The short answer is because eternal death is experienced by God *humanly*.

But!—and here we return to our initial observation and connect it with the second—to put it this way implies no christological "separation," no compartmentalization of suffering and death in the so-called human "nature" alone. T. F. Torrance is well known for his criticism of a direction in thought he refers to as the "Latin Heresy," i.e., all "dualistic" patterns of thought that would render the work of Christ something "external" to his "person."[20] Barth says something similar at this point.[21] "[I]n His own person He has made an end of us as sinners and therefore of sin itself by going to death as the One who took our place as sinners. In His person, He has delivered up us sinners and sin itself to destruction."[22] The novelty in this reconstruction of classical Reformed soteriology lies, in part, in the emphasis placed on the destruction of sinners and of sin itself. In death, Christ is

16. *CD* IV/1, 245.
17. *CD* IV/1, 247.
18. *CD* IV/1, 247.
19. *CD* IV/1, 253.
20. T. F. Torrance, "Karl Barth and the Latin Heresy," in *Karl Barth, Biblical and Evangelical Theologian* (Edinburgh: T&T Clark, 1990), 213–40.
21. It is only similar because Barth tries to avoid the use of metaphysical categories. He uses instead the language of history and of our "state" to describe this "within." "He humbles Himself to our state . . . in order to change that state from within." And: "He did not take the unreconciled state of the world lightly, but in all seriousness. He did not will to overcome and remove it from without, but from within." See *CD* IV/1, 216, 237.
22. *CD* IV/1, 253.

not merely the guilt-bearer; he is *the* sinner and it is *the* sinner (the "being of sin") that is destroyed. But that is only part of the novelty. The most important element in this construction is to be found in the conviction that all of this takes place *in the person* of the Mediator. The "man of sin" has been killed, extinguished, removed—*in him*. Barth everywhere seems to suggest that because the object of this action is human, it is a human experience. But he also tends at times to equate the "person of the union" with the Son of God, making this human experience to be the experience of the triune God in his second mode of being. So there is no consignment of suffering and death to the human "nature" alone. It is God *as human* who conquers eternal death. And he does so in himself, by making himself the subject of this human experience.

We come then to the cry itself. What is its significance? How does Barth understand it? The answer given by Barth is "the limitless anguish of separation."[23] Lest it be thought that the "separation" in question is christological—a sundering of the unity of the so-called "natures" into two discrete units—we have just seen that this is *not* what Barth has in mind. I will return to that point in just a moment. For now, I would like to underscore the fact that Barth conceives of death in God-abandonment as a very real experience on the part of Jesus.[24] If it is "eternal death" to which the Son *as human* is subjected, then "separation" has to be the very heart of the matter. In German, the phrase here translated is: *In der grenzlosen Qual der Gottesferne*.[25] "*Qual*" means "torment or agony"; "*grenzlosen*" is "having no end, limitless, without boundaries." That, for Barth, is the experience that gives rise to the cry of derelection. And again: though this is a human experience, it is not one that leaves God untouched or unaffected in the depths of his being as God. There can be no "separation" of the natures here. In another context, he protests against a certain "Greek conception of God, according to which God was far too exalted for His address to men and women, His incarnation, and therefore the reconciliation of the world and Himself, to mean anything at all for Himself, or to in any way affect His Godhead. In other words, He was the prisoner of His own Godhead."[26]

---

23. *CD* IV/1, 253.

24. *CD* IV/3, 414: "No, He is not mistaken. There is a reason for this dreadful question. It corresponds exactly to the situation. . . . God has never forsaken, and does not and will not forsake any man as He forsook this man. And 'forsook' means that He turned against Him as never before or since against any."

25. *KD* IV/1, 278.

26. *CD* IV/2, 84–85.

The experience of death in God-abandonment does not leave the Godhead unaffected because it is the experience of the Son, because it is taken up into his own life and made to be his own. In this is the divine self-humiliation: that the Son receives the human experience of eternal death into himself, not killing death on contact as Bruce Marshall has suggested,[27] but embracing it, making himself to be its true and proper subject. It is this, Barth says in his *Credo*, "that makes the cross the Cross, that is the cursed tree; . . . [that] makes the inconceivable way that is trodden in death the descent into hell, i.e. the sinking into that despair: 'My God, my God, why have you forsaken me?'"[28]

So how does Barth understand the "limitless separation"? Put more pointedly: Who is it that departs from whom in his view? Some "post-Barthian" theologians have answered (quite rightly) that the Father departs from the Son but in doing so have identified the second person of the Trinity with the man Jesus as such, moving away from even the logic of Chalcedon (and not just its categories). Those who do stand closer to Hegel than Barth finally did. Where the second person is identified with Jesus (full stop), there abandonment of the man Jesus would have to be an unqualified abandonment of the Son. The Hegelian formulation "God against God"[29] was originally intended to describe this possibility. Hegel's second person was a human being. But this is a possibility that Barth rejects. To speak of "God against God" against the background of this model would, in his view, introduce contradiction into God's own being: a rift between the person of the Father and the person of the Son. Barth's objection is clear.

> God gives Himself, but He does not give Himself away. He does not give up being God in becoming a creature, in becoming human. He does not cease to be God. . . . And when He dies in His unity with this man, death does not gain any power over Him. . . . He makes His own the being of man in contradiction against Him, but He does not make common cause with it. He also makes His own the being of man under the curse of this contradiction, but in order to do away with it as He suffers it. He acts as Lord over this contradiction even as He subjects Himself to it.[30]

---

27. Bruce D. Marshall, "The Cry of Dereliction and the Impassibility of God," in *Divine Impassibility and the Mystery of Human Suffering*, ed. James F. Keating and Thomas Joseph White, OP (Grand Rapids: Eerdmans, 2009), 258.
28. Barth, *Credo* (New York: Charles Scribner's Sons, 1962), 90.
29. *CD* IV/1, 184.
30. *CD* IV/1, 185.

So: if "separation" is real and yet is not an event between God and a man (full stop), then a rather different christological ontology is required.

But Barth also rejects another possibility—one that maintains that death in God-abandonment is an event not between God and the man Jesus but one between the eternal Father and the eternal Son defined as distinct (metaphysically grounded) subjects. On this view, the Father is understood to be one subject, the Son is a second subject in the triune Godhead, such that the one can act upon the other. Most social Trinitarians fall into this camp. But this, too, is a solution Barth rejected, and for precisely the same reason. For this solution too results in a rift in the being of the triune God. So: the eternal Son *as such* is not the subject who subjects himself to death on the cross.

We have already caught sight of the alternative. The alternative is to set aside *both* the equation of the second person of the Trinity with an *independent* (which is to say, a metaphysically rather than a christologically grounded) understanding of the Logos asarkos *as well as* the equation of the second person of the Trinity with a human being. The subject who utters the cry of dereliction is the Son *as human*. Put another way: the second person of the Trinity is Jesus Christ, the God-human in his divine-human unity. That much, it seems to me, Barth clearly says. It is the God and Father of our Lord Jesus Christ who abandoned him.[31] On this showing, the initial answer given to the problem of the christological subject is that he is "Jesus Christ," the God-human in his divine-human unity and neither the Logos *simpliciter* nor the man Jesus *simpliciter*. He is the "whole Christ" made actual in the one history.

The unresolved problem bequeathed to us by Barth is that of understanding this divine-human unity in such a way that "separation" can be a real experience in the God-human while not destroying that unity (even if only for the duration of the "three days"). What precisely is the relation of the so-called human "nature" to the person of the union? And what role does this relation play in the constitution of the christological "person" as person? It is proper to "name" the christological subject "Jesus Christ" (the one God-human in his divine-human unity). But it is quite another thing to explain that unity more closely, and to explain this event in the trinitarian

---

31. *CD* IV/3, 413: "[T]his Elect of God as such must be the Rejected of God, delivered up into the hands of the unrighteous and unholy, and, as ordained by Him, suffering and dying as a malefactor, not apart from but with and according to His good and merciful and kind but death-dealing will. The consequence is His not unjustifiable cry of pain which no arts of exegesis should be employed to mitigate: 'My God, my God, why have you forsaken me?' (Mk. 15:34)."

terms that would make best sense of it. Barth, I would say, becomes a wee bit shy at the point of explanation.

Before departing from Barth, I would like to draw your attention to one more aspect of his theology of the cross that will bring him more closely into conversation with José Saramago. Barth says, "the great and inconceivable thing is that He [the Son of God] acts as Judge in our place by taking upon Himself, by accepting responsibility for that which we do in this place. . . . He . . . gives Himself . . . to the fellowship of those who are guilty . . . and . . . makes their evil case His own."[32] "Accepting responsibility": Barth does not mean this in quite the sense that is needed, in my judgment. God, for Barth, "accepts" responsibility for the evil *we* have done. He takes it upon himself as something added to him that would not otherwise have been his. But it seems to me that this formulation is finally inadequate for addressing the case Saramago brings against the Christian God. Saramago is saying that the Christian God (should he exist) *is* guilty; that it was his eternal plan of redemption that made sin and evil necessary, that God should take responsibility not because he feels compassion for us but because he truly is responsible for all that has taken place. Confronted with Saramago's challenge, it seems to me, no other answer will do but death in God as a self-imposed act of public acknowledgment of the evil that was, in a very real sense, necessary to the accomplishment of the ends of God's love. Such an acknowledgment is, I would say, a moral obligation.

Beyond Barth

The exegete's question of how much of Psalm 22 is relevant for interpreting the cry of dereliction rests normally on the misguided effort to interpret Jesus's words in the light of the situation of the psalmist. That is to put matters the wrong way around, it seems to me. As Jürgen Moltmann rightly says, "[I]t is not right to interpret the cry of Jesus in the sense of Ps. 22, but more proper to interpret the words of the psalm here in the sense of the situation of Jesus."[33] Seen in this light, the question of whether these words were actually uttered by Jesus or constituted a later, post-Easter interpretation of the church matters little. Either way, it is the situation of Jesus to which

---

32. *CD* IV/1, 236.
33. Jürgen Moltmann, *The Crucified God: The Cross of Christ as the Foundation and Criticism of Christian Theology* (New York: Harper & Row, 1973), 150.

attention is being drawn. What comes to the lips of a man dying in agony and despair says little or nothing about their original significance. Jesus is not doing exegesis from the cross. He is giving expression to the depths of his own feeling with regard to the intimacy of his relation to the one he had long referred to as "my Father," to his long-established sense of calling, to his sheer powerlessness as one from whom even the Spirit is now departing.

Moltmann's great insight is that it is the deity of the one Jesus called his Father which is at stake in this cry. It is not so much a cry of "personal distress, but is . . . a call upon God for God's sake."[34] Jesus's person, Moltmann contends, has been identified by him so completely with his cause or mission, that rejection by his Father would be tantamount to a rejection of himself as the Father of this man, of himself as God. The cry "My God, my God, why have you forsaken me?" is thus identical with "My God, why have you forsaken *Yourself*?"[35] It is the deity of God which is at stake in the cross of Christ.

As a historical reading that seeks to understand the death of Christ in the light of the life he lived, this reading seems to me to be a very plausible one.[36] But it is also necessary—and to his credit, Moltmann sees this—to read the history backwards; to understand the cross in light of the resurrection. The resurrection is, without any doubt, an eschatological event. Resurrection is not restoration to an original state. It is "new creation" (2 Cor. 5:17).[37] It is the transfiguration of finitude since death is no longer proper to finite, created existence once it takes place. It is the "end" of history in the midst of history. That much should be clear.

But seen in the light of resurrection, the cross too is an eschatological event. The Gospels of Mark and Matthew make this especially clear. Luke does so as well, though he eliminates a fair bit of the scandal of the cross

---

34. Moltmann, *The Crucified God*, 150.

35. Moltmann, *The Crucified God*, 151.

36. Less plausible, precisely as a historical reading, is Moltmann's attempt to portray the rejection of Jesus by his Father along the lines of "God against God." Whether this depiction can be justified depends on a lot of factors, most of them strictly theological (christological and trinitarian). That "the cross of the Son divides God from God to the utmost degree of enmity and distinction" is a state that reflects the equation of the second "person" of the Trinity with a human being as such and the employment of a quasi-Pannenbergian ontology of the future in which being flows from the future into the past in order to posit a rift in the eternal relation of the Son and the Father. These moves raise questions about how Jesus can still be God in his death or how such a death can be redeeming. See Moltmann, *The Crucified God*, 152.

37. Moltmann, *The Crucified God*, 176.

through his elimination of the cry of dereliction. The death of Christ is encompassed in the narrative set forth in Mark by portents of judgment and, with that, the death of the old aeon and the birth of the new. The darkness that covers the land from the sixth to the ninth hour calls to mind Amos 8:9, which depicts the Day of the Lord as a Day of Wrath, of judgment. Adela Yarbro Collins suggests a link here with the cup of wrath spoken of in Psalm 75:8 and Isaiah 51:17, 22—from which Jesus prays to be delivered, and then accepts as his calling—in Mark 14:36.[38] The tearing of the Temple veil that coincides with Jesus breathing his last evokes the thought not only of an expansion of God's reign (as the centurion's confession in Mark 15:39 suggests) but also, and more importantly, a definitive act of self-disclosure, the "apocalypse" of God in the death of Christ. For where God is revealing himself, defining himself, telling us what it means to be "God," there God is *fully* present—thus justifying the Pauline claim that "God was in Christ" (2 Cor. 5:19).[39] God is revealed in the event of the cross as the one who comes to his people in powerlessness, in a judgment that falls upon himself as the just Judge who takes full responsibility for that evil and sin which are the consequence of creating a finite, as yet untransfigured world. He is himself the "crucified God." Matthew adds to the picture thus far painted with the help of Mark that an earthquake took place at the precise moment of the tearing of the curtain; rocks were split and tombs were opened and the bodies of many saints were raised from the dead (Matt. 27:51-52). This is an act of vindication,[40] an anticipation of the definitive vindication of the Son that would take place in his own resurrection. But before vindication comes judgment and death.

I do not think that Matthew's depiction of Jesus's surrender of his spirit has to be reduced to an act of returning to the Creator the life or spirit given to him as created;[41] the surrender of life includes, I would contend, the final departure of the Holy Spirit as would be appropriate given that the eschatological wrath of God rests fully upon him. The Spirit which was given to Jesus in his baptism in the Jordan, the Spirit which empowered his extraordinary works and suffused him with compassionate love for others, which had trained him in the ways of justice (Heb. 5:8), had already begun to depart from him in the Garden of Gethsemane; to pull back, as it were.

---

38. Adela Yarbro Collins, *Mark: A Commentary* (Minneapolis: Fortress, 2007), 751.
39. Cf. Moltmann, *The Crucified God*, 192.
40. W. D. Davies and Dale C. Allison, *Critical and Exegetical Commentary on the Gospel according to Saint Matthew*, vol. 3 (Edinburgh: T&T Clark, 1997), 629.
41. Davies and Allison, *Matthew*, 3:628.

That abandonment is now made complete, and Jesus's death takes place in the absence of the Father's presence to him in the power of the Holy Spirit.

And if that much is right, we now have an answer to the trinitarian side of the question bequeathed to us by Barth. What takes place in God-abandonment is the withdrawal of the Holy Spirit who had indwelt Jesus and, with that, the absence of the Spirit from the human consciousness of the one God-human, an event that the Son of God *receives* into his own life. The unity of the christological person is preserved *in* the event of separation in that the one who *receives* this most extreme of human experiences into his own life is God in his second mode of being. And he is not overcome by this reception because: (a) it is a human experience *in* God, and (b) there is more to God than just this one mode of being. Ontological receptivity is made, on this model, to be the modality of the Son of God's relating to the Son of Man, and the unity of the christological subject is clarified by seeing one of the so-called "natures" as receptive and the other as active.

The Relation of God to Sin and Evil

The mystery of God's relationship to sin and evil is great. For those who are committed to the notion that nothing happens in this world that falls outside the will of God, the fact that there is such a relation is inescapable. But even those committed only to the idea of an exhaustive divine foreknowledge are confronted with the very same intractable problem. For if God knew in advance all that would happen as a consequence of his creative activity and went ahead and created anyway, then surely he bears responsibility for all that happens; a responsibility that transcends and embraces what we think of as a more direct responsibility for all the particular acts performed by particular agents in the history of the world. The stakes are heightened still further for "supralapsarians," of course, since common to every version of that idea (including Karl Barth's, it has to be said) is the conviction that creation exists for the sake of redemption. And since there can be no redemption without something from which to be redeemed, the negative side of reality belongs to the overall positive aim as its shadow side, so to speak.

My own view—and I can only speak personally at this point—is that God wills all things in willing himself. In an act so immediate that it can only be called the eternal life-act of God (i.e., the very "living-ness" of God), God knows himself perfectly and comprehensively and, in doing so, wills what he is. Notice that the act of "will" here in view is understood to be a necessary act. It is *not* a "necessity" imposed from without but one that arises from the beauty, the majesty, the sheer perfection of that which is known by God in knowing himself. What this demonstrates, parenthetically, is that there is indeed a kind of "willing" (willing in its highest form, I would say) that involves *no choice among options.* God does not first have to search himself, to acquire information about himself or engage in a process of deliberation before willing himself. In that he knows himself perfectly and comprehensively "at a glance," so to speak, he wills himself. Neither God's self-knowing nor God's self-willing requires "time" to be accomplished; both are immediate. They are as "immediate" as the trinitarian processions and, in fact, as Thomas Aquinas astutely observes, God knows himself in his Word and wills himself in his Spirit. So the activities we call the divine self-knowing and the divine self-willing simply *are* the generation of the Son and the breathing forth of the Spirit.

But what, then, is it that God knows and wills in knowing and willing himself? What is the "nature" of the God known and willed in this immediate way? My own answer would be: He knows and wills his own nature as self-giving, self-donating, self-emptying love (Phil. 2:7). Again, though no choice among options is involved in this knowing and willing, the act itself could not be more *personal.* For it is a reflexive, self-conscious act which, in its occurring, defines what it means to be a "person." God is, as Barth once argued, more personal than we, not less. God is more personal because "no other being exists absolutely in its act."[42] I would only add to that the observation that God's eternal life-act is "person-forming." In being an act of self-knowing and self-willing, it is an act of self-love which is the source of all things in its superabundance. In this way, the life-act of God is "person-forming" both as it looks inward (toward the processions) and outward toward that which will be created.

And make no mistake: *necessarily* to will himself as self-giving, self-donating, self-emptying love contains in itself a relation to an other. And since that which is other than the Maker of heaven and earth can only be "finite," the love of God for himself as self-giving love necessitates the existence of the finite, *and of the finite understood initially only in its "otherness" from God.* The finite understood only in its "otherness" includes its extreme limit, which is death. So physical "death" at least is, I would say, the necessary outworking of the love of God for the self-giving love that God is.

I could make the same point by saying that God knows all things in

---

42. *CD* II/1, 271.

knowing himself in an immediate act of intuition. In knowing all things, God knows comprehensively and exactly *what he will do* before he ever does it. But if he knows immediately what he will do in knowing himself, then he could not possibly postpone, as it were, the act of willing creation and redemption. Election cannot be a contingent act in the sense of a divine choosing among options. A contingent act of willing would put God in the position of knowing in himself what he is going to will in a subsequent, allegedly contingent act *before that subsequent act of will has occurred*, which is sheer nonsense. If God already knows what he is "going to will" in knowing himself, then it has been willed in his self-willing and there can be no second act in pretemporal eternity.

But that has to mean, then, that God has a *necessary relation* to the finite. If God is indeed self-emptying love, then the love of God "necessarily" overflows. Again, such a claim does *not* make God "dependent" upon creation. Nor does it mean that God acts out of need, that somehow there is a deficiency in God's being until he does in time what he does. We are already there, in the self-emptying love which realizes itself in overflowing. But the fact that we are there, in our finitude and sinfulness, means that the love of God contains, in its very nature, the seeds of death, sin, and misery.

A Liveable Decision

I can only speak for myself in conclusion. You can consider what I am about to say a personal confession of faith, however provisional and however awkwardly stated. It is hard, indeed, the hardest thing of all, to worship a God whose very love for us brings us pain and suffering. But I find that I can live with this much more easily if I think that the way taken to the transfiguration of the conditions of finite "otherness" had necessarily to lead through an initial act of creation (with the misery that ensued in its wake) than I can with the thought that all of this has happened as a consequence of a "free decision" (a contingent election that might have been otherwise). Such an answer probably would not have satisfied Saramago. But my goal here was not to satisfy him or those who agree with him, but to give the only answer I could live with to his justified protest.

10 The Self-Witness of the Risen Jesus

Karl Barth's Reading of the Emmaus Road Story

BEVERLY ROBERTS GAVENTA

The episode narrating Jesus's encounter with two disciples on the road to Emmaus is one of Luke's most beloved stories. Commentators consistently remark on its quality, terming it "exquisite" (Marshall) or "pastoral" (Johnson) or even "hauntingly beautiful . . . a masterpiece of Luke's artistic theology" (Karris).[1] Connections are posited between this account and the earlier feeding miracles in the Gospel; connections are also posited between it and the meal scenes in Luke's second volume.[2] Clues are found here to Luke's interpretation of Scripture.[3]

Yet it would be difficult to find a treatment of the Emmaus road encounter as capacious or provocative as that of Karl Barth in the *Church Dogmatics* III/2.[4] That passage appears as part of a larger discussion under the heading,

---

1. I. Howard Marshall, *The Gospel of Luke: A Commentary on the Greek Text*, New International Greek Testament Commentary (Grand Rapids: Eerdmans, 1978), 890; Luke Timothy Johnson, *The Gospel of Luke*, Sacra Pagina 3 (Collegeville: Liturgical, 1991), 398; Robert Karris, "Luke 24:13-35," *Interpretation* 41 (1987): 57; quoted in Heidi J. Hornik and Mikeal C. Parsons, *Illuminating Luke: The Passion and Resurrection Narratives in Italian Renaissance and Baroque Painting* (New York: T&T Clark, 2008), 119.

2. Joel B. Green, *The Gospel of Luke*, New International Commentary on the New Testament (Grand Rapids: Eerdmans, 1997), 849; John T. Carroll, *Luke: A Commentary*, New Testament Library (Louisville: Westminster John Knox, 2012), 487.

3. Richard B. Hays, "Reading Scripture in Light of the Resurrection," in *The Art of Reading Scripture*, ed. Ellen F. Davis and Richard B. Hays (Grand Rapids: Eerdmans, 2003), 216-38.

4. *CD* III/2, 468-74. Further references to the *Church Dogmatics* will appear in the text in parentheses.

"Jesus, Lord of Time." Here Barth addresses the boundaries of human life within the limitlessness of God's own eternal time. He engages Bultmann's program of "demythologizing" as it applies to Easter faith,[5] but he is not engaged only with Bultmann. He also engages Oscar Cullmann's *Christ and Time* for its understanding of salvation history and, from the point of view of scholarship on Luke-Acts, the disagreement with certain constructions of salvation history is the more interesting and enduring element in the exegetical section (for reasons that I hope will become clear below).

Barth's Interpretation

Over the years I have found Barth's exegesis profoundly instructive and, indeed, encouraging, although I make no claim to expertise. My interest centers in the Romans commentary, but it extends well beyond that explosive volume.[6] Especially in the course of work on a commentary on Romans, I have often found his exegetical comments in the *Dogmatics* to be extraordinarily fruitful. For example, in his discussion of "The Determination of the Rejected" in II/2, Barth makes connections between the handing over of Jesus in the Gospels, the handing over of Jesus in Romans 4:25 and 8:32, and the "handing over" of humanity to powers of sin and death in Romans 1 (II/2, 458–506). Similarly his discussion of the relationship between God's own glory and human glory reflects Paul's argument far better than do the usual arguments for theosis or deification (II/1, 666–77).

Despite those and other such experiences of learning from Barth the exegete, this is my first attempt to unpack a section of his exegesis, that is, to follow his trail step by step, rather than reading for his treatment of a particular text or theme—reading rather than raiding. As I trust will become clear, I find once again that his work is both sound and provocative.

Yet I confess that I also find working through this section just a bit

---

5. The demythologizing controversy is familiar territory, and I shall leave it aside except to observe that David Congdon's recent book on Bultmann's hermeneutics threatens to upend much of what we have taken for granted about Bultmann and Barth in relationship to one another. See *The Mission of Demythologizing: Rudolf Bultmann's Dialectical Theology* (Minneapolis: Fortress, 2015).

6. Gaventa, "A Word of Gratitude," in *I (Still) Believe: Leading Biblical Scholars Share Their Stories of Faith and Scholarship*, ed. John Byron and Joel N. Lohr (Grand Rapids: Zondervan, 2015), 83–92; and "Reading for the Subject: The Paradox of Power in Romans 14:1–15:6," *Journal of Theological Interpretation* 5, no. 1 (2011): 1–12.

maddening. The section assigned me comes to barely more than five pages of fine print, and yet it happily troops readers across a wide swath of the New Testament before arriving at the Emmaus road story. Just as we catch a glimpse of his thinking about one passage, he takes another path altogether. Experienced exegete that I am, I think I know how to trace an exegetical argument, yet mapping his journey through the exegetical terrain is more than a bit challenging.

Perhaps this brief confession applies especially to those of us trained in a certain kind of biblical criticism, where one learns to make fine distinctions between materials. One does not leap from the Acts of the Apostles to 1 Peter to Hebrews to Romans without at least a brief pause, a word of explanation, even a footnote or two. Not every use of the language of "today" or "now" that Barth adduces in support of his claim about the present life of Jesus actually serves his purposes. Sometimes a Greek *nun* is just a *nun*. I say this simply by way of confirming Francis Watson's observation that, while Barth's exegesis is extraordinarily rich, it is of course subject to the same human limitations as the work of any exegete.[7]

In the specific section I have been invited to address, Barth is establishing the relationship between the past, present, and future of Jesus by way of introducing what he will have to say about the bounded character of human life. He begins with Revelation 1:8, "I am [he that] is" (III/2, 468). As he goes on to say, this "today," with its fulfillment and its "intimate connexion [*sic*] with the name and history of the man Jesus, is the content of the apostolic message and the meaning of the life of the apostolic community" (III/2, 469). "The Church's 'today' is likewise the acceptable year, the great Sabbath, the fulfilled time of the man Jesus." In one sense, there is no past of Jesus, if by that we mean past time, something that is over. In another sense, there is very much the past of Jesus, which is always with us.

Immediately, if also predictably, Barth denies the possible inference that he intends some sort of Christ-mysticism. Since "the history of Jesus itself becomes history again; past time becomes the time of His renewed presence." Here he cites several Gospel texts, including Matthew 18:20 ("Where two or three are gathered together in my name, there am I in the midst of them") and 28:20 ("Lo, I am with you always, even unto the end of the world"). He finds curious confirmation for this point in Paul's letters also,

---

7. Francis Watson, *Text and Truth: Redefining Biblical Theology* (Grand Rapids: Eerdmans, 1997), 247. Watson's comment comes in a discussion of James Barr and Karl Barth on natural theology, in which Watson makes a strong argument in support of Barth's position.

where "what belongs to the past" is not Jesus but our own lives, insofar as they "have not been lived in the Spirit and therefore in Him." After all, Paul himself is "the man who lives, yet lives no longer" as we learn from Galatians 2:20. Not only is Jesus alive; he is the one who makes others to live. This, for Barth, is the connection between the resurrection of Jesus and Pentecost. It bridges the gulf between Jesus's past and the apostles' present, as their time is assumed into his (III/2, 470).

Barth then turns to the story of Paul's conversion in Acts as evidence of his argument about the present role of Jesus. In Paul's conversion, Jesus continues to be the agent, the "acting subject." Invoking both Galatians 1 and the Acts accounts, Barth contends that Paul's commission comes from the living Jesus. He goes on to say that this is the reason Paul's conversion is so important for him and so "scandalous and strange" to Paul's "non-Christian hearers." "The Jesus of that earlier time is still at work" and "the life and work of the apostles is wholly and utterly dependent on His presence" (III/2, 471).

At this point Barth takes up the Emmaus road account, which he describes as "an indispensable commentary on all the other Easter narratives." As the two disciples talk with Jesus, they speak "about the enacted life and death of Jesus as though it were a matter of past history." They had hoped that Jesus would be the one to redeem Israel, but that hope is now past. They even speak of the women's report as a matter of the past. Not even the presence of Jesus or his interpretation of Scripture prompts them to understand Jesus as something other than an event of the past (III/2, 472).

It is only when Jesus breaks bread, "the very action He had performed on the night of His own passion and death," that the "full power of the earthly life of Jesus" "was now made manifest." For Barth it is important that what is revealed to them is the "earthly life of Jesus" *in* their own present. "The historical Jesus as such had removed the veil of the merely 'historical' from their eyes and came to them as the Lord, the same yesterday and today." It is important to reiterate this point: it is not simply the breaking of the bread in and of itself that Barth takes to be the moment of revelation but the fact that Jesus *reveals himself* through that moment (III/2, 472). That is to say, the disciples do not *deduce* who Jesus is; it is made known to them by Jesus himself.

Not surprisingly, this emphasis on Jesus's own role in the revelation at Emmaus recurs elsewhere in the *Church Dogmatics*. In "The Determination of the Elect," commenting on Jesus's role, Barth writes: "It is because Jesus is Himself both the content and proclamation of Scripture that He makes the disciples what they could not be of themselves—witnesses to the content of Scripture, and therefore His witnesses" (II/2, 433). "The Homecoming of the Son of Man" elaborates on this point regarding all the Easter encounters. "The execution and termination as well as the initiative lie entirely in [Jesus's] own hands and not in theirs.... He controls them, but they do not control Him" (IV/2, 145).[8]

In "Jesus, Lord of Time," Barth's reading of the Emmaus account then becomes the lens with which he looks back briefly at the preface to Luke's Gospel but then forward to Acts 1 and beyond. The Easter period is "simply a revelation of the first history [of Jesus] which dispels the errors, prejudice and blindness of the apostles and the community" (III/2, 473). The section continues with a reflection on the intertwined roles of Evangelist and Apostle, concluding that the present "is filled by the past of Jesus, because this past has not remained the past but irrupted into the present; because He has made himself present, and thus made the present His new time" (III/2, 474).

Barth's Interpretation in Conversation with Lukan Scholarship

Barth opposes his reading to Oscar Cullmann's argument in *Christ and Time* that the New Testament authors understood time to be an "ascending line" in which the Christ event is inserted as the center of a linear development.[9] The shadow of Cullmann's *Christ and Time*, with its notion of Jesus as the center of time, has lingered long in New Testament interpretation. It continues to have influence, especially in some popular notions of Pauline theology. As tempted as I am to linger over that question here, it is important to deal specifically with Barth's reading of the Emmaus road story because, as I see it, Barth's reading of the Emmaus road story and its implications stands over against several major readings of Luke and Acts in the last half-century, an anticipatory warning that went unheeded.

The most influential interpreter of Luke-Acts in the second half of the twentieth century was surely Hans Conzelmann, whose *Die Mitte der Zeit* appeared in 1953, only a few years after this volume of Barth's *Church Dogmatics*. In *Die Mitte der Zeit*, published in English under the far more prosaic

---

8. Of course, the distinction between divine and human initiatives is scarcely new in the *Church Dogmatics*, having been pivotal to Barth's Romans commentary. My point here is simply the importance it plays in his interpretation of the Emmaus encounter.

9. *Christ and Time: The Primitive Christian Conception of Time and History* (Philadelphia: Westminster, 1950). William Baird provides an instructive orientation to Cullmann and his influence in *History of New Testament Research*, 3 vols. (Minneapolis: Fortress, 2013), 476–88.

title *The Theology of St. Luke*,[10] Conzelmann argued that Lukan salvation history should be understood as consisting of three periods of time. There is the period of Israel (which continues through the ministry of John the Baptist), the period of Jesus's ministry, and the period of the church. In Conzelmann's view, Luke addresses a community faced with a crisis of hope because of the delay of Jesus's parousia. Luke pushes the return of Jesus into the distant future and replaces Jesus's return with the work of the church. The church becomes the "necessary medium of the [gospel] message,"[11] which effectively compensates for Jesus's absence. Jesus is in heaven, at God's right hand. The Spirit becomes the link that connects this absent Jesus with the present ecclesial community.[12] The influence of Conzelmann can be traced in important work on Luke-Acts through the 1960s and 1970s, particularly in the commentary of Ernst Haenchen, which was for many years a standard in classrooms and in scholars' studies.[13]

Conzelmann's periodization of Lukan history has fallen by the scholarly wayside,[14] but its replacements have been no more congenial to Barth's argument. Charles Talbert, for example, distanced himself from Conzelmann's redaction-critical approach in favor of an approach to Lukan theology shaped by a study of literature contemporaneous with Luke. He concluded that Luke produced—and would have been understood by his contemporaries as producing—an account of the founding of a community, consisting of the story of the founder and that of his successors. Although the apostles are not quite "successors" of Jesus in Talbert's view, they do "make key decisions" from Jerusalem, which is central to the "control" of Christian missions.[15]

What troubles me with such approaches is this: they assume, along with Conzelmann, that Jesus is absent from the book of Acts. In an essay on the Christology of Acts, C. F. D. Moule provides a classic formulation of this view: "More consistently than in any other New Testament writing, Acts presents Jesus as exalted and, as it were, temporarily 'absent,' but 'repre-

---

10. (New York: Harper & Row, 1951).
11. *Theology of St. Luke*, 225.
12. *Theology of St. Luke*, 184.
13. *The Acts of the Apostles: A Commentary* (Philadelphia: Westminster, 1971).
14. John T. Carroll helpfully surveys the varying critiques of Conzelmann as well as providing his own constructive treatment in *Response to the End of History: Eschatology and Situation in Luke-Acts*, Society of Biblical Literature Dissertation Series 92 (Atlanta: Scholars Press, 1988).
15. *Reading Acts: A Literary and Theological Commentary on the Acts of the Apostles* (New York: Crossroad, 1997), 1-17, quotations on 9.

sented' on earth in the meantime by the Spirit."[16] This quotation takes us well into the late twentieth century's scholarly assumptions concerning Acts. Given that Luke's Gospel closes with an Ascension scene and the book of Acts begins with a parallel account, the Ascension has been assumed to be as pivotal theologically as it is literarily. Further, Luke's account appears to emphasize not simply Jesus's departure but his enduring absence. In Acts, after all, we read that Jesus is taken from the sight of the apostles, that they stare into heaven and watch him go, that the two angelic messengers specifically announce, "This Jesus who was taken from you into heaven will return in the same way you watched him go into heaven." And Peter's sermon in Acts 3 seems to underscore this point when it refers to "the Messiah appointed for you, that is, Jesus, who must remain in heaven until the time of universal restoration that God announced long ago through his holy prophets" (3:20–21).

Reading this passage alongside the other Gospel endings only emphasizes the peculiarities of the Lukan version.[17] Mark and John have no departure scenes as such. John closes with repeated assurances of the reliability of the Evangelist's witness. Mark repeats the claim that Jesus will be waiting for the disciples in Galilee. Matthew concludes with an appearance by the resurrected Jesus in which he emphatically declares, "I am with you always, to the end of the age" (28:20).

If Acts is read primarily through the Ascension, and especially if this Ascension scene is interpreted through the other Gospel endings, then it is entirely possible (although not necessary, as I will argue below) to assume—along with Conzelmann and much of Lukan scholarship—that Jesus is absent, that the parousia is delayed indefinitely, and that the church's role is to serve in Jesus's stead.

One result of such readings is the assumption that the subject matter of the Acts of the Apostles is the church and its leaders. It is utterly commonplace to find Acts treated as history (whether good or bad history) of *the church*, with very little consideration given to the role of the risen Jesus within the church. In effect, many have read the book of Acts much as the two on the Emmaus road "read" the story of Jesus, as if it were finished.[18]

---

16. "The Christology of Acts," in *Studies in Luke-Acts: Essays Presented in Honor of Paul Schubert*, ed. Leander E. Keck and J. Louis Martyn (Nashville: Abingdon, 1966), 159–85, quotation on 179.

17. On the Lukan Ascension scenes, see especially Mikeal C. Parsons, *The Departure of Jesus in Luke-Acts: The Ascension Narratives in Context*, Journal for the Study of the New Testament Supplement Series 21 (Sheffield: JSOT, 1987).

18. Richard B. Hays makes a similar comment about the Christology of the Third Gos-

And this is where I find Barth's account of the Emmaus road event most illuminating.

Reading Acts with Karl Barth's Reading of Emmaus

Barth's claim is that the Emmaus road story serves as the key to understanding all the resurrection accounts. Here I want to broaden that question to ask what happens if we take Barth's account of the Emmaus road as the fulcrum for our understanding of Acts. I focus on Acts in particular because of Barth's own discussion, which moves forward to the Ascension and to the story of Paul's conversion in Acts. In addition, he concludes the section with a discussion of the roles of the evangelist and the apostle in a way that seems to be especially relevant to understandings of the Gospel and Acts.

The Presence of the Absent Jesus

First, Barth's reading of the Emmaus account may help us see that Jesus is not in fact "absent" from the pages of Acts.[19] Even before we arrive at the Ascension itself, the preface to the book claims that the first book narrated "the things that Jesus *began* to do and to teach" (1:1), which is more than a subtle hint that Jesus is not absent. The NRSV renders that statement as things that Jesus *did* and *taught*, obscuring the clear meaning of the Greek, which is that the Gospel of Luke is only the beginning. And in fact Jesus does continue to act throughout Luke's second volume.

At Pentecost, Peter announces it is Jesus who pours out the Spirit (Acts

---

pel: "In short, most NT critics have ascribed to Luke a Christology remarkably similar to that of the Emmaus travelers!" See his *Reading Backwards: Figural Christology and the Fourfold Gospel Witness* (Waco, TX: Baylor University Press, 2014), 57.

19. I have written about this particular issue elsewhere and without reference to Barth, although I think Barth's reading is sustained throughout Acts ("Learning and Relearning the Identity of Jesus," in *Seeking the Identity of Jesus: A Pilgrimage*, ed. Beverly Roberts Gaventa and Richard B. Hays [Grand Rapids: Eerdmans, 2007], 148–65). See also the earlier essay by Robert O'Toole, "Activity of the Risen Jesus in Luke-Acts," *Biblica* 62 (1981): 471–98; and the more recent work of Matthew Sleeman, *Geography and the Ascension Narrative in Acts*, Society for New Testament Studies Monograph Series 146 (Cambridge: Cambridge University Press, 2009).

2:33). In Stephen's vision in Acts 7, he sees Jesus "standing," which may indicate that Jesus is preparing to receive him into heaven (7:56). In Acts 9, Jesus appears *both* to Saul and to Ananias, directing events from both sides. When Peter heals Aeneas in Acts 9, he claims, "Jesus Christ heals you" (9:34). Addressing the Ephesian elders later in the book, Paul asserts that he received his ministry "from the Lord Jesus" (20:24). When Paul defends himself in Jerusalem, he recounts his conversion, adding that Jesus directed him to flee from Jerusalem (22:18–21). Perhaps the most important text to consider comes at the high point of Paul's final defense speech in Caesarea. As he recounts again his conversion and his faithfulness to his mission, Paul sums up his preaching. He has declared "that the Messiah would suffer, that as the first of those resurrected from the dead he would proclaim light both to the people and to the Gentiles" (26:23). It is not Paul but the risen Jesus himself who preaches light to Jew and Gentile alike.

It appears that for Luke, if not for some of his interpreters, Jesus can be in heaven and on earth at the same time.

Lukan Ecclesiology

It is scarcely an exaggeration if I say that readers of all sorts—whether sophisticated, learned exegetes or "ordinary" lay folk—understand the book of Acts to be about the church and its leadership. Luke's portrait of the church is taken as a model for imagining and reimagining the church in the present. Various aspects of church leadership are derived from vignettes in the book of Acts. Peter and Paul are presented as Luke's heroes. Whether or not readers are directly informed by Conzelmann and his heirs, the net effect is consistently to read Acts much as Conzelmann would have us do—namely, with very little room for the work of the risen Jesus.

Yet consider again that earlier summary of Jesus's work in the book of Acts. Jesus is the one, according to Peter, who pours out the Holy Spirit at Pentecost (2:33), which empowers the church for its witness in Jerusalem. Jesus is specifically identified in Acts 9 (and again in 22 and 26) as the agent of Paul's conversion. Jesus is the agent in healing (9:34) and the one preaching light to Israel and the Gentiles (9:34). Jesus is the one who speaks to Paul, strengthening and protecting him during his long stay in Corinth (18:9–10). Not *was* but *is*. These are not recollections of the ministry of Jesus in Galilee and Judea, but actions of the living Jesus from Jerusalem to Rome. They appear to indicate that Luke's real concern is less with establishing the church and its authority than with showing its witness to and through the agency of its *living* Lord.[20]

That the church is not in charge of itself or under the leadership of any human "leader" or "hero" is confirmed by other developments in the narrative, quite apart from specific reference to the risen Jesus. One instance is especially important, and that concerns the mission to the Gentiles. Despite the promise of the risen Lord that the apostles would be his witnesses "in Jerusalem, in all Judea and Samaria, and to the ends of the earth" (Acts 1:8), Peter assiduously resists preaching the gospel to Cornelius and his household (10:1–48). When he finally is persuaded to do so, he still does not offer baptism until the Holy Spirit, apparently impatient with such stalling about, baptizes the gathered Gentiles and forces Peter's hand (10:44–48). Peter then has to defend himself, not once but twice, to believers in Jerusalem (11:1–18; 15:6–11). This is hardly an instance of the church's "leadership." It is barely even an instance of obedience.[21]

Other examples could be adduced, but I hope my point is clear. Reading forward from the encounter with the living Lord at Emmaus, we may be able to appreciate more fully Luke's understanding of the church. For Luke, the church's "leaders" are better termed "witnesses." Their witness is to another and their work extends the work of Jesus. It has no authority in and of itself.

To be sure, this is not a competition for power or authority between the risen Jesus and his church. Yet there is also no church here acting as an independent agent in carving out and carrying out its mission.

Resurrection Epistemology

The living lordship of Jesus helps us see the church's role more clearly, but perhaps of prior importance: the living lordship of Jesus also simply enables humanity *to see*. That is, reading through Emmaus with Barth highlights the issue of epistemology. Barth's argument about the resurrected Jesus being the historical Jesus, the one who is past and present and future, could as easily have been made from other resurrection stories. He had made it decades

---

20. To be sure, Luke also speaks of the agency of the Holy Spirit, as at Pentecost (2:1–4, 14–21) and often elsewhere (e.g., 4:31; 8:15–16, 29, 39; 13:1–4). Luke apparently does not see the work of Jesus and the Spirit as mutually exclusive. See Gaventa, *Acts*, Abingdon New Testament Commentaries (Nashville: Abingdon, 2003), 33–38.

21. See further Gaventa, *From Darkness to Light: Aspects of Conversion in the New Testament* (Philadelphia: Fortress, 1986), 107–25; *Acts*, 162–75.

earlier in his commentary on 1 Corinthians 15.[22] What the Emmaus story allows him that those other accounts might not is precisely the question of epistemology.

As Barth recounts the journey to Emmaus, he emphasizes initially what the two disciples understood. They discussed everything that had happened "as though it were a matter of past history" (III/2, 471). "Jesus is no more than a bit of past history," Barth continues (III/2, 472). They narrate to Jesus the Easter message of the women, but this also "is still the object of mere recollection, and of very dubious recollection at that." They persist in this view of the Jesus of history even as Jesus himself rebukes them and even when he explains Scripture to them. It is only when he breaks bread that they see in this present action the presence of the Risen Jesus. Barth puts it very carefully: "[T]he historical Jesus as such had removed the veil of the merely 'historical' from their eyes and came to them as the Lord" (III/2, 472). If I am reading this passage correctly, for Barth what is crucial here is not the breaking of the bread as such, but Jesus's own role. I realize that way of putting things threatens to involve me in centuries of controversy over the Eucharist, but that is not my intention. My point is that, for Barth, what marks the revelation to the two nameless disciples is nothing more or less than Jesus's own action. Jesus is the one who removes the veil, *permitting* their eyes to see.

This is, of course, one of Luke's best-known motifs, the giving of sight.[23] To mention only a few key passages, the giving of sight or vision begins with the infancy narrative, with Zechariah's prophecy that God would send "dawn from on high" and "light to those who sit in darkness" (1:78–79). Simeon's prophecy reinforces this claim with the language of Isaiah that Jesus will be "light for revelation to the Gentiles" (2:32). And, as I have already noted, in Paul's culminating defense speech in Acts 26, he identifies Jesus himself as the proclaimer of light both to Israel and to the Gentiles (26:23).

This light, this seeing of Jesus as salvation, as the living Lord, is not a self-enclosed, isolated event. It extends to include the ways in which other

---

22. As A. Katherine Grieb makes clear in "Last Things First: Karl Barth's Theological Exegesis of 1 Corinthians in *The Resurrection of the Dead*," *Scottish Journal of Theology* 56, no. 1 (2003): 49–64.

23. For important recent work on this topic, see Brittany E. Wilson, "Hearing the Word and Seeing the Light: Voice and Vision in Acts," *Journal for the Study of the New Testament* (forthcoming 2017); "Sight and Spectacle: 'Seeing Paul' in Acts," in *Characters and Characterization in Luke-Acts*, ed. Frank E. Dicken and Julia A. Snyder (London: Bloomsbury T&T Clark, forthcoming).

people are known as well. A single story tells the whole tale. The story of the "bent over" woman in Luke 13 opens with an extended description of the woman, as her neighbors see her. She is "a woman with a spirit that had crippled her for eighteen years. She was bent over and was quite unable to stand up straight" (13:11).[24] These are the narrator's words, presumably describing what the neighbors see. Yet, at the end of the story, Jesus says she is a "daughter of Abraham" (13:16). In effect, Luke's Jesus is not only healing the woman but teaching his audience (both in the story world and among Luke's hearers/readers) *how to see* who this woman is. This is not simply information gathering; it is epistemology.[25]

Barth does not introduce 2 Corinthians 5 at this point in his argument, although he does reference it earlier and he could well have done so here. Paul's assertion in 2 Corinthians 5:16 that we no longer know Christ *kata sarka*, "in a merely human way," does not stand alone. It is coupled immediately with the claim that we no longer know *anyone* in a merely human way. If the historical Jesus is risen and present and continues to open eyes, then it is not only Jesus that we recognize but one another.[26]

Reading in the Presence of Jesus

There is, to be sure, room here for critiquing Barth's reading. The Emmaus road story may be one of Luke's crowning glories as a storyteller, but is it the lens through which we are to understand all the resurrection narratives? That is a somewhat difficult case to make exegetically. Yet, as I think my comments make clear, there is a sense in which Barth gets at the subject far better than most exegetes have done.

The most obvious argumentative move to make at this point is to lament the impoverishment of New Testament scholarship in its Enlightenment captivity. There continues to be a functional agnosticism in much biblical scholarship. In some quarters that functional agnosticism is a by-product of a conscious disinterest in theological claims. What fascinates some of our

---

24. On this passage, see especially Mikeal C. Parsons, *Body and Character in Luke and Acts: The Subversion of Physiognomy in Early Christianity* (Grand Rapids: Baker, 2006), 83-95.

25. See further Gaventa, "Learning and Relearning the Identity of Jesus."

26. The classic argument about this passage and its role in Pauline epistemology remains that of J. Louis Martyn in "Epistemology at the Turn of the Ages," in *Theological Issues in the Letters of Paul* (Nashville: Abingdon, 1997), 89-110.

colleagues is the study of the cultural products of religion or their power to shape communities, and so forth. I respect those concerns and the light they shed on early Christianity. In other quarters, there is a genuine concern that discussion of theology in biblical texts quickly renders them bodiless abstractions and thus irrelevant to "real" life. Nonetheless, it remains the case that Nils Dahl's claim that we have neglected the God factor in New Testament theology has been far more often quoted than it has been addressed constructively.[27]

I am willing to concede that point, yet that is an all-too-easy target. Biblical scholars are not the only ones who walk with the two on the Emmaus road and talk about Jesus as an event of the past. Have systematic theologians done better? Is there not in the desire for clarity, for orderly thought, for system, also that urge to hold the gospel at bay? To render it into an object that can be discussed and argued and analyzed, to find it smaller, more controllable, more malleable? None of us is innocent on this point.

So, instead of repeating well-worn laments regarding the weaknesses of our fields, let me ask what happens if Barth's interpretation of the Emmaus road story serves as our hermeneutic for reading, not just the world of the resurrection narratives or even the world of theological scholarship, but the world, by which I mean the whole human population?

We might begin with our reading, by which I mean now our understanding of, the church. Barth's reading challenges all of us who care about the life of the church to understand who is in charge of it, to be more modest. Perhaps even more hopeful. I have read his words again and again as I prepared this chapter. And it was in that context that I looked at the now infamous Pew report on religion in America.[28] The analogy narrates itself: How many of us and our sisters have taken that report to indicate the demise of Christianity? We read it as if the Christian faith itself were on life support, and our job is to find ways of resurrecting it. We read it as if the pollsters were in charge of the world rather than simply being in charge of a few questions. Perhaps the Emmaus road encounter, read together with the narratives of Acts, should remind us that the historical Jesus *continues* to be present in and with his witnesses.

Let me expand that point a bit further, thinking not just about the im-

---

27. See Nils Alstrup Dahl, "The Neglected Factor in New Testament Theology," in *Jesus the Christ: The Historical Origins of Christian Doctrine*, ed. Donald H. Juel (Minneapolis: Fortress, 1991), 153–63.

28. http://www.pewforum.org/religious-landscape-study/.

plications for our understanding of the church but of all humankind. As I indicated earlier, Barth makes much in this section of the presence of the living Jesus in the conversion of Paul, not only in the Acts accounts but the remarks Paul makes in Galatians 1 and 1 Corinthians 15 as well. Perhaps the most startling evidence for that presence comes when, in Acts 9, Jesus asks, "Why do you persecute *me*?" (9:4).[29] That identification of the disciples, whom Saul is at that point pursuing, with the risen Lord not only identifies Jesus as Lord, but it also identifies the disciples as belonging to Jesus. When Saul is forced to reassess Jesus, he must also reassess Jesus's disciples. His way of knowing them is as corrupt as his way of knowing Jesus.

We need not reach all the way into Acts (or Paul's letters) for this point; we have only to go back to the encounter on the Emmaus road. Barth makes much, as I have indicated, of the fact that the two disciples who meet Jesus speak about him in the past tense. Included in their remarks to the risen Jesus is the fact that some women found the tomb to be empty and they saw angels who declared Jesus to be alive (Luke 24:22-24). When the risen Jesus does cause them to see who he is, they also see that the women's testimony was in fact reliable. The women—whose speech had been dismissed—were the ones who knew what time it was. What Cleopas and his companion learn concerns not only the identity of Jesus; it concerns also the identity of humanity in its fullness. The implications here are unlimited, encompassing not only gender but race, age, ability, religion, and sexuality. The implication of Barth's reading—which I take to be entirely consistent with the witness of the Gospels—is that the crucified Jesus is Lord of history and Lord also of our ways of thinking about one another.

My deep hope is that we will receive eyes with which to see this passage again—in our time—with all its urgent claims on our world.

---

29. Barth does not specifically invoke this text.

11 The Sum of the Gospel

Barth's Intracanonical and Intertextual Interpretation of paradidōmi

SHANNON NICOLE SMYTHE

The impetus for this chapter is the conviction that analysis of Barth's revolutionary doctrine of election cannot be divorced from the theological exegesis undergirding it. Indeed, I would wager that it is Barth's engagement with the biblical text that funds his joyful insistence that election, of all the words that can be said or heard, is "the sum of the Gospel," the best word of all.

Investigation into Barth's correctives to the classical formulation of the Reformed doctrine is not a new topic.[1] Indeed, the most important fea-

---

1. See, for example, G. C. Berkouwer, *The Triumph of Grace in the Theology of Karl Barth*, trans. H. R. Boer (London: Paternoster, 1956); Donna Bowman, "Karl Barth's Doctrine of Election," in *The Divine Decision: A Process Doctrine of Election* (Louisville: Westminster John Knox, 2002), 13–72; John E. Colwell, *Actuality and Provisionality: Eternity and Election in the Theology of Karl Barth* (Edinburgh: Rutherford House Books, 1989); Oliver D. Crisp, "The Letter and the Spirit of Barth's Doctrine of Election: A Response to Michael O'Neil," *Evangelical Quarterly* 79, no. 1 (2007): 53–67; Matthias Gockel, *Barth and Schleiermacher on the Doctrine of Election: A Systematic Theological Comparison* (Oxford: Oxford University Press, 2007), 104–97; Colin Gunton, "Karl Barth's Doctrine of Election as Part of His Doctrine of God," *Journal of Theological Studies* 25, no. 2 (1974): 381–92; Robert Jenson, *Alpha and Omega: A Study in the Theology of Karl Barth* (Edinburgh: Thomas Nelson, 1963); Paul K. Jewett, *Election and Predestination* (Grand Rapids: Eerdmans, 1985), 47–56; Bruce L. McCormack, "Grace and Being: The Role of God's Gracious Election in Karl Barth's Theological Ontology," in *Orthodox and Modern: Studies in the Theology of Karl Barth* (Grand Rapids: Baker Academic, 2008), 183–200; "The Sum of the Gospel: The Doctrine of Election in the Theologies of Alexander Schweitzer and Karl Barth," in *Orthodox and Modern*, 41–61; Suzanne McDonald, "Barth's 'Other' Doctrine of Election in the *Church Dogmatics*," *International Journal of Systematic Theology* 9 (April 2007): 34–47; *Re-Imaging Election: Divine Election as Representing God to Others & Others to God* (Grand Rapids:

tures in his reworking of election have provided much fodder for scholarly discussion and debate.[2] Yet too often these studies do not consider Barth's theological exegesis, even though it is well established that his theology is consistently funded by his exegetical work.[3] While not all studies of Barth's doctrine of election have passed by the vast amount of scriptural study that accompanies it,[4] more can be done. In this chapter I argue that Barth's synthetical interpretation of some key New Testament occurrences of the Greek verb *paradidōmi*, translated by Barth as to "hand over" or "deliver," located

---

Eerdmans, 2010), 31–84; Douglas R. Sharp, *The Hermeneutics of Election: The Significance of the Doctrine in Barth's Church Dogmatics* (Lanham, MD: University Press of America, 1990); Katherine Sonderegger, *That Jesus Christ Was Born a Jew: Karl Barth's Doctrine of Israel* (University Park: Pennsylvania State University Press, 1992); and Anthony C. Yu, "Karl Barth's Doctrine of Election," *Foundations* 13, no. 3 (1970): 248–61.

2. For a more comprehensive compilation of the debate on Trinity and Election see Michael T. Dempsey, ed., *Trinity and Election in Contemporary Theology* (Grand Rapids: Eerdmans, 2011). For a sampling on the question of Barth's rejection or adherence to universalism see J. D. Bettis, "Is Karl Barth a Universalist?" *Scottish Journal of Theology* 20 (1967): 423–36; Crisp, "On Barth's Denial of Universalism," *Themelios* 29, no. 1 (2003): 18–29; Hunsinger, "Hellfire and Damnation: Four Ancient and Modern Views (1998)," in *Disruptive Grace: Studies in the Theology of Karl Barth* (Grand Rapids: Eerdmans, 2000), 226–49; McCormack, "So That He May Be Merciful to All: Karl Barth and the Problem of Universalism," *Karl Barth and American Evangelicalism*, ed. Bruce L. McCormack and Clifford B. Anderson (Grand Rapids: Eerdmans, 2011), 227–49.

3. Barth himself states that the basic rule of all church dogmatics is "that no single item of Christian doctrine is legitimately grounded, or rightly developed or expounded, unless it can of itself be understood and explained as a part of the responsibility laid upon the hearing and teaching Church towards the self-revelation of God attested in Holy Scripture. Thus the doctrine of election cannot legitimately be understood or represented except in the form of an exposition of what God Himself has said and still says concerning Himself. It cannot and must not look to anything but the Word of God, nor set before it anything but the truth and reality of that Word" (*CD* II/2, 35). George Hunsinger pointed out that "[i]n fact, it has been estimated that the Index volume to Barth's great dogmatics includes roughly 15,000 biblical references and more than 2,000 instances of exegetical discussion." George Hunsinger, "Postcritical Scriptural Interpretation: Rudolf Smend on Karl Barth," in *Thy Word Is Truth: Barth on Scripture*, ed. George Hunsinger (Grand Rapids: Eerdmans, 2012), 30. See also James A. Wharton, "Karl Barth and His Influence on Biblical Interpretation," *Union Seminary Quarterly Review* 28 (1972): 5–13, on page 6.

4. Some examples are: Mary Kathleen Cunningham, *What Is Theological Exegesis? Interpretation and Use of Scripture in Barth's Doctrine of Election* (Valley Forge, PA: Trinity Press International, 1995), 19–49; David F. Ford, *Barth and God's Story: Biblical Narrative and the Theological Method of Karl Barth in the Church Dogmatics* (Eugene, OR: Wipf & Stock, 2008 [reprint]), 72–93; Jewett, *Election and Predestination*, 47–56; and Sharp, *The Hermeneutics of Election*.

in the lengthy small print section concluding §35.4 in *Church Dogmatics* II/2, is a key biblical source for his reconstruction of election in its ontological, forensic, and ethical aspects.[5] Closer analysis of the dynamic interplay between these various New Testament instances of *paradidōmi*, which Barth calls "no mere semantic accident,"[6] provides crucial biblical support for some of the most far-reaching claims of Barth's doctrine of election.

I develop this argument in three stages. In my first section I characterize Barth's theological ontology through the interpretation he gives to the divine handing-over of Jesus spoken of in the Pauline collection. My second section considers the forensic framework of election in light of Barth's insights regarding the connection between the divine handing-over of Jesus and Jesus's handing-over of himself, as well as the understanding Barth has of the negative divine handing-over of humanity. The third section shows how the ethical aim of election comes to the fore in light of the forensic-ontological framework of the divine *paradidōmi* and the interplay Barth finds between the handing-over of Jesus by Judas, Jesus's handing himself over, and the apostolic calling to hand-over or deliver the tradition (*paradosis*). In conclusion, I consider not only Barth's intracanonical method of exegesis but also how his dogmatic reflections on the intertextuality of *paradidōmi* help further the church's missionary vocation.

One important matter must be mentioned before going any further, and it has to do with Barth's use of Judas as a representative figure for Israel in the *Church Dogmatics*. As has been rightly pointed out, while Barth was insistent, following Romans 9–11, that "God's covenant with Israel is irrevocable," he still "kept too much anti-Judaic baggage in his theology," of which the typological use of Judas as representative of Israel is a prime instance. Barth's retention of these elements "cannot be followed by Christian theology today."[7] Yet even as Barth is no supersessionist, his reading of the figure

---

5. Stephen N. Williams's observation applies here: "Barth often takes up theological positions prior to his detailed exegetical discussions, and we have to resist the temptation to think he has stitched up the issue before coming to Scripture, for he does eventually, at least putatively and frequently, seek to ground—and not simply to bolster—his theological convictions in biblical exegesis." Williams, "Karl Barth on Election," in *The Election of Grace: A Riddle without a Resolution?* (Grand Rapids: Eerdmans, 2015), 192.

6. *CD* II/2, 482 (535). Pages from the *KD* will follow pages cited from the *CD* in parentheses. Unless otherwise noted, all italics are restored from the original German.

7. Hunsinger, "After Barth: A Christian Appreciation of Jews and Judaism," in *Conversational Theology: Essays on Ecumenical, Postliberal and Political Themes, with Special Reference to Karl Barth* (London: Bloomsbury T&T Clark, 2015), 95. Hunsinger advocates for soft supersessionism, which he defines as a non–anti-Judaic Christian response in which

of Judas remains deeply troubling.[8] For this reason, my discussion of Barth's theology of the individual who is the rejected one elected, or Judas, shall assume that Judas is Everyman and will draw no connection to Judas as a representative figure for the Jewish community.[9] In taking this approach, I am not only following Barth's own insistence that Christian mission to Jews is a contradiction in terms but also highlighting a concept central to all of Barth's theology, namely, that in Judas "*all* flesh passes under judgment" even as divine grace "surpasses all rejection."[10]

Theological Ontology and the Divine Handing-Over

The foundational element of Barth's revision of election is naming Jesus Christ the electing God and the elected human.[11] God's self-determination to bear the name of Jesus reveals that the material content of election is the covenant of grace.[12] Unlike much traditional exegetical work done to support the doctrine of predestination, Barth includes and then pushes beyond Ephesians 1:3-4, which is seen as the ground for understanding Jesus as the basis of humanity's election by God. More foundationally, Barth closely examines the prologue to the Gospel of John in order, through exegesis of John 1:1, 2, and 14,[13] to sustain an argument that Jesus Christ is himself the

---

Judeaophilia is governed by a center in Christ and love for Christ. Hunsinger, "After Barth: A Christian Appreciation of Jews and Judaism," 93-107.

8. Sonderegger, "Israel," in *The Westminster Handbook to Karl Barth* (Louisville: Westminster John Knox, 2013), 119. As Sonderegger so profoundly puts it: while Barth passionately discovered Israel for Christian theology, "to discover *Judaism* for Christian theology is a task left for other theologians to complete. It remains a high and urgent calling." Sonderegger, "Israel," 120.

9. On Judas as Everyman, see Sonderegger, *That Jesus Christ Was Born a Jew*, 122.

10. Sonderegger, *That Jesus Christ Was Born a Jew*, 133.

11. First, "in so far as He is *God*, we must obviously—and above all!—ascribe to Him the active determination of electing." Second, "in so far as He is *human*, the passive determination of election is also necessarily proper to Him." *CD* II/2, 103, rev. (110).

12. McCormack, "Grace and Being," 189.

13. Jüngel looks briefly but carefully at the exegetical moves made by Barth in his reading of John 1 within his doctrine of election in order to support his description of God's being in becoming. Eberhard Jüngel, *God's Being Is in Becoming: The Trinitarian Being of God in the Theology of Karl Barth*, trans. John Webster (Grand Rapids: Eerdmans, 2001), 95-96. For two other helpful examinations of the moves made by Barth in this treatment of John 1, see the essay by Paul Dafydd Jones, "The Heart of the Matter: Karl Barth's Christological Exegesis," in *Thy Word Is Truth: Barth on Scripture*, ed. George Hunsinger (Grand Rapids:

subject of election and that God's decision for the incarnation thus has "an eternal bearing on the divine life."[14] God, already in eternity, "in an act of unconditional self-determination . . . has ordained Himself to be the bearer of this name,"[15] to be, in other words, the God of love and mercy to humanity that we see in Jesus Christ.[16] In place of speculation about an abstract absolute decree of God, the covenant God makes with humanity is the beginning of all the works of God.[17] In contrast to the Reformed tradition's account of election, which "failed to point to the person of the Son, Jesus Christ, as the Subject of the act"[18] of eternal election, election for Barth is an explanation of what occurred in the reconciling history of Jesus Christ. Election is first a historical event and then also a decision in pretemporal eternity "made by God strictly *in anticipation of* the event that took place at Golgotha."[19] In other words, what God elects in eternity is precisely the history of Jesus Christ. The lived history of Jesus Christ crowds out any notion of a secret, absolute decree of God.[20] The unchanging being of God is constituted by

---

Eerdmans, 2012), 173–95, esp. 179–85, and the chapter by Aaron T. Smith, "The Spirit of Election and Obedience," in *A Theology of the Third Article: Karl Barth and the Spirit of the Word* (Minneapolis: Fortress, 2014), 199–216. For a critique that Barth's reading of John 1 "ranges far outside the immediate confines of the text" see Williams, "Karl Barth on Election," 197–98.

14. Jones, "The Heart of the Matter," 184. Jones's essay supports mine in that he shows how "Barth allows his ontology to be controlled by the particulars of the biblical record" (191).

15. *CD* II/2, 100 (108).

16. In other words, "election is the event in God's life in which he assigns to himself the being he will have for all eternity." McCormack, "Grace and Being," 189.

17. "In the beginning it was the choice of *the Father* to establish this covenant with man by giving up His Son for him, that He Himself might become man in the fulfillment of His grace. In the beginning it was the choice of *the Son* to be obedient to grace, and therefore to offer up Himself and to become man in order that this covenant might be made a reality. In the beginning it was the resolve of *the Holy Spirit* that the unity of God, of Father and Son should not be disturbed or rent by this covenant with man, but that it should be made the more glorious, the deity of God, the divinity of His love and freedom, being confirmed and demonstrated by this offering of the Father and this self-offering of the Son." *CD* II/2, 101–2, rev. (109).

18. *CD* II/2, 75 (81).

19. David W. Congdon, "*Apokatastasis* and Apostolicity: A Response to Oliver Crisp on the Question of Barth's Universalism," *Scottish Journal of Theology* 67, no. 4 (2014): 467.

20. "[I]n the primal and basic decision in which He *wills to be* and actually *is* God, in the mystery of what *takes place* from and to all eternity within Himself, within His triune being, God is none other than the One who in His Son or Word elects Himself, and in and with Himself elects His people." *CD* II/2, 76, rev. (82).

God's decision to turn toward the human race in Jesus Christ in self-giving love. There is "no height or depth in which God can be God in any other way."[21]

Moving beyond John 1, Barth gives additional scriptural support, by way of an analysis of a collection of divine and human *paradidōmi* clauses in the New Testament, for understanding "the election of Jesus Christ and His community."[22] He begins with the handing-over of Jesus by Judas in the passion narratives,[23] turning next to the apostolic handing-over of the tradition in Luke 1:1; Romans 6:17; 1 Corinthians 11:2, 23; 15:3; and Jude 3, pausing at the terrible divine "delivery" of humanity by God in Romans 1:24, 26, and 28, before finally considering the event of the positive divine *paradidōmi* spoken of in Romans 4:25 and 8:32; Galatians 2:20; and Ephesians 5:2 and 25. This final cluster of God handing Godself over happens "before" any of the others[24] and is the historical revelation of the gracious being of God. Barth connects this divine handing-over formula within the Pauline collection to the "*original* and *authentic paradounai*"[25] in the prologue to John's Gospel. "Delivery, handing-over, abandonment by God are themselves included in and necessarily result from the fact that God wills to make man participant in the eternal life by giving Himself to be his Covenant-partner."[26] The basis for the Pauline divine *paradidōmi* formula ultimately resides in John 1:14, where the incarnation is the primary instance of the "real and original handing-over of Jesus" and the instantiation of the decree of God's eternal love.[27] Further support of this connection is the fact that Romans 8:35; Galatians 2:20; and Ephesians 5:25 relate the divine handing-over "so emphatically

---

21. *CD* II/2, 77 (83).

22. *CD* II/2, 458 (508). For a discussion of some possible NT exegetical difficulties with Barth's notion of election "in Christ" see McDonald, *Re-Imaging Election*, 66–69.

23. Specifically, Barth observes that in John 18:3–4, Judas was "merely a spectator" in Jesus's arrest and that in the synoptic account he simply identified Jesus with his kiss, which shows that Jesus was "handed over by one of His own, by one of His disciples and apostles, from within the Church." *CD* II/2, 460 (510).

24. "Clearly the necessity and power and meaning of all delivery are established in this *first* and radical delivery, in which God, in the person of Jesus, or Jesus as the Son of God, made Himself the object of delivery. It is not permissible to understand any other delivery except with reference to this one (without prejudice to its special meaning). All other delivery looks either to or from this. It has its reality in what happened here. It is impossible to interpret it apart from its connection with this event." *CD* II/2, 489, rev. (543).

25. *CD* II/2, 491, rev. (545).

26. *CD* II/2, 491 (545).

27. *CD* II/2, 490 (545).

The Sum of the Gospel

to the divine *agapan*."[28] The "decree of God's eternal love, in which the Father sent the Son and the Son obeyed the Father,"[29] necessarily overflows in history in the divine positive *paradidōmi* in which God's will is revealed through God's willingness "to deliver Himself into the situation of impotence in face of the power by which man is overborne."[30] Thus, the condition for the possibility of the divine willing "His own handing-over" is the triune decision for incarnation.

Barth's Word Study of *Paradidōmi* in §35.4 of *CD* II/2

References to Judas handing over Jesus. See Barth, *CD* II/2, 459–60.	References to the apostolic handing-over of the tradition. See Barth, *CD* II/2, 483.	Examples of the terrible divine "delivery" of humanity by God. See Barth, *CD* II/2, 484–85.	Examples of the event of the positive divine handing-over of Godself. See Barth, *CD* II/2, 489–90.	Examples of the technical meaning of *paradidōmi* in the New Testament. See Barth, *CD* II/2, 480–81.
Mark 3:19; Matthew 10:4; Luke 22:21; John 6:64	Luke 1:1–2; Romans 6:17; 1 Corinthians 11:2; 11:23; 15:3	Acts 7:42; Romans 1:24, 26, 28	Romans 4:25; 8:32; Galatians 2:20; Ephesians 5:2; 5:25	Matthew 5:25; 18:34; 4:12; 24:10; Mark 1:14; Acts 21:11; 28:17; 21:1; 12:4

Forensicism and the Divine Handing-Over

Barth's *paradidōmi* word study provides an exegetical basis for the modification Barth makes to a forensic construal of justification and the atonement, which are closely related to election for Barth. In Barth's hands, forensicism is deeply ontological. McCormack suggests that at "the very root of forensic thinking [is] the recognition that human being is the function of a decision which gives rise to a willed relation. Human being is the function of a decision God *made* in eternity past in his electing grace. And it is a function of a decision God *makes* in time in justifying the ungodly. The former is the ground of the latter; the latter actualizes the content of the former in time."[31]

---

28. *CD* II/2, 491 (545).
29. *CD* II/2, 491 (545).
30. *CD* II/2, 491 (546).
31. Bruce McCormack, "What's at Stake in Current Debates over Justification: The

Barth's reading of the divine handing-over provides the biblical basis for his modified forensicism by setting forth the formal framework of covenant ontology in its divine and human aspects. The divine decision for the historical event of the divine handing-over, enacted by God and Jesus, replaces the older Protestant conception of imputation. The divine verdict of acquittal, the heart of justification, is actualized not only in the original divine handing-over of the Word become flesh but also in the historical instance of God handing Jesus over to the event of Golgotha as well as in Jesus freely handing himself over to sin and death for us.[32]

Beginning again with positive instances of the divine *paradidōmi* in the biblical text, Barth locates Romans 4:25 in its particular context, noting that it comes at the climax of an illustration of faith and divine justification in the story of Abraham. Barth's interpretation of the passage highlights that the faith that justifies is faith in the resurrecting God who handed over Jesus for our acquittal.

> The faith which Paul says justifies the believer is faith in Him who raised our Lord Jesus Christ from the dead. This God of Abraham has ascribed justification to us in the fact that Jesus *was delivered* by God *for the removal of our trespasses*, and then raised from the grave that we might be clothed with His righteousness. The handing-over of Jesus by God creates the indispensable preliminary condition for the positive thing which we receive in faith.... [I]t removes the obstacle which prevents God from acquitting us as a just Judge. With the handing-over of Jesus our trespasses are taken away.[33]

Paul's focus on the God who justifies in Romans 4:25 is likewise the subject in 8:32, where the forensic framework again comes to light. In "the delivery (in which God does violence to Himself as once — but very differently — He had done to Abraham at the time of Isaac's sacrifice) there is accomplished by the One who alone can be their *Judge* that which purifies them from every

---

Crisis of Protestantism in the West," in *Justification: What's at Stake in the Current Debates*, ed. Mark Husbands and Daniel J. Treier (Downers Grove, IL: InterVarsity Press, 2004), 115.

32. Hence Jüngel suggests that "Barth understands justification precisely from the viewpoint of election as God's self-justification. For God's choice 'from all eternity ... to take to Himself and to bear man's rejection is a prior justification of God in respect of the risk' to which he resolved to expose man by confronting him with nothingness and sin ([*CD* II/2], p. 165)." Jüngel, *God's Being Is in Becoming*, 93, n. 71.

33. *CD* II/2, 489, rev. (543).

accusation, and makes any future accusation *irrelevant (gegenstandslos)* from the very outset."[34] Both passages indicate that the event of handing-over in the divine life takes place within a forensic framework. As Judge, God deals with sin by choosing delivery to reprobation for Godself and mercy for us, the ones who stand accused.

Moving outside of Pauline passages, Barth's investigation of a handful of *paradidōmi* passages in Matthew, Mark, and Acts reveals that "'delivery' is the handing-over or transfer from a free or relatively free person to the confining power of those who wish him harm, and from whom he must expect harm."[35] Based on these passages, Barth suggests a definition of the technical meaning of handing-over as "to be delivered up in powerlessness to [a] strange and hostile overwhelming power. To 'hand over' is to deprive a powerful person of his freedom, so that his power is not merely damaged but is as such destroyed, and he has no option but to submit to that which is inflicted on him."[36] Such a decision for the divine deprivation of power and freedom is seen in the fact that in justification, God's declaration of our innocence has its basis in God's love. God's love is manifested in the eternal decision of God to enter into the covenant of grace with us, which entails not only the handing-over of Jesus but also of Jesus giving himself up for us.[37] "Concretely, the sending of the Father and the obedience of the Son are simply this divine *paradounai*."[38] The technical definition of handing-over, derived as it is from

---

34. *CD* II/2, 489, rev. (543).

35. *CD* II/2, 481 (534). Barth looks at Matthew 5:25, 18:34, 4:12, 24:10; Mark 1:14; Acts 21:11, 28:17, 27:1, and 12:4.

36. *CD* II/2, 490 (544). Corroborating Barth's definition is the fact that when this verb is used in the LXX it is overwhelmingly in the context of the handing-over of an individual(s) to the "power of another agent," 115. Beverly Roberts Gaventa, "God Handed Them Over," in *Our Mother Saint Paul* (Louisville: Westminster John Knox, 2007), 113–23. For a brief but helpful study of Paul's use of the *paradidōmi* tradition as it refers to Jesus in Galatians 1 and 2 and Romans 4 and 8, see the work of Victor Paul Furnish, "'He Gave Himself [Was Given] Up . . .': Paul's Use of a Christological Assertion," in *The Future of Christology: Essays in Honor of Leander E. Keck*, ed. Abraham J. Malherbe and Wayne A. Meeks (Minneapolis: Fortress, 1993), 109–21.

37. "The forgiveness of their sins must have its basis in the fact that God 'gave up' His Son, that *Jesus 'gave up' Himself* for them." *CD* II/2, 490, rev. (544). "This '*for us*,' which is so strongly emphasized by Paul, obviously shows us in what sense this handing-over is the eternal will of God." *CD* II/2, 493, rev. (547).

38. *CD* II/2, 491 (545). Barth continues: "If it is truly the will of the Father to send His eternal Son, and the will of the Son to obey His eternal Father in the execution of this mission; if it is truly the will of God to give Himself to man in such seriousness and fullness that He Himself becomes what man is—flesh, a bearer of human unworthiness and incapacity—

the biblical instances of handing-over in the Gospels and Acts, makes plain the theological ontology embedded within Barth's forensic thinking. God, in handing-over Jesus, made an offering of his freedom to his love. The divine *paradounai* is the divine offering of freedom to divine love.[39] "So great is His *love* that He regarded it as worthy of this offering."[40] In such an offering, God remains faithful to us but also to himself. "He—who in this situation is both the offended and the accuser, both judge and law—is free to order it according to His good-pleasure, and He employed this freedom of His in such a way that in its ordering He willed to suffer that which we ought to have suffered."[41]

The forensic nature of the divine handing-over is deeply ontological; it not only creates God's verdict of acquittal on humanity but it also brings about the real transformation of guilty humanity. Unlike the old accusation that forensic justification leads to a kind of legal fiction, by replacing the concept of imputation with the outcome of God's decision for the divine handing-over, no such charge can be made. As God's gracious saving action, the divine *paradidōmi* effectively creates new humanity. "This obstacle to the covenant between God and man is actually removed. . . . He does not merely execute judgment upon sin. He takes it upon Himself and suffers it so that there can be no further question of suffering it ourselves."[42] Using the language of Romans 8:29-39, God's delivery of Jesus purifies us from every accusation such that there is no longer a future basis for any condemnation. God's declaration of our innocence, based on God's active decision to be handed over for us and in our place, is nothing shy of the powerful love of God that effectively creates a new beginning and new life for humanity.

Barth also draws a connection between God's love and the negative

---

then this means that it is the will of God to deliver Himself into the situation of impotence in face of the power by which man is overborne, giving Himself not merely to the constraint of the limitation of creaturely life, but to the curse of human guilt, to the rejection of the life of man as it is ruled and determined by his sin, abandoning Himself to the utter opposite of His own divine form of existence." *CD* II/2, 491 (545-46).

39. On this same point, see also Jones, "The Heart of the Matter," 184-85, and Gaventa, "God Handed Them Over," 122.

40. *CD* II/2, 491, rev. (546).

41. *CD* II/2, 493 (548). Here is an instance of what Congdon calls Barth's "necessity *within divine freedom*." He explains that by necessity in this context Barth is speaking of a "necessity within the *singularity* of the divine decision," a necessity "that occurs in a contingent historical event and is inseparable from this contingency. It is the necessity not of immanent logic but of transcendent, eschatological action." Congdon, "*Apokatastasis* and Apostolicity," 470-71.

42. *CD* II/2, 494 (549).

instances of the divine handing-over of humanity in Romans 1:24, 26, and 28. The revelation of God's wrath, as seen in the action of handing-over humanity to the "authority of a power which is too great for them—the power ... of their enemy"[43] and to "abandonment to Satan,"[44] has as its aim the gracious divine eschatological possibility of faith. In faith in Jesus Christ we cannot consider lost any of those who are handed over by God. "If there is light for them, and hope, it can only be because and if there is an *eschaton*, a limit, by which even their inescapable bondage is hemmed in *from outside*."[45] This *eschaton* is the objective handing-over of Jesus. "From this *end* He wills to make a fresh beginning with them."[46] The wrath of God set forth in Romans 1:17–3:20 is but the reverse side of God's righteousness. Therefore it judges absolutely as an annihilating sentence whose action abandons sinful humanity and "burns them right down to faith, as it were, that there it may promise and give them ... both freedom and justification."[47] So also, in Galatians 2:20, it is the self-giving of Christ that brings Paul "fundamentally and finally into liberty, not merely forbidding but making it quite impossible for him to return to bondage under the Law's accusation."[48] In Ephesians 5:2 and 25, which parallel Philippians 2:6–7, it is the love of Christ on display in his giving himself up for us that makes necessary the exhortation of Christians to be followers of God and to love one another in self-sacrificial ways.

Ethics and the Divine and Human Handing-Over

For Barth, humanity's election has its teleological goal in vocation. Barth draws out this connection by highlighting that the apostolic handing-over of the tradition (*paradosis*) is one that corresponds to the divine handing-over.[49] In this way, Barth's covenant ontology has an ethical

---

43. *CD* II/2, 484 (538).
44. *CD* II/2, 485 (539).
45. *CD* II/2, 496, rev. (552).
46. *CD* II/2, 488, rev. (541).
47. *CD* II/2, 487 (541).
48. *CD* II/2, 489–90 (544).
49. *CD* II/2, 498 (554). Barth defines the "*true* and *proper*" apostolic handing-over as an echo of the divine handing-over in this way: "As the praise of God by creation is related to the praise which God Himself has prepared for His Son in the glory of His resurrection, so that which the apostles will and do is related by their *paradounai* to that which God Himself has decreed from all eternity, and accomplished in time, with His delivering up of Jesus Christ." *CD* II/2, 498, rev. (553).

shape.⁵⁰ The determination of the elect, for both the individual and the community, is actively to participate in the love, activity, and work of the triune God by sharing in Jesus's own mission.⁵¹ Election is election to be an active apostle in service to God and correspondence to Jesus. It is election to the vocation of witness and the ministry of reconciliation by which the elect enact a positive instance of the apostolic ministry of handing-over the message of Jesus. Whereas the traditional doctrine of predestination ends with a word about the elect going to heaven, Barth's insistence on Jesus Christ as the electing God and elected human leads him instead to consider the life-content of the elect, emphasizing their employment as missionary witnesses to the living God in Jesus Christ. Just as the whole history of Jesus Christ is an event not for himself nor for his own sake but for "the reality and revelation of the will of God on behalf of an unlimited number"⁵² of others, so the task of the Christian is to have an active, living faith that recognizes the "supremacy of the elect Jesus Christ in face of the rejected" and "denies the actuality and asserts the passing of the existence of the rejected."⁵³

The intersection of the elect and the rejected occurs where the elect must proclaim to those whose life corresponds to Judas's handing-over of Jesus that the "election of Jesus Christ is the beginning of all the ways and works of God which controls even their life."⁵⁴ This places a limit and boundary on the rejected, as she has "no truth of her own."⁵⁵ Confronted with the proclamation of the gospel, the rejected is but "a shadow which yields and dissolves and dissipates, being clearly limited by God."⁵⁶ The individual Christian or the community of faith who makes this proclamation demonstrates the positive instance of the human handing-over of Jesus, thus reversing the negative handing-over of Jesus by Judas. The connection between election and vocation are again seen in the fact that Barth "understands the event of election in Jesus Christ to be inseparable from one's

---

50. McCormack, "What's at Stake in Current Debates over Justification," 113.

51. Daniel Migliore highlights that for Barth "Christian life is a *participatio Christi* in the active, agential, ethical sense of free and glad participation in the service of Jesus Christ and his work of reconciliation." Migliore, "*Participatio Christi*: The Central Theme of Barth's Doctrine of Sanctification," *Zeitschrift für Dialektische Theologie* 18, no. 3 (2002): 291.

52. *CD* II/2, 421 (466).
53. *CD* II/2, 454 (503).
54. *CD* II/2, 454 (504).
55. *CD* II/2, 453 (503).
56. *CD* II/2, 454 (504).

The Sum of the Gospel

existential participation in it as an apostolic witness."[57] Just as God is what God does, so also true humanity is what Jesus does. In this vein, "[w]hat we are essentially is a divine act which establishes a covenantal relation—a relation which perdures and makes us to be what we are even when, in our perversity, we choose to live on the basis of a lie rather than the truth."[58] Thus the essence of a human being "is that which God has chosen us to be in entering into covenant with us."[59] God has chosen us in Christ to join in God's missionary work in the world by our lived witness. We have been elected to witness to those who are like Judas even as we are reversing the work of Judas.

Yet Barth also highlights the legitimate place of the rejected in God's work of salvation. Indeed, the handing-over of Jesus by Judas *fulfilled* God's decision to choose reprobation for Godself in order that humanity might be chosen in Christ for the vocation of proclamation. Barth proposes that the "whole significance of the apostolate . . . depends upon the fact that" Judas handed over Jesus "as it was decreed to be necessary in the counsel of God."[60] At the same time, Jesus Christ also objectively does away with Judas's negative delivery. This does not downplay Judas's guilt nor does it make Judas an example of *apokatastasis*.[61] Rather, it introduces the figure of Paul, who represents the apostle who fulfills his election to witness, replacing Judas as an apostle by reversing the negative human *paradidōmi* to a positive one.[62] As Barth sees it, the textual interplay of the *paradidōmi* of Judas and Paul is only possible in light of Jesus, whose decision to hand himself over is the powerfully unattainable prototype of both that therefore

---

57. Congdon, "*Apokatastasis* and Apostolicity," 466. "By locating the existence of the human person in correspondence to the existence of Jesus Christ, [Barth] aims to be more truly existential than the existentialists. The existentiality of human beings is grounded in the *existentiality of God*." Congdon, "Theology as Theanthropology: Barth's Theology of Existence in Its Existentialist Context," in *Karl Barth and the Making of Evangelical Theology*, ed. Clifford B. Anderson and Bruce L. McCormack (Grand Rapids: Eerdmans, 2015), 30–66. For more on this topic, see also Congdon, *The Mission of Demythologizing: Rudolf Bultmann's Dialectical Theology* (Minneapolis: Fortress, 2015).

58. McCormack, "What's at Stake in Current Debates over Justification," 115.

59. McCormack, "What's at Stake in Current Debates over Justification," 114.

60. *CD* II/2, 461 (511).

61. "The problem of *apokatastasis* is therefore inseparable from the question of apostolicity." Congdon, "*Apokatastsis* and Apostolicity." 477.

62. Sonderegger is helpful here. Judas "may be *the* sinner of the New Testament, but more, he is the living declaration of justification by grace alone." Sonderegger, *That Jesus Christ Was Born a Jew*, 122.

makes the situation between the elect and the rejected an "open situation of *proclamation*."⁶³

The apostolic *paradosis* is therefore "plenipotentiary in character" because "all the gracious light of the commission and ministry in which sinful [humans] may proclaim the Gospel to other sinful [humans] is only the reflection of the radiance of the eternal mercy in which God willed to take sinful [humanity] to Godself, and actually did take [them] to Godself by the handing-over of God's Son."⁶⁴ In view of the divine *paradidōmi* as the prototype of the human witness of handing-over, the ethical telos of Barth's covenantal ontology is understood as our existential participation in Christ's history of handing himself over for the sake of humanity.

Scriptural and Human Witness to Jesus as Victor

It bears mentioning that Barth "states his conclusions before providing his proofs."⁶⁵ The fact that Barth's doctrine of election in its most important ontological, forensic, and ethical dimensions is parsed according to an analysis of the recurrence of a single Greek word tells us that his revision of election is based in large part on his *paradidōmi* word study.⁶⁶ It will not do, for example, simply to dismiss Barth's doctrine of election with the argument given by Stephen Williams in his Kantzer lectures that it is based on an interpretation of John 1:1–2 ranging "far outside" "the theological language and explicit internal theological pattern" of the text.⁶⁷ For Barth, Jesus the Victor is the one to whom the whole Bible as a canon bears witness. As he sees it, Scripture must be interpreted in relation to its true subject matter. In this way, the important role played by the *paradidōmi* of Judas in the passion narratives of Jesus is seen first in its prototype in the divine *paradidōmi* and second in its apostolic counterpart in the positive human *paradidōmi* of Paul. This is both a canonical and a theological interplay. Insofar as there is a theological relationship between textual interplay of the *paradidōmi* of Judas and Paul grounded in the divine *paradidōmi* of Jesus, so also there is

---

63. *CD* II/2, 480, rev. (533).
64. *CD* II/2, 497 (552).
65. Williams, "Karl Barth on Election," 192.
66. Jones corroborates this claim: "[N]otice again that it is attention to the biblical record that stimulates Barth's formulation of finely grained doctrinal claims." Jones, "The Heart of the Matter," 190.
67. Williams, "Karl Barth on Election," 197–98.

an important canonical conversation between Gospel and Pauline letters in light of the witness of Jesus. Both canonical reflections are mutually informed by the indissoluble unity of their witness to the past and present of Jesus.[68] Theologians and biblical scholars seeking to norm theology to the witness of Scripture should take note of Barth's synthetical method of reforming doctrine through intracanonical conversation and intertextuality.[69] Following Barth, as well as the instruction of Pope Francis,[70] pastors seeking to preach the gospel should begin again at the beginning by considering the role of word studies in illuminating the good news.

Finally, regarding the church's proclamation of the divine handing-over, Barth's theological exegesis of New Testament instances of *paradidōmi* serves the missionary purpose of putting the rejection of Judas always before the church so that "the story of Judas Iscariot and what follows at Gethsemane and Golgotha, will *not* be repeated."[71] The goal of the missionary proclamation is to make the rejected individual "powerless in face of the overwhelming power of Jesus."[72] The powerlessness of the rejected is the affirmation of the power of God to overcome their rejection. The rejected individual "is not determined by God merely to be rejected. [She] is determined to hear and say that [she] is a rejected [human] *elected*,"[73] in light of the eschatological victory of Jesus. The church must recognize

---

68. "The importance of any one biblical voice for theological understanding or ethical praxis is focused or qualified by its relationship to the other voices that constitute the whole canonical chorus." See Robert W. Wall, "Canonical Contexts and Canonical Conversations," in *Between Two Horizons: Spanning New Testament Studies and Systematic Theology*, ed. Joel B. Green and Max Turner (Grand Rapids: Eerdmans, 2000), 176.

69. As I see it, Barth's methodology agrees in part with a canonical approach to reading Scripture in that both envisage a conversation with the New Testament's pluriform subject matter "that is more complementary than adversarial" where the purpose is clarification of the common ground of diverse witnesses. Wall, "Canonical Contexts and Canonical Conversations" (179–80). Wall continues: "[T]he canonical interpreter seeks to relate the different ideas of particular biblical writers and canonical units together in contrapuntal yet complementary ways, to expose the self-correcting (or 'prophetic') and mutually-informing (or 'priestly') whole of New Testament theology" (180).

70. See sections 145–53 of Pope Francis's Apostolic Exhortation Evangelii Gaudium to the Bishops, Clergy, Consecrated Persons and the Lay Faithful on the Proclamation of the Gospel in Today's World, online, http://w2.vatican.va/content/francesco/en/apost_exhortations/documents/papa-francesco_esortazione-ap_20131124_evangelii-gaudium.html#III.%E2%80%82Preparing_to_preach, accessed on June 18, 2015.

71. *CD* II/2, 500, rev. (555).

72. *CD* II/2, 501 (557).

73. *CD* II/2, 506, rev. (563).

every encounter with "Judas" as a possible encounter with "Paul,"[74] a redeemed Judas, a person who might "discover anew her and his calling to be an apostolic participant in Christ's mission."[75] Whatever the future of the rejected may be, "it will take place under the power of the proclamation of this handing-over, in the situation which is not merely kept open by this proclamation, but is kept open in the wholly disparate relationship of the two powers."[76] Therefore the church must deliver itself to the ministry of witnessing to the sum of the gospel by proclaiming the divine *paradidōmi*.[77] It must have the posture of a servant[78] in obedient correspondence to Jesus's servanthood, which reveals the being of God who hands over divine freedom to self-giving love,[79] thereby overcoming the negative power of the rejected. In its corresponding deliverance, the apostolicity of the church is

---

74. What I have in mind here is similar to what Barth describes as the difference between an "active Christian"—what I am here calling a "Paul"—and a "virtual Christian"—what I am here calling a "Judas." The difference is between those who are living into their new humanity in Christ and those who are already included in Christ even as their "ignorance and unbelief" means that they are outside him and without him. Barth clarifies that this "ontological connection is the legal basis of the *kērygma* which forms the community and with which the community is charged." Barth, *CD* IV/2, 275 (305).

75. Congdon, "*Apokatastasis* and Apostolicity," 479-80.

76. *CD* II/2, 505 (561). In Barth's own conclusion to his exegetical investigation of *paradidōmi* and the question of the will and intention of God for the rejected, he has this to say: "The answer can only be as follows. He wills that he too should hear the Gospel, and with it the promise of his election. He wills, then, that *this Gospel should be proclaimed to him. He wills that he should appropriate* and live by the hope which is given him in the Gospel. He wills that the rejected *should believe*, and that as a believer, he should *become* a rejected man elected." *CD* II/2, 506, rev. (563).

77. "Mission is the abundant fellowship of active participation in the very glory that is the life of God from and to all eternity. It is life in the community of reconciliation moving out in solidarity with the world in active knowledge that God died for it, too. It is the response of doxology as we follow the Spirit's lead as captives in the train of the living glorious Lord, the Lamb that was slain." John G. Flett, *The Witness of God: The Trinity, Missio Dei, Karl Barth, and the Nature of Christian Community* (Grand Rapids: Eerdmans, 2010), 297-98.

78. Barth lifts up the figure of Mary of Bethany in John 12, for whom Jesus's own self-offering is a prototype, as an example of the kind of action the apostles should imitate in their call to "the special subjective cleansing of those who already are objectively clean." *CD* II/2, 473-74 (525-26).

79. Barth posits that "obedience to Jesus Christ necessarily leads us to believe, without any reservations, that our fellow-men belong to God." Barth, "The Christian Message in Europe Today," in *Against the Stream: Shorter Post-War Writings 1946-52*, ed. Ronald Gregor Smith (New York: Philosophical Library, 1954), 179.

dynamic not static.[80] The church must become like Paul again and again as we seek to align our mission with God's will that all humanity, rejected and elected in Jesus Christ, be summoned again and again to faith and to the mission of Paul.

---

80. Flett argues that "[a]postolicity is the concrete criterion of the church's visible service to God and humanity." *The Witness of God*, 290.

12 What's in Those Lamps?

A Sermon on Matthew 25:1–13

FLEMING RUTLEDGE

Jesus said, "Then the kingdom of heaven shall be compared to ten maidens who took their lamps and went to meet the bridegroom. Five of them were foolish, and five were wise. For when the foolish took their lamps, they took no oil with them; but the wise took flasks of oil with their lamps. As the bridegroom was delayed, they all slumbered and slept. But at midnight there was a cry, 'Behold, the bridegroom! Come out to meet him.' Then all those maidens rose and trimmed their lamps. And the foolish said to the wise, 'Give us some of your oil, for our lamps are going out.' But the wise replied, 'Perhaps there will not be enough for us and for you; go rather to the dealers and buy for yourselves.' And while they went to buy, the bridegroom came, and those who were ready went in with him to the marriage feast; and the door was shut. Afterward the other maidens came also, saying, 'Lord, lord, open to us.' But he replied, 'Truly, I say to you, I do not know you.' Watch therefore, for you know neither the day nor the hour."

MATT. 25:1–13

Here in the middle of the so-called "long green season," or "ordinary time," here at the very moment of the summer solstice, this will be an Advent ser-

---

This sermon was delivered in Miller Chapel, Princeton Theological Seminary, on June 22, 2015, five days after the massacre of nine parishioners of Emanuel A.M.E. Church, Charleston, South Carolina, who were gathered for Bible study.

mon. As Karl Barth wrote many times, the church has no other time in this world but that of Advent—"the time between," as he often called it. Advent is the time of both "waiting and hastening," a verse from Second Peter that Barth loved to quote: "waiting for and hastening the coming of the day of God" (2 Pet. 3:12). Advent is the dialectic between the waiting and the hastening, the faithful confidence that strains forward toward the day and the long endurance that is required to wait for it. There is no other time given us in this life than this time, the time between the first coming of our Lord in humility and his second coming in glory. This is a strong theme in the Gospel of Matthew.

Many things have changed. When I was a Sunday school student growing up, this parable was called "The Wise and Foolish Virgins." Now it's called "The Wise and Foolish Bridesmaids." I guess bridesmaids aren't virgins any more. Fifty plus years ago, when my classmates and I were getting married, a lot of us actually *were* virgins (that was a good thing, in my opinion).

Many things have also changed in the world of biblical interpretation. When you have preached largely from the Epistles and the Old Testament for the past twenty years, as I have, and you come back to the Gospels for the first time in a while, you forget how disconcerting it can be to use some of the biblical commentaries. Take today's parable, for example. When you look it up in scholarly commentaries, you find all kinds of disputes—who is meeting whom and where, were they lamps or torches, would shops be open at night, does this parable actually go back to the historical Jesus, etc. Not only is this very discouraging for the preacher, it can actually lead away from the point of the parable. How refreshing it is for us preachers to turn to Barth's expository passages!

And there is yet another thing that has changed in the last fifty years. When I was young, the creedal confession that "he will come again in glory to judge the living and the dead" used to be rejected out of hand by virtually all progressive American Christians. Today, the eschatological, even apocalyptic atmosphere of the New Testament has finally begun to percolate down into the local congregations. Perhaps we are beginning to realize that if Christian faith is going to have any guts, it simply cannot be satisfied with exclusively human hope.

Two days ago, the principal of the Goose Creek School in Charleston, where one of the murdered churchgoers was an admired track coach, said, "Our society is broken, pretty much, but there will be a time when these times will be made right." Notice the use of the passive voice, "*will be made right.*" There is a divine agency behind this making-right, and that agency cannot be overcome by the principalities, or by the powers, or by things present or things to come (Rom. 8:38–39). That is what chapters 24 and 25 of Matthew point to. They are oriented toward the triumph of God in the second coming of Christ.

The various parables and sayings of these two chapters offer a remarkably rich and varied picture. We have the long discourse which is Matthew's version of the synoptic Apocalypse. Then we have the parables of the thief in the night, the faithful and unfaithful servants, the ten bridesmaids, the money in trust (the "talents"), and finally the Last Judgment. All of these are appointed for the Advent season. And then, "When Jesus had finished all these sayings, he said to his disciples, 'You know that after two days the Passover is coming, and the Son of man will be delivered up to be crucified'" (Matt. 26:1–2). Matthew has arranged this link between the Last Judgment and the crucifixion in a most artful and intentional way.

Now about those ten young women. The reason it still makes sense, biblically speaking, to think of them as virgins is that Paul writes to the Corinthian church as follows: "I betrothed you to one husband, to present you as a chaste virgin espoused to Christ" (2 Cor. 11:22). Virtually all interpreters agree that the ten bridesmaids represent the church—the community of professing Christians. That is why the bride does not appear in the story. If there was a bride, the symbolism would become bifurcated, with two different figures representing the church. In this parable, the *bridesmaids* are the virgin church, and the bridegroom, Jesus Christ, is arriving to sweep them up into his triumphal procession.

As we all know, the image of a wedding festival is a primary image—perhaps *the* primary image—of the kingdom of heaven (as Matthew calls it). Whatever the marriage customs may have been in first-century Judea, it is clear that the most important characteristic of the celebration is its untrammeled joyousness. In the story, the arrival of the bridegroom is intended to signal the beginning of the feast. Until he comes, it is all anticipation.

Anticipation is thrilling, for a while. The excitement about what is just around the corner heightens the sense of coming fulfillment. Everyone feels supercharged. This lasts for an hour, two hours—then the waiting becomes tedious. Why is he late? Three hours, and the nagging question arises, what if he does not come at all? Darkness has fallen. More hours go by. No one can stay at a pitch of anticipation forever. The young women begin to grow sleepy; their oil lamps begin to burn low. Suddenly the electrifying cry arises, "He's coming!" The lights of the procession approach in the night. The bridesmaids leap to their feet, grab their guttering lamps, trim them, and pour in their reserves of oil. Except that five of them have no extra; they wail, "Our lamps are going out!"

Some have suggested that the five wise virgins are selfish because they would not share. That is a moralistic reading of the story. As one interpreter says acerbically, "Better to greet the bridegroom with five lights than no lights at all." The foolish five rush off to the shops, but it is too late. The five whose lamps are brilliantly burning go into the wedding feast with the bridegroom and the five who were unprepared have the door shut against them.

We could be here for the rest of the day debating the ultimate destiny of the foolish five. Barth famously wrote that we are permitted to hope for a salvation that will reach to all. That is why one woman in Charleston—a woman prepared—said directly to the killer, "May God have mercy on your soul." The important thing about this parable right now is to think about what it means for the church to be ready for the coming of her Lord. What does it mean for us, all these weary and discouraging hours, and days, and years that he does not come, and it appears that he never will, and the church grows slack?

What's in those lamps? What does it mean to be ready at all hours of the night? What does it mean to be "the community of the last times" (*CD* III/2, 508)? In Luke's Gospel, Jesus says "Let your loins be girded and your lamps burning" (Luke 12:35). The emphasis is on being supplied and ready. On the night of the Passover, the children of Israel are commanded: "[Eat with] your loins girded, your sandals on your feet, and your staff in your hand; and you shall eat in haste" (Exod. 12:11). Does this mean we always have to gobble down our dinner standing up? Of course not. No one can be awake all the time. All ten of the bridesmaids went to sleep. Human frailty is accounted for; God understands our weakness. Perpetual alertness is not what is wanted; what is wanted is that stored-up emergency supply to last while "according to his promise, we wait for new heavens and a new earth in which righteousness dwells" (2 Pet. 3:13).

This confidence in the "great gettin' up morning" has strengthened the congregation of Emanuel A.M.E. Church in Charleston, South Carolina—known to many as "Mother Emanuel." When I started struggling with this sermon ten days ago, I wondered how in the world I was going to illustrate it. Little did I know that something would happen that would show forth the Advent church, assaulted by darkness, but rising up with all its lamps burning, and with plenty of extra oil for the long, long haul ahead.

When Eric Harris and Dylan Klebold shot up the Columbine High School in 1999, there were some troubling stories about local Christian youth groups. Before the blood was even dry, it seemed, youth leaders began asking the traumatized students whose friends were dead, "Do you forgive Eric and Dylan?" This sort of premature, even invasive, call for forgiveness should never be inflicted on anyone, let alone young teenagers who have just experienced the unimaginable. It is very difficult even for much older Christian people to navigate the passage between justice and mercy. Ordinarily we might do well to mistrust such premature offers of forgiveness.

Last week in Charleston, however, was different. To be sure, it is important not to romanticize or idealize the black church, or any church. All Christian groups are riven by sin just like all other groups. But the black churches have suffered so extremely, and so unjustly, for so long, that they have achieved a maturity that seems almost superhuman. The members of "Mother Emanuel" Church who lost their pastor, their relatives, and their friends in a bloody, hateful assault are not teenagers unaccustomed to suffering, crime, violence, and death. These are adults who have seen ugliness in human character that white people cannot even comprehend. Many of them have been learning "the mind of Christ" (1 Cor. 2:16) for decades. They were being conformed, as a group, to his likeness. Therefore they had a readiness, as a *community* of believers, that cannot develop the same way in isolated *individuals*.

I heard a long interview on NPR with an African American pastor in South Carolina. The interviewer simply could not comprehend what he was saying to her. She kept saying, "But how can you forgive? How can you be like this?" All weekend, the mystification of the reporters was notable. They kept asking the same question over and over: "How can you forgive Dylann Roof?" They could not understand it. The radio and TV people kept using well-worn phrases like "the triumph of the human spirit" and "the goodness of the American people." No, the pastor on NPR said, it is *our faith*. What we have seen in the members of Mother Emanuel Church and the other black churches is neither the triumph of the human spirit nor the goodness of the American people. It is a cloud of witnesses to the victory of the limitless love of the One who will come again to set all things right.

Barth testifies that the oil of the lamps is the witness of the Spirit in the waiting church (*CD* III/2, 505-6). That is what we are seeing in this response of the Mother Emanuel members. They are so practiced, through regular worship, Bible study, and prayer that they do not need to run out to the store in the middle of the night to buy more oil. They have been in the middle of the night for a long time. They do not need any well-meaning, immature counselors to tell them to forgive Dylann Roof. It is part of their DNA as a

Christian community. They have been storing up oil for generations. On Friday night, they were standing out in the courtyard of their horribly violated church, and they were singing "Let my little light shine." When the church reopened for worship yesterday, one of the ministers said that people kept asking why, and how, but "those of us who know Jesus, we can look through the window of our faith, and we see hope, we see light."[1]

Maybe the best clue to the inner meaning of this parable of the lamps and the oil can be found in just two words. The parable tells us that when the bridegroom arrived, "those who were ready went in with him to the marriage feast." *With him!* The five who were prepared, who stored up a supply of oil in anticipation of the great banquet, see the lighted procession approaching them with the glorious Bridegroom at its head. "Come, good and faithful servants, enter into the joy of your Master." We *accompany him*, we enter his eternal wedding banquet *with him, at his side*, cleansed from all our accumulated misdoings, freed from our bondage to the power of sin, in fellowship with the Lord Jesus in all his splendor, the one who has loved us even unto death and hell, who comes again to receive those who belong to him.

"With him!" "Beloved . . . it does not yet appear what we shall be, but we know that, when he appears, we shall be like him, for we shall see him as he is" (1 John 3:2, KJV).

AMEN

---

1. John Eligon and Richard Fausset, "Defiant Show of Unity in Church That Lost 9," *The New York Times*, June 22, 2015. It is almost unknown for *The New York Times* to quote someone using the name of Jesus in a confessional context except when the speaker is African American. Sermons given at the funerals of well-known white people are often quoted, but the quotations are always generic. References to Christ are not included. I have noticed this for decades. Therefore the witness of the black church is all the more important to us all.

Contributors

Richard Bauckham served as professor of New Testament studies at St. Andrews University in Scotland until 2007. He is now senior scholar at Ridley Hall, Cambridge. Among his many writings are *God Crucified, Jesus and the Eyewitnesses,* and *Gospel of Glory: Major Themes in Johannine Theology.* A fellow of the British Academy and a fellow of the Royal Society of Edinburgh, he is currently working on a commentary on the Gospel of John.

Kendall Cox is lecturer in religious studies at the University of Virginia. A PhD graduate of UVA, her dissertation is entitled "Prodigal Christ: The Parable of the Prodigal Son in the Theologies of Julian of Norwich and Karl Barth."

Beverly Roberts Gaventa is emerita professor of New Testament at Princeton Theological Seminary and now serves as distinguished professor of New Testament at Baylor University in Waco, Texas. Her many writings include *From Darkness to Light: Aspects of Conversion in the New Testament, Mary: Glimpses of the Mother of Jesus,* and a commentary on *The Acts of the Apostles.* She is also editor of *Apocalyptic Paul: Cosmos and Anthropos in Romans 5–8* and *The New Interpreter's Bible One-Volume Commentary.*

Eric Gregory is professor of religion at Princeton University and chair of the Council of the Humanities. He is the author of *Politics and the Order of Love: An Augustinian Ethic of Democratic Citizenship* and a number of seminal articles on ethics and political theology. Recipient of Princeton's President's Award for Distinguished Teaching in 2007, he is currently writing a book tentatively titled *What We Owe Strangers: Globalization and the Good Samaritan*.

Willie James Jennings is associate professor of systematic theology and Africana studies at Yale Divinity School. He is the author of *The Christian Imagination: Theology and the Origins of Race*, for which he received the prestigious Grawemeyer Award in Religion in 2015. He is preparing a commentary on the book of Acts and a book with the title *Unfolding the World: Recasting the Christian Doctrine of Creation*.

Paul Dafydd Jones is associate professor of religious studies at the University of Virginia. He is the author of *The Humanity of Christ: Christology in Karl Barth's Church Dogmatics*, and is coeditor of the forthcoming *Oxford Handbook of Karl Barth*. He is at work on a new book titled *Patience: A Theological Exploration*.

Bruce L. McCormack is the Charles Hodge professor of systematic theology at Princeton Theological Seminary. Author of *Karl Barth's Critically Realistic Dialectical Theology* and *Orthodox and Modern: Studies in the Theology of Karl Barth*, he is also editor of *Engaging the Doctrine of God* and several volumes on Barth's theology, including *Karl Barth and the Making of Evangelical Theology: A Fifty-Year Perspective*. He serves as director of the Center for Barth Studies at Princeton Seminary.

Daniel L. Migliore is the Charles Hodge professor emeritus of systematic theology at Princeton Theological Seminary. Among his writings are *Faith Seeking Understanding: An Introduction to Christian Theology*, *The Power of God and the Gods of Power*, and most recently, a commentary on *Philippians and Philemon*. He is also editor of *Commanding Grace: Studies in Karl Barth's Ethics*.

Jürgen Moltmann is professor emeritus of systematic theology at Tübingen University. One of the most influential theologians of the past half-century, he is the author of numerous books, including *Theology of Hope*, *The Crucified God*, *The Church in the Power of the Spirit*, *The Trinity and the Kingdom*, *The Coming God*, and, most recently, *The Living God and the Fullness of Life*.

Paul T. Nimmo holds the Kings Chair of systematic theology at the University of Aberdeen in Scotland. He is the author of *Being in Action: The Theological Shape of Barth's Ethical Vision* and *Karl Barth: A Guide for the Perplexed*. Coeditor of the forthcoming *Oxford Handbook of Karl Barth*, he also serves as an editor of *The International Journal of Systematic Theology*.

Fleming Rutledge, a nationally known preacher, served on the clergy staff at Grace Church in Manhattan. She is the author of several volumes of sermons, including *And God Spoke to Abraham: Preaching from the Old Testament* and *Not Ashamed of the Gospel: Sermons from Paul's Letter to the Romans*. Her most recent book is *The Crucifixion: Understanding the Death of Jesus Christ*.

Shannon Nicole Smythe, a PhD graduate of Princeton Theological Seminary, is assistant professor of theological studies at Seattle Pacific University. She is the author of *Women in Ministry: Questions and Answers in the Exploration of a Calling* and *Forensic Apocalyptic Theology: Karl Barth and the Doctrine of Justification*.

Index of Authors

Allen, Michael, 92
Allison, Dale C., 169
Ambrose, Colin M., 46
Amyraut, Moyse, 1
Anderson, Clifford B., 188, 199
Anselm of Canterbury, 111
Aquinas, Thomas, 35, 45, 142–43, 171
Arndt, W. F., 71
Augustine, 36, 41, 42, 43, 45, 54–55, 84–85, 108, 114

Bailey, Kenneth E., 87
Baird, William, 177
Baker, Denise, 111
Baker, J. Wayne, 7
Balthasar, Hans Urs von, xxiii–xxiv, 89–105, 129, 149
Barnett, Michael, 51
Barr, James, 175
Battles, Ford Lewis, 130
Bauckham, Richard, xxi–xxii
Bauer, W., 71
Becht, Michael, 89
Bender, Courtney, 52
Benjamin, Walter, 38
Benoit, D., 15
Bergner, Gerhard, xiii
Berkouwer, G. C., 120, 187

Bernard of Clairvaux, 111
Bettis, J. D., 188
Biggar, Nigel, 53
Bizer, Ernst, 2, 132
Blowers, Paul M., 128
Boer, H. R., 187
Bonhoeffer, Dietrich, 34
Bouchard, Larry, 120
Boulton, Mathew Myer, 132
Bovon, François, 144
Bowman, Donna, 187
Braaten, Carl E., 124
Bretherton, Luke, 51
Bromiley, Geoffrey W., 16
Brown, Raymond E., 128
Bruun, Mette B., 114
Bultmann, Rudolf, 84, 144–45, 174
Burnett, Richard, 104
Busch, Eberhard, xiii, xx, 57, 105, 110, 123
Bynum, Caroline Walker, 113
Byron, John, 174

Caird, G. B., 42
Calvin, John, 1–2, 11, 13–15, 47, 130–34, 139, 143, 146–47, 149
Camosy, Charles C., 35
Canlis, Julie, 132

INDEX OF AUTHORS

Carroll, John T., 173, 178
Casey, Michael, OCSO, 111
Chalamet, Christophe, 139
Chaucer, Geoffrey, 110
Clough, David, 38, 43, 49
Coakley, Sarah, 97–98, 120, 121
Codevilla, Angelo M., 57
Colledge, Edmund, 111
Collins, Adela Yarbro, 169
Colwell, John E., 187
Congdon, David, 174, 191, 196, 199, 202
Constas, Nicholas, 128
Conzelmann, Hans, 177–78, 181
Cowell, Alan, 57
Cox, Kendall, xxiv–xxv
Crawford, Emma, 151
Crisp, Oliver D., 187, 188
Crossan, John Dominic, 40
Crouch, James, 144
Cullmann, Oscar, 174, 177
Cunningham, Mary Kathleen, xiii, 22, 188

Dahl, Nils Alstrup, 185
Daley, Brian E., SJ, 129
Danker, F. W., 71
Davies, Oliver, 99
Davies, W. D., 169
Davis, Ellen F., 173
Davis, Stephen T., 121
Deaton, Angus, 51
Dempsey, Michael T., 188
DeVries, Dawn, 135
Dicken, Frank E., 183
Diem, Hermann, xiii
Dodd, C. H., 41
Donahue, John R., SJ, 40
Durand, Marie, 15

Ebeling, Gerhard, 122
Edmondson, Stephen, 131
Eicher, Peter, xiv
Eligon, John, 209
Elser, Ashleigh, 139

Fangmeier, Jürgen, xx

Fanon, Frantz, 12
Fausset, Richard, 209
Favre, A., 15
Fedler, Kyle, 133
Fitzmyer, Joseph, 40
Flett, John G., 202, 203
Ford, David, 120, 188
Fout, Jason A., 97
Foxgrover, David, 133
Francis, Pope, 201
Frei, Hans W., 48, 115, 120
Furnish, Victor Paul, 195
Fürst, Walther, 16

Gagnon, Robert A. J., 42
Gaventa, Beverly Roberts, xxvi, 174, 180, 182, 184, 195, 196
Geiger, Max, xx
Gerhardt, Paul, 2, 5–6
Gherardini, B., 110
Gibson, David, 22
Gignilliat, Mark S., xiii–xiv
Gingrich, F. W., 71
Gockel, Matthias, 187
Gollwitzer, Helmut, 86, 108–9
Gomarus, Franciscus, 1
Green, Garrett, 51
Green, Joel B., 173, 201
Greene-McCreight, Kathryn, 115
Greggs, Tom, 119
Gregory, Eric, xxii
Grieb, A. Katherine, 183
Grobel, Kendrick, 145
Guder, Darrell L., 122, 130
Guder, Judith J., 130
Gunton, Colin, 187
Gustafson, James, 35

Haddorff, David, 37
Haenchen, Ernst, 178
Harnack, Adolf von, 85, 107
Hauerwas, Stanley, 35, 120
Hays, Richard B., 173, 179–80
Hector, Kevin W., 35, 119, 135, 136
Hegel, G. W. F., 35, 165
Henreckson, David, 55

Index of Authors

Heppe, Heinrich, 2, 132
Higton, Mike, 40, 41, 42
Hilary of Poitiers, 142
Hill, Edmund, 85
Hooker, Thomas, 36
Hooper, Walter, 36
Hornik, Heidi J., 173
Hoskyns, Edwyn C., xv, 127
Huber, W., 7
Hunsinger, George, xii, xx, 37–38, 46, 115, 119, 120, 122, 140, 188, 189–90
Husbands, Mark, 194

Jeffrey, David Lyle, 42
Jenkins, Jacqueline, 106
Jenkins, Willis, 52
Jennings, Willie James, xxii–xxiii
Jenson, Robert, 187
Jeremias, Joachim, 40
Jewett, Paul K., 187, 188
Johnson, Adam, 134
Johnson, Luke Timothy, 173
Jones, L. Gregory, 120
Jones, Paul Dafydd, xii, xxv, 46, 93, 119, 121, 134, 190, 191, 196, 200
Jones, Serene, 132
Juel, Donald H., 185
Julian of Norwich, xxiv–xxv, 106–23
Julicher, Adolph, 41
Jüngel, Eberhard, 119, 122, 150, 190, 194

Kähler, Martin, 124
Karris, Robert, 173
Keating, James F., 165
Keck, Leander E., 136, 179
Kelley, Robin D. G., 59
Kelsey, David H., 120
Kendall, Daniel, SJ, 121
Khorschide, M., 3
Kierkegaard, Søren, 50
Kilby, Karen, 91, 93
King, Martin Luther, Jr., 13
Kleinig, John, 39
Koester, Helmut, 144
Konrad, Johann-Friedrich, xiii

Laansma, Jon C., 161
Leitch, James W., xiv
Lewis, Alan, 117
Lewis, C. S., 36
Lincoln, Andrew, xiv
Lindars, Barnabas, 128
Lindbeck, George, 115
Lohr, Joel N., 174
Lombard, Peter, 143
Longenecker, Bruce, 42
Loser, Werner, 89, 100
Louth, Andrew, 128
Lubac, Henri de, 110
Luther, Martin, 10–11, 45, 149

MacKenzie, Ross, 134
Mackintosh, H. R., 134
Madigan, Kevin, 143–44
Malherbe, Abraham J., 195
Mangina, Joseph, 38, 48
Marshall, Bruce D., 165
Marshall, I. Howard, 173
Martyn, J. Louis, 179, 184
Maximus the Confessor, 128–30
McCormack, Bruce L., xiv, xv, xxv–xxvi, 115, 119, 141, 161, 187, 188, 191, 193, 198
McCosker, Phillip, xiv
McDonald, Suzanne, 187, 192
McFague, Sallie, 122
McKenny, Gerald, 35, 37, 97
McNeill, John T., 130
Meeks, Wayne A., 195
Migliore, Daniel L., xxiii–xxiv, 104, 198
Milem, Bruce, 99
Milton, John, 2
Molnar, Paul, 38, 92, 119
Moloney, Francis J., 30
Moltmann, Jürgen, xx–xxi, 1, 7, 11, 13, 98, 167–68, 169
Morrison, A. W., 130
Moule, C. F. D., 178–79
Muller, Richard, 135

Nelson, Dana D., 62
Neufeldt-Fast, Arnold, 150

INDEX OF AUTHORS

Niebuhr, Reinhold, 34
Nimmo, Paul T., xiv, xxiii, 37, 119, 138
Nuth, Joan, 111
Nygren, Anders, 36

O'Collins, Gerald, SJ, 121
Ogden, Schubert, 145
Olevian, Caspar, 7
O'Toole, Robert, 180
Otten, H., 3
Outka, Gene, 36–37, 51

Paddison, Angus, xiv
Parker, T. H. L., 130
Parsons, Mikeal C., 173, 179, 184
Pearson, Lori, 135, 137
Pelikan, Jaroslav, 149
Placher, William C., 122
Pontiero, Giovanni, 156
Pullan, L., 142

Rawls, John, 39
Redeker, Martin, 135
Redfield, Peter, 52
Ricoeur, Paul, 115–16
Rindge, Matthew, 40
Rose, Matthew, 37
Rotelle, John E., 85
Roukema, Riemer, 41
Rutledge, Fleming, xxvii

Sanday, W., 142
Saramago, José, xxv–xxvi, 155–60, 167, 172
Saunders, Thomas Bailey, 107
Scanlon, Larry, 110
Schlatter, Adolf, 19, 30
Schleiermacher, Friedrich, 35, 130, 134–39, 147
Schmitt, Francis, OSB, 111
Schnucker, Robert V., 133
Schrenk, G., 7
Sen, Amartya, 39
Sharp, Douglas R., 188
Shuster, M., 135
Silano, Giulio, 143

Singer, Peter, 35
Sleeman, Matthew, 180
Smend, Rudolf, xx
Smith, Aaron T., 191
Smith, Ronald Gregor, 202
Smith, Ted A., 38
Smythe, Shannon Nicole, xxvi–xxvii
Snyder, Julia A., 183
Solis, Gabriel, 59
Sonderegger, Katherine, 188, 190, 199
Soskice, Janet, 113
Spearing, A. C., 110
Spearing, Elizabeth, 110
Stancaro, Francesco, 131
Stenning, H. J., xv
Stewart, J. S., 134
Strauss, D. F., 136
Swain, Scott, 92
Swietek, Francis, 111
Sykes, Stephen W., 32

Talbert, Charles, 178
Tanner, Kathryn, 120
Taves, Ann, 52
Taylor, Charles, 38, 51–52
Teske, Roland, 41
Theodor of Beza, 1, 2
Thiemann, Ronald F., 49, 120
Thomas, John Newton, 123
Thomson, G. T., 132
Thomson, Judith, 39
Ticciati, Susannah, xiii
Torrance, David W., 130, 134
Torrance, T. F., 92, 130, 134, 163
Treier, Daniel J., 161, 194
Turner, Denys, 99, 110, 111
Turner, Max, 201
Tylanda, Joseph, 131

Valentini, Laura, 39
Vetter, Harold R., 5
Vincent, Isabel, 57
Vogelsang, E., 11
Von der Ruhr, Mario, 151

Wailes, Stephen L., 85

Index of Authors

Walker, Adrian, 149–50
Wall, Robert W., 201
Walter, Peter, 89
Washington, James M., 13
Watson, E. W., 142
Watson, Francis B., xiv, 175
Watson, Nicholas, 106
Watson, Philip, 36
Weber, Max, 2, 11
Webster, John, xiv, 37–38, 53, 55, 119, 150, 190
Weil, Simone, 151
Weinberg, Gerhard L., 57
Weiss, Thomas G., 51
Werpehowski, William, 37

Wesley, John, 2
Wharton, James A., xvii, 188
White, Thomas Joseph, OP, 165
Wieser, Thomas, 123
Wilken, Robert Louis, 128
Williams, Rowan D., 32
Williams, Stephen N., xii–xiii, 189, 191, 200
Wilson, Brittany E., 183
Wilson, Mary F., 139
Wolf, Ernst, 11
Woodard-Lehman, Derek Alan, 37
Woolf, Virginia, 153

Yu, Anthony C., 188

Index of Subjects

Abraham, 194
Advent, 204–6
Agape, 36–37
Agape: An Ethical Analysis (Outka), 36–37
Analogical reading: definition of analogy, 88; parable of the lost son, xxiv, 86–89, 106, 109–10, 117–18
Apokatastasis, 199
Athanasius, 130, 137
Atonement, doctrine of: and Barth's doctrine of election (the divine handing-over), 193–95; and Barth's exposition on the compassion of Jesus Christ (Matthew 9:36), 75–77; Barth's juridical language in, 149–50; christological interpretations of the parable of the lost son, 114–15; Julian of Norwich's gloss on parable of the lost son, 112–13, 118–19
Augustine, 36, 54–55; and parable of the Good Samaritan, 41, 42, 43, 45, 54–55; and parable of the lost son, 84–85, 108, 114

Balthasar, Hans Urs von: on the father's primal act of kenosis (self-emptying), xxiv, 90–92; and parable of the lost son, xxiii–xxiv, 89–105; understanding of human freedom, xxiv, 99–104
Black churches, 208–9
Bonn lectures (1933), 16, 17–20, 24–25, 26–27. *See also* Johannine Prologue
Bridesmaids, parable of the ten wise and foolish, xxvii, 204–9

Calvin, John: doctrine of predestination, 1–2, 11, 13–15; Gethsemane in the thought of, 130–34, 139, 143, 146–47, 149; and parable of the Good Samaritan, 47
Chalcedon: "definition" of, 128, 141; four adjectives of, 121, 146. *See also* Trinity/trinitarian theology
Christ and Time (Cullmann), 174, 177
The Christian Faith (Schleiermacher), 134–37
Church Dogmatics (Barth), xv–xx; on the compassion of Jesus Christ, xxiii, 67–79; criticism of Kierkegaard's *Works of Love*, 50; debate with Bultmann, 84; on difference between the Synoptics and Gospel of John, xix; on divine mercy and grace, 46–47, 78–79; doctrine of predestination/

Index of Subjects

doctrine of the election of grace, 1–15; on dogmatic theology, xii–xiii; the Emmaus road story and self-witness of the risen Jesus, 173–77, 183; fundamental features of Barth's exegesis, xvi–xx; Gethsemane prayer, 127, 139–53; Good Samaritan parable, 42–51; Jesus's cry of dereliction, 162–67; Jesus's revelation of the love between the Father and Son, 32–33; the Johannine Prologue, 19, 20–24, 25–26, 27–28; lost son parable, 82, 83–89, 94–96, 106–10, 116–18; the love commandments, 43–46; outline of evangelical history in the Synoptic Gospels (the synoptic *Geschichte*), 124–27, 139; story of the rich young ruler, 59–65; on three phases of exegesis, xvi; trinitarian theology, 92

Church Dogmatics I/1, 27–28, 121
Church Dogmatics I/2, xvi, xix, 42–51
Church Dogmatics II/1, 78–79
Church Dogmatics II/2, 1–15, 59–65
Church Dogmatics III/1, 25–26
Church Dogmatics III/2, 173–77, 181, 183
Church Dogmatics IV/1, 84, 92, 124–27, 139–53, 162–67
Church Dogmatics IV/2, xxiii, 50, 67–79, 82, 83–89, 94–96, 106–10, 116–18
Church Dogmatics IV/3, 32–33
Clement of Alexandria, 40–41
Columbine High School massacre (1999), 207–8
Compassion of Jesus Christ (Matthew 9:36), xxiii, 67–79; analysis, 74–79; *Church Dogmatics* IV/2, 67–79; the crowds as object of Jesus's compassion, 72–73, 74–77; exegesis, 71–74; on the inseparable connection between the person and the work of Jesus, 73–74; insights for atonement theory, 75–77; insights for theological anthropology, 74–75, 76; Jesus as good shepherd (whom the crowds do not recognize), 73, 75, 76–77; relationship between compassion of Jesus and compassion of God, 77–79; the setting, 68–71; the term for compassion (*Ebarmen/splanchna*), 71–72, 77, 78, 79; the true human being Jesus Christ, 68–70

Counter-Reformation, 13
Covenant: covenant partnership, 62–63; human freedom and concept of, 7
Credo (Barth), 165
Cyril of Alexandria, 130, 137

De Doctrina Christiana (Augustine), 41
Die Freude Gottes (Gollwitzer), 86
Die Mitte der Zeit (Conzelmann), 177–78
Docetism, 130
Dyothelitism, 128–32, 137–38, 140–41

Election, doctrine of: and the apostolic handing-over of the tradition (*paradosis*), 197–200; and atonement, 193–95; Barth's doctrine of, xiii, xxvi–xxvii, 20–22, 89, 118–19, 126, 187–203; Barth's theological ontology and the divine handing-over, 190–93, 196; *Church Dogmatics* II/2, 126, 189, 191, 192–93, 194–200, 201–2; election of Jesus Christ, 8–11; God's election of grace and political theology, 11–15; God's election of grace as the sum of the Gospel, 3–6; and "God's overflowing glory," 9–10; implications for Christian missions, 201–3; Jesus Christ as subject of election, 190–93; the Johannine Prologue, 20–22, 192–93; Julian of Norwich's gloss on the lost son parable, 112–13, 118–19; and the lost son parable (christological interpretation), 112–13, 118–19; the *paradidōmi* (handing over) passages in the New Testament, xxvi–xxvii, 187–203; and predestination (the election of grace), xx–xxi, 1–15, 198; theological problem of God's freedom of choice/communicative

219

INDEX OF SUBJECTS

freedom, 6–7; theological problem of God's will and God's nature, 7; and vocation, 197–200. See also *Paradidōmi* (handing over)

Emanuel A.M.E. Church (Charleston, South Carolina), massacre of nine black parishioners at, xxvii, 204–9

Emmaus road story (the self-witness of the risen Jesus), xxvi, 173–86; the "absent" of Jesus in Acts (and presence of), 178–81; Barth's account as fulcrum for understanding Acts, 180–84; Barth's interpretation in conversation with Lukan scholarship, 177–80, 184–85; *Church Dogmatics* III/2, 173–77, 183; and Conzelmann's periodization of Lukan salvation history, 177–78; and Cullmann's notion of Jesus as the center of time, 174, 177; Jesus's revelation of himself through breaking bread, 176–77, 183; and Jesus's role in the giving of sight, 183–84; and Lukan ecclesiology, 181–82; and Paul's conversion in Acts, 176, 181; reading in the presence of Jesus, 184–86; relationship between the past, present, and future of Jesus, 175–76; and resurrection epistemology, 182–84

The Epistle to the Romans (Barth), xiv–xv, 127

Ethics, contemporary Christian: and Barth's interpretation of the parable of the Good Samaritan, 34–38; disconnect between developments in Barth studies and, 35–36; and the doctrine of election (the divine/human handing-over), 197–200; and global justice debates, 52–55

Exegesis, Barth's commitment to, xv–xx; assumption of diversity and unity of biblical witness, xviii–xix; assumption of the actuality and contemporaneity of the subject matter of Scripture, xix; attention to the narrative form that witness takes, xvii–xviii; christocentric readings, xvi–xvii; the connection between exegesis and dogmatics, 125–27; fundamental features of, xvi–xx; "post-critical" interpretation and importance of a "tested and critical naivety" on the part of the interpreter, xix–xx; and requirement of imagination, xvi

Forensicism and doctrine of election (the divine handing-over), 193–97

Freedom, divine: and doctrine of the election of grace, 6–7; God's freedom of choice/communicative freedom, 6–7; God's self-willing and self-knowing, 170–72

Freedom, human: Balthasar's reading of parable of the lost son, xxiv, 99–104; Barth's interpretations of the parable of the lost son, xxiv, 82–83, 99–104; and concept of covenant between God and the elected, 7; and story of the rich young ruler, 64

Gethsemane prayer, xxv, 124–54; the answer/non-answer Jesus receives from the Father, 144–47, 151; Barth on Christ's human nature, 129–30; and Barth's christological actualism, 140; Calvin's interpretation, 130–34, 139, 143, 146–47, 149; *Church Dogmatics* IV/1, 127, 139–53; consequences of, 150–53; and dyothelitism, 128–32, 137–38, 140–41; four dimensions of Jesus's personal actions at Gethsemane, 141–53; Jesus's decision to open himself to sin/to God's rejection of sin, 147–50; Jesus's lack of knowledge of what the Father requires of him, 141–44; Maximus the Confessor's interpretation, 128–30; Schleiermacher's interpretation (neglect of Gethsemane), 134–39, 147

Good Samaritan, parable of the, xxii, 34–55; Barth's approach and contemporary Christian ethics, 34–38;

Index of Subjects

the church and question of ecclesio-centrism in Barth's interpretation, 48; *Church Dogmatics* I/2, 42–51; and contrast between reading as example and as allegory, 40–42; and current discussions of humanitarian aid and global justice, 38, 39, 51–55; and divine grace, 46–47; and the love commandments, 43–46; in modern scholarship, 38–42; moral and existential interpretations (distinctions between), 40; secular readings, 39

The Gospel according to Jesus Christ (Saramago), 155–60

Grace, divine: divine freedom and the election of grace, 6–7; divine mercy and, 12, 78–79; and parable of the Good Samaritan, 46–47; and predestination (doctrine of the election of grace), xx–xxi, 1–15, 198. *See also* Predestination, doctrine of

Historical-critical scholarship, xv, xvii, 39–42, 104, 115, 160
Historical Jesus, Barth on, xvii, 152, 176, 182–85
Holy Spirit, 97
Humanitarian aid, 38, 39, 51–55

"In the Name of God the Almighty" (1941 lecture), 58
Irenaeus, 40–41
Islam, 3

Jesus's cry of derelicton, xxv–xxvi, 155–72; *Church Dogmatics* IV/1, 162–67; and eternal death, 163–64; God's acceptance of responsibility for the evil we have done, 167; the Gospels on the cross in the light of resurrection, 168–69; the "limitless anguish of separation" and death in God-abandonment, 164–66, 170; Matthew's depiction of Jesus's death and surrender of his spirit, 169–70; Moltmann on, 167–68; and the mystery of God's relationship to sin and evil, 170–72; the passion of Jesus as the "passion of God himself," xxv–xxvi, 162–63; Saramago's dramatic retelling, xxv–xxvi, 155–60, 167, 170; the Son of God as subject of (as the one cries out), 162–63

Jesus Seminar, 39–40
Jewish community: Judas and, 189–90; refugees in wartime Switzerland, 57
Johannine Prologue, xxi–xxii, 16–33; and Barth's doctrine of election, 20–22; and Barth's doctrine of the Trinity, 20, 32; Barth's exegetical assault on notion of a *Logos asarkos*, 22–24; Bauckham's assessment of Barth's interpretation, 28–33; *Church Dogmatics*, 19, 20–24, 25–26, 27–28; the literary structure and Barth's failure to attend to, 28–29; Münster lectures and Bonn lectures, 16, 17–20, 24–25, 26–27; the point of the Prologue and Barth's failure to acknowledge, 31–33; the relationship to Genesis 1:1–5 and Barth's neglect of, 29; the term *ho Logos* as verbal placeholder for Jesus Christ, 17–20, 30, 31; the term *houtos* as referring to Jesus, 18–19, 21, 24, 26, 30–31; the verb "became" (*egeneto*), 26–28; verse 3 (on creation through the Word), 24–26; verse 14 (the Word became flesh), 26–28; verses 1–2 (the Word (*Logos*) as verbal placeholder (*Platzhalter*) for Jesus Christ), 17–24, 29, 30–31, 32; the word "flesh" (*sarx*), 27, 28; word study of divine and human *paradidōmi* clauses, 192–93
John the Baptist, 30, 178
Judas, *paradidōmi* of, 189–90, 192, 198–202
Julian of Norwich: account of atonement and election, 112–13, 118–19; on divine motherhood, 113; on parable of the lost son, xxiv–xxv, 106–7, 110–23

INDEX OF SUBJECTS

Justice, global: and doctrine of the election of grace, 11–15; and parable of the Good Samaritan, 38, 39, 51–55

Justification: and doctrine of election (the divine handing-over), 193–97; and God's election of grace, 9; and parable of the lost son, 117

Karl Barth Conference at Princeton Theological Seminary (2015), xiv

Last Judgment, 206

Lost son, parable of the, xxiii–xxv, 80–105, 106–23; Balthasar's focus on the action of the father, xxiv, 90–92, 94; Balthasar's reading, xxiii–xxiv, 89–105; Balthasar's trinitarian theology, 91–99, 100, 105; Balthasar's understanding of human freedom, xxiv, 99–104; Barth's analogy between the way of the son and the way of Jesus Christ, xxiv, 86–89, 106, 109–10, 117–18; Barth's christocentric reading, xxiv, 83–89, 114–19; and Barth's doctrine of reconciliation, 80, 83, 89, 106–10, 116–18; Barth's "indirect" exegesis, 85–86; Barth's message of joy, 81–82, 104; Barth's 1917 sermon on, 81–83; Barth's references to the Holy Spirit, 97; and Barth's trinitarian theology, 92–99, 105; Barth's understanding of human freedom, xxiv, 82–83, 99–104; and Christology in the mode of parable, xxiv–xxv, 116–23; *Church Dogmatics* IV/2, 82, 83–89, 94–96, 106–10, 116–18; and the command-obedience relationship, xxiv, 80, 92–98; comparing Barth and Balthasar, xxiii–xxiv, 80–105; comparing Barth and Julian of Norwich, xxiv–xxv, 106–23; doctrines of election and the Trinity, 118–22; identification with the lost son (as human sinners), 82; intrabiblical or intertextual readings, 115–16; Julian of Norwich's reading, xxiv–xxv, 106–7, 110–23; Julian on divine motherhood, 113; Julian's account of atonement and election, 112–13, 118–19

Maximus the Confessor, 128–30

Mercy, divine, 77–78, 200; grace and, 12, 78–79; parable of the Good Samaritan, 46–47. *See also* Compassion of Jesus Christ (Matthew 9:36)

Moltmann, Jürgen, on Jesus's cry of dereliction, 167–68

Münster lectures (1925–26), 16, 17–20, 24–25, 26–27. *See also* Johannine Prologue

Origen, 40–41

Paradidōmi (handing over), xxvi–xxvii, 187–203; the apostolic handing-over of the tradition (*paradosis*), 197–200; Barth's theological ontology and the divine handing-over, 190–93, 196; doctrine of election and *paradidōmi* passages in the New Testament, xxvi–xxvii, 187–203; and the eschaton, 197; ethics and the divine/human handing-over, 197–200; forensic framework of the divine handing-over, 193–97; implications for Christian missions, 201–3; Jesus Christ as subject of election, 190–93; the Johannine Prologue, 192–93; of Judas, 189–90, 192, 198–202; the positive human *paradidōmi* of Paul, 192–93, 194–95, 196–97, 200–202; scriptural and human witness to Jesus as Victor, 200–203. *See also* Election, doctrine of

Paul: conversion and Barth's interpretation of the Emmaus road story, 176, 181; positive human *paradidōmi* of, 192–93, 194–95, 196–97, 200–202

Pentecost, 180–81

Pew report on religion in America (2012), 185

Index of Subjects

Philo of Alexandria, 24
Predestination, doctrine of: and Barth's doctrine of the election of grace, xx–xxi, 1–15, 198; Barth's reaction to Calvinist/Reformed doctrines, 1, 2–3; and Barth's theology of the cross, 8–9; Calvin, 1–2, 11, 13–15; *Church Dogmatics* II/2, 1–15; double predestination (rejection of), xxi, 3, 8–11, 118; Julian of Norwich, 111, 112; Luther, 10–11. *See also* Election, doctrine of: Barth's doctrine of
Prodigal son parable. *See* Lost son, parable of the

Reconciliation, doctrine of, xviii; and christocentric reading the lost son parable, 80, 83, 89, 106–10, 116–18
A Revelation of Love, "Example of the Lord and Servant" (Julian of Norwich), 106–7, 110–14
Rich young ruler, story of the, xxii–xxiii, 56–66; and Barth in neutral Switzerland during World War II, 56–59, 63–64; Barth's exegesis as challenge to the church today, 65–66; and Barth's notion of freedom, 64; the call to covenant partnership, 62–63; *Church Dogmatics* II/2, 59–65; and contemporary banking practices, 63, 66; and economic anthropology, 65–66; and white Christian masculine subjectivity, 62, 65–66

Safenwil pastorate, xiv, 81–83
Saramago, José, xxv–xxvi, 155–60, 167, 170. *See also* Jesus's cry of derelection
Schleiermacher, Friedrich, 134–39, 147
Self-emptying, God's: Balthasar's reading of the lost son parable and primal act of kenosis, xxiv, 90–92; and the mystery of God's relationship to sin and evil, 171–72

"Sermon on the Preparation for Dying" (Luther), 10–11
Sin: Barth's account of original, 75; and Barth's juridical language in his exposition of atonement, 149–50; Gethsemane prayer and Jesus's decision to open himself to, 147–50; the mystery of God's relationship to, 170–72
Sixth Ecumenical Council (680–681), 130
Staupitz, Johann von, 10–11
Stoicism, 24, 29
Supralapsarianism, 4, 148, 170
Switzerland during World War II, 56–59, 63–64
Synoptic *Geschichte*, 124–27, 139

Temptation narratives, 144–45
Theo-Drama (Balthasar), 89–93, 99–100
Trinity/trinitarian theology: Balthasar's interpretation of the lost son parable, 91–99, 100, 105; and Barth's doctrine of election, 95–96, 118–19; Barth's interpretation of the lost son parable, 92–99, 105, 118–22; Barth's understanding of the divine-human unity, 165–67, 170; Chalcedon "definition," 128, 141; the command-obedience relationship, xxiv, 80, 92–98; Johannine Prologue and the *Logos* as verbal placeholder for Jesus Christ, 20, 32; Julian of Norwich on, 113, 118–19; and the "limitless separation" in Jesus's cry of derelection, 165–67, 170

Virgins, parable of the. *See* Bridesmaids, parable of the ten wise and foolish

"Why I Am Still a Christian" (Balthasar), 90
Works of Love (Kierkegaard), 50
World War II, 56–59, 63–64

Index of Scripture References

OLD TESTAMENT

Genesis
1	xiii, xxii
1:1	18
1:1–5	29
2–3	116
2	xiii

Exodus
12:11	207

Leviticus
19	37

Deuteronomy
6	37
32	109a

1 Samuel
25	xiii

Psalms
22	161, 167
33:6	29
75:8	169
100:5	14

Isaiah
40:4–5	13
51:17	141, 169
51:22	169
53	116

Ezekiel
34:2–6	73

Amos
8:9	169

Malachi
1:2–3	118

NEW TESTAMENT

Matthew
4	158
4:12	193, 195
5:25	193, 195
9:36 NRSV	67–79
9:36a	71
10:4	193
10:22	14
11:27	95
12:39f	145
18	46
18:20	175
18:34	193, 195
22	37
24	206
24:10	193, 195
25	50, 206
25:1–13	204–9
26:1–2	206
26:36–46	128, 138
26:39	128
27:46	153, 161
27:51–52	169
28:20	175, 179

Mark
1:11	95
1:14	193, 195
1:15	146
3:19	193
8:31	152
10:17	60
10:17–22	56–66
10:17–31 NRSV	xiii, 59–60
10:18	60
10:19	60
10:20	61
10:21	61

Index of Scripture References

10:21–22	61	24:22–24	186	17:2	27
10:23–25	64			17:4–5	95
10:28	65	**John**		18:1	128
12	37	1	44, 161	18:3–4	192
14:32–42	128	1:1	xxi, 17–20, 21, 23–24,	18:11	95
14:35	161		27, 30, 190	21:24	30
14:36	169	1:1c	19		
15:34	162, 166	1:1–2	17–24, 30, 200	**Acts**	
15:39	169	1:1–13	26	1:1	180
		1:1–14	xxi, 83	1:8	182
Luke		1:1–18	16–33	2:1–4	182
1	70	1:2	xxi, 18–19, 20, 21,	2:14–21	182
1:1	192		23–24, 26, 30–31, 190	2:33	180–81
1:1–2	193	1:2–8	18	3	179
1:52–53	12	1:3	18, 21–22, 24–	3:20–21	179
1:78	71, 79		26, 27, 30	4:31	182
1:78–79	183	1:4	20	7	181
2:32	183	1:5	30	7:42	193
2:52	136, 137, 143, 146	1:6	26	7:56	181
4:18	11	1:7	30	8:15–16	182
10	44, 50	1:10–11	27	8:29	182
10:25–37	34–55	1:12	26	8:39	182
10:29	46	1:13	27	9	181, 186
10:34	39	1:14	17, 18, 22, 26–28,	9:4	186
12:35	207		110, 113, 116, 190, 192	9:34	181
13	184	1:14–18	31	10:1–48	182
13:11	184	1:17	xxi, 18, 19	10:44–48	182
13:16	184	1:18	xxi, xxii, 31	11:1–18	182
15	46, 108	1:30	30	12:4	193, 195
15:1–2	108, 109	3:2	30	13:1–4	182
15:2	117	3:6	27	15:6–11	182
15:3–7	106	3:16	95	18:9–10	181
15:8–10	106	4:47	30	20:24	181
15:11–32	80–105, 106–23	6:11	95	21:1	193
15:12–24	108	6:50	30	21:11	193, 195
15:20	113	6:58	30	22	181
15:24	103, 109, 118	6:64	193	22:18–21	181
15:25–32	108	6:71	30	26	181, 183
15:31–32	104	7:40	30	26:23	181, 183
15:32	103, 109	7:41	30	27:1	195
19:10	114	8:15	27	28:17	193, 195
22:21	193	9:8	30		
22:32	14	10:17	95	**Romans**	
22:39–46	128	12	202	1	174
22:43	144	12:21	30	1:5	97
22:44	144	12:27	128	1:17–3:20	197

INDEX OF SCRIPTURE REFERENCES

1:24	192, 193, 197
1:26	192, 193, 197
1:28	192, 193, 197
3:25	134
4	195
4:25	9, 174, 192, 193, 194
5	112
5:14	109
5:14f	116
5:20	111
6:17	192, 193
8	195
8:29–39	196
8:31–39	10
8:32	174, 192, 193, 194
8:35	192
8:38–39	206
9–11	189
9:13	118
11:33	2
11:35	2
11:36	113
13:10	43

1 Corinthians

1:9	14
1:26–27	12
1:28	12
1:29	12
2:16	208
8:6	24
11:2	192, 193
11:23	192, 193
13:12	57, 99
15	183, 186
15:3	192, 193
15:22	116
15:55	10

2 Corinthians

1:22	15
5	184
5:16	184
5:17	168
5:19	169
5:19 KJV	128
5:21	116, 142, 148
11:22	206

Galatians

1	186, 195
2	195
2:20	95, 176, 192, 193, 197
3:13	142, 149

Ephesians

1	161
1:3–4	190
1:3–5	xxi
1:14	15
5:2	192, 193, 197
5:25	192, 193, 197

Philippians

1:6	14
2:5–11	83
2:6–7	112, 123, 197
2:6–11	116
2:7	171
4:7	135

Colossians

1	161
1:15	69
1:15–17	113
1:16	24

1 Thessalonians

1:3	14

1 Timothy

1:5	43
2:5 KJV	126

2 Timothy

2:13	7

Hebrews

1	161
1:2	24
4:15	136
5:7–9	146
5:8	132, 169
10:32	14
12:2	14

James

5:7	14

2 Peter

3:12	205
3:13	207

1 John

3:2 KJV	209

Jude

3	192

Revelation

1:8	175
1:9	14
2:2	14
13:8	147
13:10	14
19:13	17

www.ingramcontent.com/pod-product-compliance
Lightning Source LLC
Chambersburg PA
CBHW032003220426
43664CB00005B/128